THE WEB OF MEANING

The Web of Meaning

The Internet in a Changing Chinese Society

ELAINE J. YUAN

UNIVERSITY OF TORONTO PRESS

Toronto Buffalo London

© University of Toronto Press 2021
Toronto Buffalo London
utorontopress.com
Printed in Canada

ISBN 978-1-4875-0813-5 (cloth)
ISBN 978-1-4875-3763-0 (EPUB)
ISBN 978-1-4875-3762-3 (PDF)

Library and Archives Canada Cataloguing in Publication

Title: The web of meaning: the Internet in a changing Chinese society /
Elaine J. Yuan.
Names: Yuan, Elaine J., 1974– author.
Description: Includes bibliographical references and index.
Identifiers: Canadiana (print) 20200412396 | Canadiana (ebook) 20200412485 |
ISBN 9781487508135 (cloth) | ISBN 9781487537630 (EPUB) |
ISBN 9781487537623 (PDF)
Subjects: LCSH: Internet – Social aspects – China. | LCSH: Social
change – China.
Classification: LCC HN740.Z9 I56 2021 | DDC 302.23/10951 – dc23

This book has been published with the assistance of the Chiang Ching-Kuo
Foundation for International Scholarly Exchange.

University of Toronto Press acknowledges the financial assistance to its
publishing program of the Canada Council for the Arts and the Ontario Arts
Council, an agency of the Government of Ontario.

 Canada Council
for the Arts
Conseil des Arts
du Canada

 ONTARIO ARTS COUNCIL
CONSEIL DES ARTS DE L'ONTARIO
an Ontario government agency
un organisme du gouvernement de l'Ontario

Funded by the Financé par le
Government gouvernement
of Canada du Canada

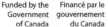 Canadä

 MIX
Paper from
responsible sources
FSC® C016245

Contents

Acknowledgments

The Web of Meaning couples together two of the most fascinating subjects of the past few decades in their fast and dizzying development: the Internet and China. Originally, the Internet was deemed universal, while China posed, at most, a special case, a local outlier, or even a threat. The enormous size and magnitude of the country's recent development are fundamentally changing this situation and forcing us to reframe our questions and preconceptions about technology and society. The challenge has become how to understand and question media technology, its rapidly developing practices, and emerging communities of meaning in the specific political, economic, and cultural configuration of Chinese society while providing answers that speak to the concerns and interests of wider audiences.

This book has been written within the context of changing perspectives about the media in China. In my efforts to meet these challenges, I have benefited from comments, suggestions, criticisms, and encouragement from many people. I would like to take the opportunity to thank the following, who have supported this book in a variety of ways during its various stages of gestation. It goes without saying, of course, that this book's errors or shortcomings are entirely my own.

Many colleagues in the Department of Communication at the University of Illinois at Chicago (UIC) were among the first to hear the initial ideas of the book and to provide feedback on the relevant empirical research. The many discussions with Jim Sosnoski helped me navigate semiotics and discourse analysis, new areas of interest that constituted the beginning of a cultural turn in my research orientation. Michael Schandorf provided valuable comments and meticulous editing of the draft proposal. Andy Rojecki and Siyuan Yin offered detailed comments on earlier drafts of some of the chapters. Kevin Sherman volunteered to help with the references. Zizi Papacharissi kindly introduced me to potential outlets for publication as the book neared completion.

The diverse network of scholars at the annual Chinese Internet Research Conferences whom I encountered over the years have also been a tremendous source of inspiration and help. My sincere gratitude goes to Ang Peng Hwa, Min Jiang, Randy Kluver, Jack Qiu, Cara Wallis, Marcella Szablewicz, Baohua Zhou, and Guobin Yang, who, together with numerous others, have worked diligently to provide not only an intellectual environment for research on the Chinese Internet but also a lively community of friendship and support.

A special shout out to my colleague Florian Schneider, the editor-in-chief of *Asiascape: Digital Asia*, whose effort to create this timely venue for research on digital communication in Asia has nurtured a growing community of researchers in the area, including myself. Zhongdang Pan and Guobing Yang, the editors of the journal *Communication and the Public*, are also among the leaders of the community, who have promoted the integration of scholarship from China with the rest of the International community.

My deep appreciation is also due to Eran Fisher and Erika Kuever, whose works provided much inspiration for my thinking about the network market, and to Jim Webster and Limin Liang, who have been very supportive with their input and comments along the way.

Many of the ideas in this book were previously aired at seminars, conferences, and workshops. These include a research seminar organized by Weishan Miao and Guohua Zeng in the Journalism and Communication Department at the Chinese Academy of Social Sciences; a presentation at the annual convention of the Association of Asian Studies in Toronto, with co-panelists Lin Zhang, Bingchun Meng, Yanning Huang, and Linliang Qian, and discussant Yongming Zhou; invited talks for the *People's Internet* project at the University of Copenhagen, a multi-nation endeavour led by Klaus Jensen and joined by Jun Liu and many other team members; an invited talk organized by Athina Karatzogianni at University of Leicester; a colloquium organized by Bingchun Meng at the London School of Economics and Political Science; a presentation at the symposium on the Digital Formations and Chinese Experiences: Creation, Appropriation, and Circulation, organized by Zhongdang Pan, Guobin Yang, and Lu Wei at the Penn Wharton China Center; an invited talk at the School of Public Policy and Management, Tsinghua University; an invited talk at EU-China Dialogue in Media and Communication Studies, Peking University; and an invited talk at the Communication Department, University of Macau.

I would like to extend my sincere gratitude to Aswin Punathambekar, Adrienne Shaw, Florian Schneider, and Lance Bennett for their valuable comments on the initial book proposal. In addition, I am deeply grateful to the institute of Humanities at the University of Illinois at Chicago, for the financial assistance that has made possible some of the fieldwork for this book. I am also indebted to May Zhao, and many other colleagues, from CTR Market Research in China for being supportive over the years and for providing the Sina Weibo data for this book project.

Some of the material presented in chapter 3 appeared in "'Privacy' in Semantic Networks on Chinese Social Media: The Case of Sina Weibo," *Journal of Communication*, *63*(6), 1011–31. Part of chapter 4 on cyber-nationalism appeared in "Public Opinion in Chinese Social Media: The Diaoyu Islands Dispute on Sina Weibo," in *The Dispute over the Diaoyou/Senkaku Islands: How Media Narratives Shape Public Opinion and Challenge the Global Order*, edited by T.A. Hollihan, 266–81 (New York: Palgrave, 2014). I would like to take the opportunity to thank James Danowski, my former colleague at UIC, for creating the powerful computer program for semantic network analysis, which I used for the analysis of privacy data. I am also grateful to Miao Feng, a resourceful graduate student of mine, for helping with collecting the data for the privacy project and with analysing the data for the piece on cyber-nationalism. And many thanks also go to Tom Hollihan, who provided the encouragement and opportunity for the research on cyber-nationalism.

Last but certainly not least, I would like to extend my warm gratitude to Peter F. Bang, or just LP, the only ancient historian who would, and has, read my manuscript from cover to cover, twice.

THE WEB OF MEANING

Introduction

The Internet has been integral to transformations in Chinese society in recent decades. The dynamics of political decentralization, market expansion, and social stratification have played out through the vast networks of technological, economic, and political connection mediated by the Internet. Implemented by the state in the 1990s mainly as technical infrastructure for economic growth, the Internet has since catalyzed the transformation of China's telecommunications industries, served as the information backbone for the growing market economy, birthed the dynamic e-commerce sector, and spawned some of the largest Internet corporations in the world, including Alibaba, Tencent, and Baidu (Tai, 2006; Y. Zhao, 2008; McKinsey & Company, 2015). In China, however, the neutral, inevitable, and benevolent image of the Internet in the economic sphere is often overshadowed by its potential political implications. Hailed as the new frontier of civil society (Tai, 2006; G. Yang, 2003; Han, 2018), the Internet provides a stage for public and political participation by the emerging social and political forces energized by economic liberalization. In response to the challenges of an increasingly pluralized and autonomous society, the Chinese government – while engaging in the controversial practice of Internet regulation – has acknowledged the importance of the Internet as "a bridge facilitating direct communication between the government and the public" (State Council Information Office, 2010; G. Yang, 2011, p. 1044).

Yet the Chinese Internet has been as much an outcome of the symbolic practices of its now more than 800 million users as it has been a creation of the state and the market (CNNIC, 2019). Despite an enormous digital divide, a slew of new social and economic constituencies now are active on the Internet. They include ethnic minority groups (Maurer-Fazio, 2012), popular religious sects (Thornton, 2010), domestic migrant workers (Qiu, 2009), homeowners (Huang & Sun, 2014), urban youth and alternative cultural groups (S.W. Chen, 2014; F. Liu, 2011; Szablewicz, 2014), same-sex communities (D. Zhang et al., 2007), people living with HIV (Zhuang & Bresnahan, 2012), rights-defence activists and NGOs (Gleiss, 2015), environmentalists (Sullivan & Xie, 2009), and cyber-nationalists (Shen & Breslin, 2010; X. Wu, 2007), as well as overseas Chinese diasporas (Ding, 2007). The everyday practices of information, communication, association, and identification of these diverse actors acquire new forms from the possibilities afforded by the Internet. In its vibrant landscape of interwoven online communities, networks, and events, the lifeworld experiences of Chinese people are constantly renewed through personal stories, popular cultures, and public sentiments. As diverging interests and changing relations crop up in multiple social domains, new social categories and representations are simultaneously produced to understand these changes. Flourishing discourses in the symbolic spaces made possible by the Internet do not simply react to changes in social identities, relations, and institutions, but also constitute, codify, and regulate those very changes (Bourdieu, 1991; Foucault, 1972, 1979; Hall, 1982).

The central proposition of this book is that the transformative role of the Internet in China lies in its capacity to mediate – to formalize, (de)stabilize, and articulate – symbolic representations of an expanding array of social actors in contemporary Chinese society. On one hand, the symbolic spaces mediated by the Internet provide defining contexts in which discourses of new social identities and relations unfold. On the other hand, these spaces acquire their forms, functions, and meanings through networked communications and interactions among actors embedded in existing political, economic, and cultural institutions. Enabling new network spaces, symbolic resources, forms of sociality, and struggles for power, the Internet has altered the cultural politics of public visibility, voice, and power. At the same time, the Internet has been decisively shaped in the process by the specific constellation of forces and cultural practices existing in China. Instead of simply a universal technology, it has developed along the contours of China's specific socio-economic transformations.

Network Privacy, Cyber-nationalism, and the Network Market

The rise of the Internet as symbolic space has coincided with a series of social developments in China, ranging from the loosening of state control over cultural and media institutions and the growing influence of market forces in cultural production to the surge of popular culture and consumer society (G. Yang, 2009; Y. Zhao, 2008). Examining the symbolic struggles underlying the changing practices and shifting relations in multiple social domains in contemporary China, *The Web of Meaning* aims to demonstrate that symbolic practice, and the cultural process it entails, constitutes changing power structures in political and economic domains by legitimizing or challenging the logics of domination within those domains.

Through three empirical cases – namely, network privacy, cyber-nationalism, and the network market – this book illustrates the dynamics and implications of the discursive reproduction of social institutions, which unfold in socio-technological contexts mediated by various forms of network communication. The case of network privacy centres on how the new conceptions of privacy are premised on the condensation of the popular discourses delineating the new private self in the Internet-mediated lifeworld. The varied privacy discourses both reflect and shape the practices and understandings of the individual negotiating their outer limits in multiple – and sometimes inconsistent – institutional contexts such as kinship, the market, or bureaucracies, each with distinctive socially and historically constructed norms and clusters of practices. In the lifeworld mediated by network media, however, these institutional norms are understood and negotiated mostly through everyday experiences and personal expressions shared on mediated networks of "direct" social relations, as opposed to "indirect" relations oriented toward the official functions of economic and political institutions such as the state or the market (Calhoun, 1992a). As reflected in rich social media discourses, privacy in diverse contexts embodies evolving social identities, roles, values, genders, and statuses, understood and constructed in a lifeworld that is no longer bound by physical or geographical proximity – that is, the cultural process of privacy conception takes place in the lifeworld extended by the Internet from the "world within reach" to the "world within mediated reach" (S. Zhao, 2006).

The case of cyber-nationalism examines the reformulation of nationalism in the symbolic space emergent in popular nationalist movements, represented by a recent wave of anti-Japan protests over the disputed territory of the Diaoyu Islands in the South China Sea. At a time when Chinese society has become increasingly fragmented, the case shows, the conventional understanding of nationalism as a unifying group identity, membership, or ideology is subject to modification. While people still rally in large numbers under Chinese identity enacted in collective cultural memories of national territorial sovereignty, the discursive space that emerged in the protests consists of different interpretive communities formed through collective expressions of sentiments and grievances about their changing social and economic positions. Established and scaled through Internet-mediated communications, such organic communities are fluid in organization and orientation, "often enabling coordinated adjustments and rapid action aimed at shifting political targets" (Bennett & Segerberg, 2012, p. 753). Such symbolic communities provide the basis for identity formation among emerging social groups in their navigation of complex social and political landscapes.

The last case examines the construction of the network market epitomized in Alibaba's rise as the world's leading online market. Far from being simply a result of market decrees crossed with network technology, the development of a network market is embedded in complex institutional contexts and cultural processes. It implies a discursive field encompassing multiple sites embedded in the most important realms of economic life – production, consumption, commodity, work, and sociability. In each of these sites, digital discourses about the role of network technology to create opportunities for a new mode of economic development reflect and shape evolving power dynamics among the players, including the state, the market, corporations, and consumers. The field has shaped the symbolic and interactional practices of participants differentially positioned in the domestic economic policymaking process and in the competitive global regime of capitalist production and consumption.

Privacy, nationalism, and the marketplace are three prominent examples of social institutions that undergo changes in contemporary China – the shifting relations between the private and the public, between various social groups *vis-à-vis* the nation-state, and between production and consumption in light of the country's transition to a market-driven consumer society. Together, the three cases serve as the basis for a broad illustration of the important cultural process of social change articulated through symbolic projects of social actors to define and pursue various interests. These cases highlight historically contingent developments playing out in part in the cultural processes mediated by network communication. On one hand, shifting frames of meaning take shape based on the existing social structures of various institutional domains; on the other hand, emergent norms are symbolically produced as actors struggle to understand and negotiate their changing positions and interests.

The Internet as Discursive Fields: A Theoretical Framework

Highlighting the centrality of the symbolic in the organization of social life, *The Web of Meaning* sets to examine the role of the Internet in symbolic formation and reproduction. Far from being simply a technical infrastructure, inherently unhindered by geographic barriers or centralized control, the Internet enables recursive interaction between cultural representations and social structures, between mediated discursive practices and the power relations in which discourses are produced (P.H. Collins, 2015). The symbolic Internet operates less as a received egalitarian public sphere structuring the deliberative activities of all eligible participants than as an array of discursive fields composed of differentially positioned social actors with widely varying access to social and symbolic resources (Habermas, 1974; Bourdieu, 1991). Originally explicated by Bourdieu ([1992] 1996, 2005) and subsequently modified by other theorists (e.g., Fligstein & McAdam, 2012; Martin, 2003), field theory proposes that society is constituted by structured spaces where different social actors compete for position. Such structured spaces are defined and configured by the distribution of capital in the form of any source of social power, whether economic, political, or cultural. Field theory thus understands existing structures of social relations as both sources and outcomes of struggles for power, which tend to reproduce hierarchies of domination and subordination (S. Liu & Emirbayer, 2016).

The symbolic spaces mediated by the Internet often take the form of a field. Structured in existing political, economic, and cultural orders, such discursive fields are constituted in the struggles of social actors vying for symbolic power to represent their own positions and interests in changing social life. While often affecting the distribution of opportunities and resources in the field, the existing political and economic structures alone can never fully determine the dynamics or the results of symbolic struggles. The process and outcome of the struggles are also contingent on the specific cultural process mediated by the socio-technological structures of network communication. Capable of facilitating social engagements "infinitely variable in closeness, content and intensity," such socio-technological structures comprise intricate layers of context and practice that fold together in time and space (Bakardjieva, 2009, p. 97; Bennett & Segerberg, 2012; Sassen, 2012). Diffuse matrices of communication and representation on the Internet take the tangible shape of a discursive field when the symbolic practices of the players take place amid the structural ruptures of existing political and economic institutions. In such a process, the political and economic positions and interests of the players are translated and reformulated in symbolic terms as resources for the expression and contestation of new relations within the structural dynamics of the discursive field. In this light, the formation of symbolic fields represents contingent, dynamic,

and relational emergences in the interaction between network communication, cultural production, and social relations. Empirical efforts are
needed to discover how symbolic practices are organized through the
constitution of network sociality in a particular institutional environment or social domain.

The field framework as an analytical strategy in *The Web of Meaning*
both complements and challenges the prevalent public sphere model.
In this book, I argue that the contemporary public sphere operates as
a series of overlapping discursive fields among which complex communicative relationships exist. Rather than based on a normative conception, discursive fields are approached as socially constructed and
characterized by lines of division and relationships of force. It is, therefore, important to consider the distribution of power, networks of communication, how issues take shape, and how influence in the discursive
fields is structured (Calhoun, 1992b). Each of the three empirical cases
of the symbolic reproduction of rapidly evolving social institutions –
privacy, nationalism, and the market – can be conceived as a discursive field comprising a different set of social actors who are compelled
to engage with the negotiation of practices, social relations, and moral
dilemmas that define the very institution (DiMaggio, 1997). This book
strives to show that the dynamics and outcomes of the symbolic struggles in the discursive fields are affected by how network communication intersects with particular social structures and cultural orders. At
the same time, the field framework provides a basis for a critique of the
power relationships embedded in the dominant symbolic characterizations of social institutions.

The Internet for Critical Discourses: Method

The premise of *The Web of Meaning* is that the role of the Internet as
discursive space in social transformation is defined in the context of
its entanglement with social institutions –"organizational and symbolic
practices that operate within networks of rules, structural ties, public
narratives, and binding relationships that are embedded in time and
space" (Somers, 1993, p. 595). Social change brings into question the
conventions, assumptions, and legitimization of social institutions. As
previously presupposed and taken-for-granted aspects of society lose
their unquestionable character, social order can no longer be assumed
in advance but must be actively sought through debates and discussions (Crossley & Roberts, 2004).

Rooted in this cultural understanding of social change, *The Web of
Meaning* sets to examine the processes and implications of discourse,

meaning, and cultural representation in particular institutional contexts. It analyses social discourses as "abstract webs of linguistically articulated meaning," components of cultural structures, underlying the political and economic orders, and produced by the symbolic practices of social actors embedded in specific social contexts (Chouliaraki & Fairclough, 1999; Schatzki et al., 2001, p. 14). The book aims to show how identity formations and power relations are mediated, negotiated, and sometimes changed through discursive practices. Moreover, it problematizes the relation between network communication and the social contexts it mediates. The dynamics of network communication affect how discursive practices are organized through particular relational networks formed by social actors embedded in specific social contexts.

For these purposes, *The Web of Meaning* has three analytical foci, each with its respective theoretical underpinning: a) symbolic practices, the social discourses they produce, and the underlying cultural structures they enact; b) the relation between symbolic practices and their political and economic contexts; and c) the particular forms of socio-technological mediation of the cultural formations through network communication. Within this analytical framework, I analyse discourses simultaneously as outcomes of symbolic practice, networked interaction, and power struggle.

The book draws samples from the vast volume of user-generated data posted on major social media sites, as well as data from online news organizations and government and corporate websites. I use formal analytic methodologies, such as topic modelling and semantic network analysis, to reduce large corpora of complex data to simpler, more easily intelligible structures of meaning. The quantitative methods help ground the critical analysis on a solid empirical base and provide more thorough and more richly validated explanations.

Sets of cultural concepts and underlying structures are further assessed by looking at how actors, both individual and collective, make practical use of the cultural meanings of these concepts. I examine discursive clues such as word choice, mixed meanings, hybrid identity statements, and shifts in political representations to plot various social locations of discursive agents in relation to their relative location within the discursive field. On the one hand, the underlying logic of symbolic expressions of different social actors provides clues to understand the changing social relations. On the other hand, it reveals how particular discourses are produced and contested within particular relational contexts and institutional arrangements (Chouliaraki & Fairclough, 1999; Lemke, 2005).

Lastly, the analysis explicates how the communicative dynamics of the discursive fields influence the outcomes of symbolic struggles. The formation of a discursive field is contingent on how communication flows are scaled up and stabilized through the socio-technical circuits of social interaction. The shape of such a socio-technical structure depends on how the technical features of network communication intersect with the particular social logic of communication among actors in a particular social context. Capable of multi-scalar interconnectivity among diverse actors, goals, and power relations, such structures may take the form of systemic social organization, communal organizations of interdependent personal relations, or culturally differentiated and discursively mediated publics and communities (Calhoun, 1992b). Conditioned on such structures, the discursive fields enable new types of articulation between the powerful and the powerless (Sassen, 2012).

Together, these three foci systematically relate discourse to its social property as an instance of mediated social practice and assess the relationships between discourse and social context (Fairclough, 1992; Lemke 2005). The analysis highlights how the characteristics of network communication affect the relation between cultural expression and social structure. A combination of both quantitative and qualitative methods helps strengthen the capacity and validity of the empirical analyses, which sets a solid ground for further critical interrogation.

Outline of the Book

The arguments presented in *The Web of Meaning* about social transformations, discursive fields, and symbolic practices are both theoretical and substantive. In the introduction, chapter 1, chapter 2, and the conclusion, the book mainly makes the theoretical arguments that changing social circumstances not only produce institutional space for new meaning systems but also create symbolic space in which new meaning systems are themselves produced. Moreover, the transformative power of symbolic practices lies in the ways in which social conditions are themselves constructed and structured by symbolic categories. Substantively, the book presents three empirical cases in chapters 3, 4, and 5. They illustrate how respective sets of social actors formulate social discourses by thematizing their social environments and debating alternative visions of social representations. The theoretical framework remains in the background throughout the substantive analyses in the empirical chapters in order to allow the concrete patterns themselves to be emphasized.

Chapter 1 highlights the cultural aspects of social change in China, emphasizes the importance of symbolic power in cultural (re)production, and locates discursive practices in structured spaces mediated by the socio-technological processes of the Internet. The chapter begins by situating social change in the realm of cultural (re)production of subjects, institutions, and knowledge. I argue that the Internet forms symbolic spaces where social actors struggle to define new concepts and categories for understanding changing social life in contemporary Chinese society.

The second part of the chapter explicates the cultural process of discursive formation through the cases of *shamate* and *diaosi*, two cultural representations that formed in the new symbolic space mediated by the Internet. The outcome of such discursive social formation depends not only on how participants in the process are embedded in the existing socio-economic structure but also on how the symbolic process is mediated by contingent network communications.

Lastly, the chapter discusses how the Internet mediates new forms of social interaction in the Chinese context. It zeros in on Internet events – contingent occurrences that gain momentum and become consequential public events as they reverberate through the network of communication. Erupting in public comments and defined by continuing public discourses during the contesting process, an Internet event exemplifies the socially embedded process of discursive practices in network communication.

The first part of chapter 2 provides a historical review of the structural transformation of the cultural realm in China, which sets the stage for the emergence of the Internet as symbolic space. The commercialization of Chinese media, the decline of the previously totalizing political ideology, the development of cultural markets and industries, the rise of popular culture, and the emergence of new conceptions of "the public" opened up opportunities for a broad range of cultural agents to forge new identities and alliances through symbolic practices.

The chapter then proposes that new dynamics of symbolic interaction can be understood with a field structure, which emerges from symbolic struggles among participants with differentially distributed symbolic resources and varying goals. Working within the field framework, the chapter goes on to explain how symbolic power is constituted in transactions with political, economic, cultural, and social capital in the new symbolic spaces mediated by the Internet in China.

Trends of market-oriented socialization and individualization at the expense of socialist collectives have greatly upset the established boundaries between the private and public realms in Chinese society. The evolving private/public relation is prominently expressed in the contested notion of privacy in the Chinese context. The rise of the Internet as mediated lifeworld enables privacy practices and discourses to work as mechanisms for socially situated processes of boundary management.

Against this backdrop, chapter 3, the book's first empirical chapter, examines the lifeworld discourses on privacy by examining a corpus of 18,000 user-generated postings on Sina Weibo, China's leading social media platform. A comprehensive network of major privacy-related concepts, constructed in a semantic network analysis, represents a structure of cultural codes underlying the multifaceted notion of privacy in the mediated lifeworld. The eleven distinct yet organically related semantic clusters represent the personal, professional, public, emotional, and spatial domains in which privacy is practised and understood in changing Chinese society. Finally, the findings are interpreted in a discussion of a rapidly evolving private realm in relation to emerging new public realms in China. Pervasive network communication turns these domains into discursive sites where new conventions and relations are contested by actors embedded in these very domains.

With the pluralization of social life, previously established notions of national identity and belonging have been opened up for contestation in China. The Internet has enabled non-state players to engage with the state, which had previously dominated the definition of the nation. Approaching nationalism as a cultural formation, chapter 4 examines how central reference points of national identity are authored and contested in popular discourses mediated by the Internet. The empirical case is built around the recent eruption of nationalist protests against Japan in the long historical territorial dispute over the Diaoyu Islands in the East China Sea. Using linguistic topic modelling methods, I trace and analyse a representative sample of 100,000 postings from Sina Weibo generated during the most turbulent period of the protests in 2012.

As the cultural and political structures that traditionally anchored the strength of nationalism as a common identity dissolve, the findings indicate, variegated reinterpretations of historical memories and contemporary experiences about sovereignty of the Chinese state have emerged. No longer predominantly a homogeneous community, even when faced with a common outside threat, the nation is subject to the imaginings and expressions of various social groups in relation to their particular socio-economic positions. The Internet event of cyber-nationalism presents a contingent discursive field where the nation as a political community and nationalism as a relational identity are contested and articulated in the symbolic struggles among various social groups.

The surge of the market into social life is one of the defining characteristics of China's post-socialist transformations in recent decades.

The rise of the Internet provides a timely opportunity for promoting a network economy in the country's post-industrial economic transition. Chapter 5 looks to Alibaba, one of the world's largest e-commerce corporations, as a case study of the role of the Internet in the development of the network market in China. The network market of Alibaba is premised on symbolic struggles over such key notions as "the Internet +," "entrepreneurship," "innovation," and "fake goods" in the discursive sites of state policies, corporate strategies, and consumer communities. It is through such struggles that the changing relations between the state and market, production and consumption, public and private spheres of life, buyer and seller identities, and global market standards and local prosumer practices are contested and legitimized.

Far from simply a top-down imposition of economic principles by the Chinese state or a neutral process where technology seamlessly merges with the market, the development of the network market involves dialectical relationships among economic structures, mediating technology, and discursive practices that construct the order of the social economic world (McGuigan & Manzerolle, 2014; Zelizer, 1988). The Internet in this case serves not only as a new infrastructure of production and consumption, but also as a discursive field where economic actors mobilize symbolic resources to promote their goals in the market.

The conclusion reiterates the argument about the role of the Internet in the cultural process of social change in China. Mediating various forms of network communication, the Internet intersects with existing intuitional contexts where the social reproduction of the private/public boundary, national identities, and market-oriented social structuring take place. The conclusion also compares the field framework with the prominent public sphere theory for understanding the Chinese Internet. Contemporary public symbolic spaces in China are characterized by differentially available symbolic resources rather than by universal accessibility prescribed by the public sphere model. Focusing on discursive processes by which social groups legitimize social order in their own interests, the field framework replaces the abstract and normative presumption of the public with analyses of the processes in which pluralistic publics take forms. With a more open, plural, and relational understanding of the public symbolic space, the field framework brings forth the power dimension in symbolic contestation.

The Web of Meaning: A New Approach

Focusing on the Internet, discursive practices, and social institutions in changing Chinese society, *The Web of Meaning* speaks to researchers and students across a range of fields including new media and the Internet studies, critical cultural studies, cultural sociology, and media economics, as well as to scholars of China in general.

The book aims to contribute to existing scholarly research on the social implications of the Chinese Internet (e.g., Tai, 2006; Han, 2018; G. Yang, 2009; Y. Zhou, 2006). Emphasizing mediated cultural practices that are mutually constitutive with changing social contexts, this book overcomes the pitfall of technological determinism that often characterizes the Internet as a utopian or dystopian force external to social process. It provides an alternative to a "Tiananmen Square" approach that looks at the Internet and social change through the limited normative lens of democratization (Leibold, 2011; Meng, 2010, p. 501). Moreover, unlike many of the edited volumes on digital media in China (e.g., W. Chen & Reese, 2015; Herold & Marolt, 2011), *The Web of Meaning* presents a systematic framework for examining the discursive reproduction of social institutions rather than simply looking at isolated cases of the political and economic effects of the Internet.

The field framework proposed by *The Web of Meaning* stands in contrast to the public sphere model that underlies much existing research on the Internet in China (e.g., Lei, 2017). While the Habermasian model tends to subsume public discourse to a presumed normative and egalitarian perspective, the field approach situates discursive practices in the conditions of their genesis and functioning by scrutinizing, through concrete empirical cases, the particular ways in which these discourses are structured by particular sets of participants. As outcomes of contestation among multiple viewpoints, public discourses are therefore invested in particular ideologies and sustain particular relations of power within society (Fairclough, 1992).

The focus on the Internet and network communication distinguishes this book from the existing body of research on Chinese media and communication in general (e.g., C.C. Lee, 2003; Shirk, 2011; Y. Zhao, 2008). Often focusing on the political economy of media institutions, such research tends to rely on an external view of power and ideology or an emphasis on social structures. Thinking in terms of the field and practices, *The Web of Meaning* approaches the Internet as new forms of communication mediating interactions between social actors who take an active part in constructing the very political, economic, and cultural structures in which they are embedded. Under this framework, the central role of the Internet in China's social transformations is exemplified not as media spectacles reflecting structural changes, but as mediated cultural processes that interact with existing institutional structures in different ways (H. Yu, 2009).

Given its focus on critical discourse and the sociology of practices, this book seeks to address topics central to scholars working in the fields of linguistics, semiotics, discourse analysis, and cultural sociology (e.g., Kong, 2014; Cao et al., 2014; Chilton et al., 2012). The field approach situates the case studies in the duality of social institutions – that is, cultural, political, and economic imperatives – and the dynamics of symbolic practices in network communication that can alter the effects of those imperatives. Applying innovative methods such as network analysis and linguistic topic modelling to examining theoretically important subjects in these fields, this book demonstrates how new data-driven approaches may serve as empirical foundations for critical cultural analysis. Moreover, due to the inclusion of rich empirical data depicting everyday experience as well as significant events on the Internet, the book hopes to appeal to general audiences, both those interested in new media technologies and those who follow contemporary China.

1

The Internet and Social Change in China

For an observer looking for clues to understand fast-changing Chinese society, some of the most telling social representations in recent years have been encoded in the rich vernacular of the Internet: for example, *tuhao*, a culturally despicable class of nouveau riche; *fuerdai*, a generation of bratty young people living off their rich parents' economic resources; *diaosi*, self-mocking underdogs (P. Yang et al., 2014); *shamate*, young migrant workers whose efforts to blend into urban life lead only to their further alienation (Lu, 2013); *shengnv*, "leftover women," who can hardly escape society's patriarchal gaze, despite their success in achieving economic independence (Fincher, 2014); and *ziganwu*, the "voluntary fifty-cent army," whose pro-government political stance makes them the target of criticism by liberal-leaning Chinese netizens (Han, 2015).

Reflecting diverse, sometimes conflicting, experiences of change, discursive portraits of new social subjects and relations such as these abound in the vibrant symbolic spaces mediated by the Chinese Internet. These social representations articulate images and knowledge about the personification of certain traits – real or imagined – by emerging social groups. By engaging with such discursive categories and imaginaries, people understand and reflect upon their own political and economic status in the rapidly changing world. As the positions and affiliations surrounding these symbolic identities further crystalize and synthesize in private and public communications, new systems of perception and action take shape. In this light, the Internet emerges as a crucial space for "social formation," where differences in socio-economic status, gender, ethnicity, and lifestyle are identified; knowledge is created; and power is enacted (Foucault, 1971).

With the gradual retreat of the Chinese state from a position of omnipotent authority and the development of a market economy as a new way of organizing social life, Chinese society has become increasingly pluralized, with an expanding scope of life experiences and the simultaneous reconstitution of social relations. Diverse modes of agency, representation, and communication parallel the growing plurality of social subjects in the fast-changing society. New ways of cultural expression and multiple concurrent symbolic sites mediated by the Internet have made various expressions of new identities and relations possible.

Indeed, the Internet has been a central stage for enunciating changes through new forms of communication. In contrast with traditional media institutions, which served as vehicles for social integration by providing common access to shared meaning in the era of mass communication (Spitulnik, 1996; Thompson, 1995), the Internet enacts a different kind of symbolic space. It is constituted by ebbs and flows of networked communication among various social actors and groups, who constantly revise and renew their responses to unfolding developments. In this light, the Internet affords new forms of sociability that take place in multiple, simultaneous, and contingent modes of associations and linkages. Numerous and diverse communicative networks, communities, and events on the Internet, mobile and flexible in spatial and temporal arrangement, private as well as public in configuration, create rich social locales and milieus for social interaction. Such Internet sociabilities offer unique opportunities for various social interests actively and interactively to pursue identity-related projects that were previously impossible and even inconceivable (Feenberg & Bakardjieva, 2004, p. 40).

Premised on a cultural understanding of social change in China, this chapter highlights the potential of social discourses, produced in pervasive communications mediated by the Internet, to contest and define social life. Taking shape in the complex flows of interaction enabled by various forms of network communication, such discourses have been outcomes of symbolic practices of actors competing to represent their own understanding of changing reality. Embodying new and versatile symbolic spaces, the Internet not only organizes various symbolic practices but also constitutes evolving relational contexts in which such practices are grounded. Drawing on some prominent empirical examples, this chapter attempts to demonstrate how viewpoints, interests, and positions can be "articulated" into discourses within fluid fields of networked communication. In later chapters of the book, this approach will be applied to analyse a set of current cases in greater detail. I shall defer until the next chapter the account of the historical development of the Internet and its operation as discursive fields in China's political economic life.

New Cultural Subjects: *Shamate* and *Diaosi*

Social discourses are harbingers of change. In times of profound transformation, many existing cognitive classifications, normative values,
and political representations no longer effectively signify the meaning
of social realities. People shift to more deliberative modes to construct
new social representations in order to interpret new stimuli. Consequently, social discourses multiply, break up, and reorganize (Chouliaraki & Fairclough, 1999; Fairclough, 1992). At such times, the "work
of categorization, i.e., of making-explicit and of classification, is performed incessantly, at every moment of ordinary existence, in the struggles in which agents clash over the meaning of the social world and of
their position within it, the meaning of their social identity, through
all the forms of benediction or malediction, eulogy, praise, congratula-
tions, compliments, or insults, reproaches, criticisms, accusations, slan-
ders, etc." (Bourdieu, 1985, p. 202).

Drawing on existing accounts of the popular discourses surrounding *shamate* and *diaosi*, two prominent cultural phenomena, this section
provides concrete examples to illustrate how discourses both reflect
and constitute elements of a changing world in the Chinese context.
The focus of the examples is on relating the discursive articulation of
these terms to the positions of social actors in both the symbolic and the
socio-economic spheres of life.

The term *shamate* is a nonsensical Chinese translation of the English
word "smart." It references a cultural style practised by a group of Chinese youths. Tracing back to Visual Kei, a Japanese music genre that
mimics the visual elements of Western glam rock, this Chinese cultural
counterpart had little to do with music but was all about elaborate hair-
styles, dramatic makeup, and flamboyant outfits (see fig. 1.1). When
it was first started in Hong Kong, a first stop for global cultural im-
ports to China, the cultural style was considered an edgy and hip cultural alternative to the urban mainstream. For that reason, the "smart"
culture spread to the mainland through the Internet, attracting young
people of different social demographics, including many rural migrant
workers new to urban life. Although, as a cultural group, its members
mainly hang out in exclusive online communities, that exclusivity did
not stop "the gaze" of the online mainstream from producing its own
hegemonic recoding of the term. Nowadays, as the colourful visual and
textual imageries of the members of *shamate* are readily available online
everywhere people care to click, the term has begun to mean something
completely different within mainstream online discourses. Journalist
Rachel Lu (2013) provided a profile of these young people in a report

Figure 1.1. *Shamates*. Source: Fair use/shangdu.com in Rachel Lu,
"Vanity Fail," *Foreign Policy*, 2 December 2013, https://foreignpolicy.
com/2013/12/02/vanity-fail/

on the subject: *shamates* are "in their late teens or early 20s, often with
less than high-school educations and few marketable skills, working
low-paying jobs in the big cities, like a barber, security guard, deliv-
eryman, or waitress." In stark contrast to the "smart" style, *shamates'*
exaggerated colourful hairdos, kitsch clothing, and cheap accessories
such as an off-brand cellphone, are anything but "smart" in the eyes
of hip city residents. Far from a trendy urban lifestyle, *shamate* has become synonymous with "cheap," "rustic," "contrived," and "uncouth"
in mainstream online discourse. No longer a subject of alternative culture, but instead an object of widespread online shunning and mock-
ing, *shamates* are relentlessly disdained and rejected by urban yuppies
and cultural elites (Lu, 2013).

The term *diaosi* has a cultural trajectory of its own. *Diaosi*, roughly
meaning "loser," originated from an online fan community dedicated
to a Chinese soccer player. That community is a popular online space
where a large number of fans, non-fans, and onlookers hang out. Differences of opinion in their sometimes heated discussions about the soccer
player, Chinese soccer, and other broad social issues, gave birth to the

term, which was meant to be a denigrating label of some fans by their opponents. As the term circulated across communities, its original context-specific signification quickly became decontextualized, and then recontextualized according to the new set of discursive relations among the interlocutors in the most current context. The term soon shed its derogatory connotation to become a self-mocking label that people voluntarily wore. While the term reached a certain level of notoriety, its meaning started to stabilize in people's efforts to interpret and reflect on it. The identity label finally became attached to a uniform image: that of a young male college graduate working a dead-end job, with little prospect of saving enough to own an apartment or a car, or to have the other basic trappings of middle-class life – and, for that reason, unable to get a girlfriend (P. Yang et al., 2014). *Diaosi* is often caricatured and contrasted with an equally exaggerated representation of an opposing imaginary – the *gaofushuai*, who is "tall, rich, and handsome" a term that usually refers to the privileged upper echelon of Chinese youth who often inherit wealth and power from their parents (Szablewicz, 2014).

A vivid graphical sketch of both male and female *diaosi* soon started to circulatete on the Internet (fig. 1.2). According to the labels on the sketch, a male *diaosi*:

- has no more than 1,000-Yuan of cash in his pocket
- wears shoes that cost no more than 800 Yuan
- had no more than three girlfriends before marriage
- has a year-end bonus that doesn't exceed 10,000 Yuan
- drinks Master Kong green tea
- wears Jeanswest 361 Degrees
- smokes cigarettes that cost less than 20 Yuan
- drives a car that cost less than 100,000 Yuan
- drinks only Chinese rice liquor and beer
- hasn't travelled long-distance in the past three to five years

The female *diaosi*:

- has never had a bikini
- doesn't wear bright nail polish
- doesn't wear matching underwear
- never wears shoes with heels over 5 cm
- hasn't changed her hairstyle for more than half a year
- has tried to lose weight for more than five months
- doesn't dare to grin broadly

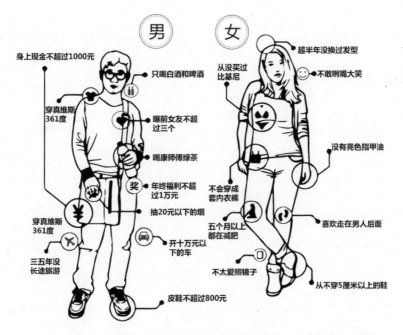

身上现金不超过1000元
只喝白酒和啤酒
穿真维斯361度
曝前女友不超过三个
喝康师傅绿茶
年终福利不超过1万元
抽20元以下的烟
穿真维斯361度
开十万元以下的车
三五年没长途旅游
皮鞋不超过800元

男   女

超半年没换过发型
从没买过比基尼
不敢咧嘴大笑
没有亮色指甲油
不会穿成套内衣裤
五个月以上都在减肥
喜欢走在男人后面
不太爱照镜子
从不穿5厘米以上的鞋

Figure 1.2. Male and female *diaosi*. Source: "Don't be too harsh on diaosi, Xiaoba tells the life story of Tuhao," sohu.com, 14 November 2013.

- always stays behind when walking with men
- doesn't like, or like too much, to look in the mirror

Both *shamate* and *diaosi* are signifiers of new subjects constituted in the dynamic symbolic processes in which various actors participate by socializing through the Internet. The communication processes have connected the otherwise heterogeneous domains of meaning, both semantic and social, into discursive totalities (Laclau, 2005). These discursive realms included networks of global cultural flow, communities of popular (sub)culture, and currents of consumerism, among others. As the two signifying terms spread across multiple domains, the terms picked up complex layers of meaning. In addition to comments from media scholars and critics, the terms also attracted the attention of powerful institutional actors during their quick promulgation. For instance, *People's Daily*, the leading organ for the Chinese Communist Party (CCP), published an editorial commentary on the *diaosi* phenomenon, warning the public of an unhealthy "*diaosi* mentality." Marketers, on the other hand, were keen to adopt the identity labels and vernacular to connect with their target consumers in promotional campaigns (Szablewicz, 2014). The terms became common yet fluid signifiers differentially employed by practitioners of popular culture, consumerism, market strategies, and official propaganda, all of which in turn contributed to their further popularity.

However fluid the terms, the imagined subjects they conjure up in the symbolic sphere are in fact deeply rooted in the economic and political structures of contemporary China. Discourses surrounding *shamate* and *diaosi* were specific symbolic projects linked with material practices embedded in power relations. They were the outcome of a symbolic struggle for people to put into words their perceptions of the economic order that they experience. Discourse both reflects and constitutes economic and political relations and power structures at various levels, ranging from class relations at the societal level to relations specific to particular institutions such as family, community, and workplace (Fairclough, 1992). While unequal distribution of wealth has reached a historical level amid China's rapid transition to a market economy in recent decades, rapid privatization and urbanization, together with rising consumerism, have led to further social and cultural stratification (Bian, 2002; Y. Zhao, 2008). The discourses about *shamate* and *diaosi* were expressions of the widening gap between social groups and increasing class friction. Whereas *shamate* embodies alienated underclass strangers living on the fringes of China's big cities, *diaosi* represents a class of urban youth, self-perceived as "underprivileged losers" with low socioeconomic status, boring lives, and a hopeless future. Established in opposition to its imaginary counterpart *gaofushuai*, the dimension of self-mockery in *diaosi* identity expressed a deep sense of disillusionment with the possibilities for upward socio-economic mobility and the hardening of social structures (Lu, 2013; Szablewicz, 2014; P. Yang et al., 2014).

Yet, representations of the economic and political reality are necessarily mediated by the symbolic space's own power structure. Discursive production requires cultural and social capital, which is always unevenly distributed among social actors (Bourdieu, 1989). The resultant discourse is the outcome of the symbolic struggle won by those who are rich in symbolic resources. The dominant players are able to elevate their existential and instrumental logics to a hegemonic position within the heterogeneous symbolic space (Latham & Sassen, 2005). In the case of *shamate* and *diaosi*, the discourses presented the growing social disjunctures in Chinese society perceived and understood through a particular lens. The middle-class urban online population cynically adopts an artificial underclass identity by depicting themselves as *diaosi* in relation to its imagined counterparts of *gaofushuai*, "the winner" and *shamate*, "the loser." *Diaosi*'s self-perceived "have-not" status, however, not only stands in contrast to the "proletariat" identity, which had been the historical subject of China's Communist social revolution (P. Yang et al., 2014), but it also eclipses the contemporary life experience of the real underclasses, who are invisible online. Therefore, these interconnected semantics, images, and understandings serve particular social groups as vehicles for representing the forms and causes of deprivation. The symbolic force of dominant social groups filled the public agenda with their own objectives in their appropriation of the language of social inequality.

Indeed, *shamate* and *diaosi* are not isolated terms but rather semantic components of cultural structures – systems of symbols and meanings that underlie social practices. In creating and articulating such terms as *shamate* and *diaosi* through their discursive practices, social actors amend and reconstitute the existing meaning systems that provided the symbolic resources for such practices in the first place (Sewell, 2015). Such cultural structures provide categories and frames of reference by which we understand economic and political orders. As the example of *shamate* and *diaosi* demonstrate, in applying the terms to understanding and critiquing a wide array of socio-political issues, social actors "set up inside and outside positions" along cultural and economic fault lines and seek emotional bonding among themselves (Meng, 2011, p. 47). As they encode and decode such terms, various social actors evaluate and identify with these positions through metaphoric, imagistic, and narrative associations in which they at the same time subject themselves to the body of knowledge and rules contained within these terms (Hall, 2001). Consequently, association among similarly socialized people and dissociation among those from different backgrounds are affirmed through such discursive practices. In this light, discourse may serve as the symbolic base on which social distinction is realized and social groups are formed.

On the other hand, discursive articulation is never total but always an "overdetermination of heterogeneous elements" (Laclau, 2005, p. 235). It is the result of a dynamic process where meaning is created through the participation of diverse, and often conflicting, social actors speaking from multiple and changing positions. Terms and images such as *shamate* and *diaosi* are elements of a floating semantic network that may be applied in different contexts, therefore taking on new meanings in the ongoing course of articulation (Szablewicz, 2014). As the term *diaosi*, for instance, was further promulgated within a wider group of constituencies on the Internet, the domain expanded enormously in places where the notion of "underprivileged losers" would come into use. Successful entrepreneurs, elite professionals, and cultural celebrities all started applying the term to refer to themselves in one way or another. In doing so, they actively participated in the symbolic game of framing desires for social mobility. As such, the term mutated into a broad identity that many of the urban mainstream are willing to wear for themselves (P. Yang et al., 2014). In their current forms, discourses of *shamate* and *diaosi* are hardly fully developed ideologies or worldviews but, instead, "meanings and values as they are actively lived and felt" (Szablewicz, 2014, p. 269). In this light, it is counterproductive to read the content of the terms too literally: "What is important is an understanding of the symbolic and social mechanisms involved in the perpetuation and evolution of the terms in the articulation process" (Szablewicz, 2014, p. 270).

Discursive Articulation

The examples of *shamate* and *diaosi* have illustrated how discourses both capture and constitute social change and how they are produced by various individual and institutional actors with specific purposes and in specific contexts. Indeed, as the product of symbolic practices, discourses take shape at multiple intertwining levels. These strata include the lifeworld of the personal as well as the propositions of the public and institutional realms of society. At the personal level, social actors make sense of who they are and what to do in life by constructing coherent life stories. Lifeworld discourses are sustained and transformed by interpersonal webs of relations (Somers, 1992, 1994). Take, for example, the rising discourse on privacy in China that manifests in the form of millions of postings about personal life on Sina Weibo, one of China's largest social media sites. The majority of these messages have to do with people's most immediate concerns regarding their social roles and personal relations in everyday life. The discourses on privacy both reflect and constitute people's understandings and practices with regard to the changing relationship between the private self and public milieus (see chapter 3).

At the public and institutional levels, discourses are attached to structural entities larger than the single individual. Such entities represent intersubjective networks or institutions, ranging from family, the "publics," and corporations, to the state and its agents (Somers, 1992, 1994). Discursive regimes such as the ideologies of neoliberalism and nationalism are crucial for institutional actors seeking to manage and regulate social and economic life in a way that favours their own interests and survival. Such discursive regimes provide institutional power with form, substance, and solidity by making their ideologies appear coherent, rational, and commonsensical to people (Kitchin & Dodge, 2011). With its dominance over the production and dissemination of public discourses, for instance, the Chinese party-state was able to mobilize the nation for its modernization project through hegemonic discourses on economic development, patriotism, and international relations in the socialist era (Cao et al., 2014).

Institutional forces, however, are not monolithic and essential entities preordained and fully formed outside of social life to shape it from a distance. They are produced and sustained through ongoing, relational, and contingent discursive and material practices of many different individual and collective actors (Kitchin & Dodge, 2011). Complex and always evolving, institutions are emerging through processes of contestation and negotiation among different competing ideas, interests, agendas, and ways of life. Consequently, discursive regimes are always in the process of taking shape, consisting of a multitude of communications and discussions, all interpreted and acted upon in diverse ways. Beneath the veneer of coherence, consistency, and stability, institutions and structures are in a constant state of metamorphosis. Never to be fixed, discourses only interact to produce a particular trajectory of interrelated sets of social representations in a specific context.

What is at issue, therefore, is articulation – the "unity" of a discourse in which diverse symbolic elements come to form more or less stable structures of meaning that underlie social practices (Chouliaraki & Fairclough, 1999). As Stuart Hall obverves, the linkage among different elements is not "necessary, determined, absolute and essential for all time." A discourse can be rearticulated in different ways. What we need to find out is under what circumstances or historical conditions a connection can be forged or made between the articulated discourse and the social forces (Hall, 1986, p. 53). The dynamic process of articulation of various discursive resources through the voices of social actors in relation to their social-economic positions is the key to understanding the meaning of social action and relations (Slack, 1996).

Social discourses take place in social networks – that is, relational settings made of "contested but patterned relations among people and institutions" (Somers, 1992, p. 610). The distinctiveness of the socio-technical features of the Internet contributes to the development of relational settings, social domains, and institutional frameworks, which

otherwise would be absent. It digitally stages large-scale complex en-
sembles of interaction, space, and organization that move beyond direct interaction at specific places (Latham & Sassen, 2005). The Internet
rescales geo-corporeal social relations and domains by temporally and
spatially shifting the relations that form the coordinates of social discourses produced at various levels.

Forms of Internet Sociality

In modern history, the social organization of symbolic practices and
interactions has long relied on the development of communication media. New forms of communication media often change the symbolic
character of social life by reorganizing the ways in which symbolic
content are produced and exchanged, as well as by restructuring the
ways in which actors relate to each other in society (Thompson, 1995,
p. 11). Mass media, for instance, in their early development alongside
modern society, played crucial roles in bringing people together across
time and space. According to Habermas, before newspapers became
fully market-driven in early modern Europe, they facilitated rational
deliberative processes, which connected voluntary personal relationships and communities to a bourgeois public sphere where social
problems were contested and decisions were made (Habermas, 1991;
Wessler, 2008). Anderson's notion of the imagined community, as another example, explains how the print media had created possibilities
for shared experience of belonging and identities in the construction
and integration of community across extra-local space (Anderson,
2006). In contrast, broadcast media such as television do not tend to
foster public discourse. As one-way means of communication, they often reach a large number of people in spatially and socially dispersed,
privatized settings rather than bringing them together as members of a
community (Calhoun, 1998a). On the other hand, TV does provide an
informational environment that contributes to the breakdown of the
socio-informational barriers that used to delineate the boundaries of
distinct social groups along the lines of age, gender, and social hierarchy (Meyrowitz, 1986).

   At the peak of the mass media era, information and symbolic content
were produced and disseminated under a highly centralized institutional model with a relatively stable set of rules, resources, and social
relations. Cultural gatekeepers such as journalists, editors, and producers played a predominant role in determining what audiences or consumers came to see and how they would see it. While audiences were
not always passive receivers in the process, there was nevertheless a

structured break between production and reception (Thompson, 1995). Consequently, media discourse and public opinion became two parallel systems, with the former exerting great power in setting the agenda for the latter (Gamson & Modigliani, 1989). Moreover, as social institutions, mass media were embedded in and affected by broader political and economic systems, which varied across different societies and times (Hallin & Mancini, 2004). In contrast to the highly commercial system in the United States, for instance, mass media in China used to be an integral part of the political system. The media system was organized in a centralized hierarchical structure comprising different levels of media outlets, which corresponded to various political and administrative levels. Within such a structure, media discourses were produced mainly by media professionals and social elites under the tight control of the party-state (Y. Zhao, 2008; see chapter 2).

The implications of the Internet for symbolic practices and social interactions contrast with those of traditional mass media. Internet-mediated communications and interactions are not organized as one single political or social institution with standard practices and procedures fully defined by pre-existing conventions and social relations (G. Yang, 2012). Instead of a monolithic medium, the Internet enables a rich terrain of human communicative activities by "remediating" all existing forms of media, from the electronic networks of the telegraph and the telephone to the audio-visual forms of radio and television (Bolter & Grusin, 1999). Nor are Internet-mediated communications the product of one single professional actor, with a high degree of distinctiveness and homogeneity, such as the kind that defined journalism (Sparrow, 1999).

As people's experiences with network technology become more expansive and more routine, all kinds of social actors congregate on networks, constantly engendering new modes of interaction and producing multiple forms of symbolic content (Newhagen & Rafaeli, 1996; Lievrouw, 2004, p. 11). People generate a rich repertoire of use by approaching the Internet from a variety of structural as well as situational motivations, needs, and ideologies. Therefore, the symbolic power of the Internet results both from its empowering features that enact contingent and contested spaces, and from forms of engagement created by individuals and social groups who take advantage of the network features. In this light, the Internet and associated network technologies have not only extended the means of symbolic expression and dissemination to a wider network of social agents, but also significantly reorganized the structure and conditions that underlie symbolic exchange and social interaction in society (Poster, 1990: 45; S. Zhao, 2006).

Symbolic practices enabled by the Internet have great implications for contemporary social life at all levels. In the lifeworld of personal and informal associations, the Internet has transformed the social domains of the self, bringing about a new "horizon of possibility" for the individual actor (Couldry & Hepp, 2018). The spatiotemporal conditions of everyday interaction and communication – the "horizon of expectation" (the time the individual can anticipate and be oriented toward) and the "space of experience" (one's sphere of immediate action) (S. Zhao, 2006) – have become both flexible and malleable. Intimate personal relations, for instance, can now be extended to a mediated reach across large geographical space. Various types of personal relations, including families, friendships, and romantic partnerships, can be maintained through diverse patterns of connection enabled by such network platforms as email, blogs, social network sites, and microblogging sites (Tong & Walther, 2011). In addition, the Internet can serve as a communal space for community association built on shared identity, common goals, and reciprocal moral obligations among members. While traditional communities form out of shared geographical locations and embodied practices, closely knit online communities can be based entirely on common interests and mutual liking (Postill, 2008). The Internet is capable of facilitating solidarity by broadening and strengthening traditional neighbourhood communities based on common cultural traits (Wittel, 2001; Rheingold, 1993). Consequently, it has become a fertile ground for lifeworld discourses.

Internet sociality also takes the form of networks. The social logic of network sociality derives from voluntary, short-term, instrumental encounters among a large number of relatively loose social connections (Postill, 2008; Wellman et al., 2003). The Internet has proven a successful medium for people to mobilize based on interest-based, one-dimensional relations such as entertainment, commerce, or work-related activity. Such social relationships are indirect, existing only through the intermediation of information technology and/or bureaucratic organizations rather than physical co-presence (Calhoun, 1998a). On a broad level, these indirect relations are crucial for system integration through large-scale organizations of modem markets, capitalist production, and the state across time and space (Giddens & Pierson, 1998). These kinds of impersonal relations are the main form of association in modern Western civil society (Taylor, 1990).

More importantly, the Internet serves crucial bridging functions between diverse and distinct modes of communication that vary widely in scope, size, and relational context over broad spatial and temporal spectrums. Internet socialities provide mechanisms for switching in and out of established modalities of sociocultural interaction. The Internet is capable of facilitating not only relatively "bounded" and stable complexes of institutions such as lifeworld communities, states, economies, and civil societies, but also emergent social events and movements (Bennett & Segerberg, 2012; Emirbayer & Sheller, 1999). The interspatial connectivity of the Internet is conducive to large-scale conversations that grow from communication organized around topically connected small communities. In this way, personal issues may be elevated into a public affair through rapid network communication. Benkler (2006, p. 259), for instance, has demonstrated how attention to social issues in the networked environment spreads from engaged groups of people via websites with heavy internal links and reaches other clusters through external links. Still more often, Internet sociality develops in a rhizomatic fashion that reflects non-linear, heterogeneous, decentralized, and fluid network connections among diverse social actors. Online opinions and comments from myriad sources, stimulated by quickly spreading memes, hashtags, and buzzwords, feed off each other – thus generating further momentum of participation (Meng, 2011). Such moments can be affective as well as behavioural in nature, engendering structures of feelings and collective consciousness among participants (Papacharissi, 2015).

Embodying the multi-layered complexity of contemporary communication, Internet sociality is fluid, porous, and interstitial. It offers flexible means of communication that can be used to construct different social spaces by sufficiently motivated actors. Examples of such Internet sociality are legion in the Chinese context. In the private realm, animated discussions about such issues as mother-daughter, family, and marital relationships, for instance, are sparked by an increased amount of available information, access to other people's life experiences, and the possibility of discussing new issues through social networks mediated by the Internet (Pissin, 2015; Ye et al., 2014). People's understandings and debates of these issues both reflect and constitute the changing institutions of family and marriage at the confluence of the lingering Confucian tradition, shifting socialist ideals, and emerging (neo)liberal doctrines in contemporary Chinese society. The Internet is also capable of enabling collective representation, identification, and mobilization by mediating specific, group-related, and interest-defined discursive practices. Taking advantage of the open-ended flow of network communication, "socially distant interlocutors" may "bridge social-network positions, formulate collective orientations, and generate psychical 'working alliances,' in pursuit of influence over issues of common concern" (Emirbayer & Sheller, 1999, p. 156). Rongbin Han

(2015), for example, demonstrated how a constituency of Internet users, who identify themselves as "the voluntary fifty-cent army," acquire and consolidate their common identity in discursive battles against regime bashers. His observations also reveal that, beyond "us vs. them" encounters between regime supporters and opponents, Internet sociality is capable of generating performative and malleable power relations among multiple actors championing plural political values, ideas, and norms (see also Perry & Selden, 2003; Bian, 2002).

The structural change of mediated sociality calls for a revision of existing analytical categories. Corporeal co-presence is no longer the benchmark for evaluating all forms of human contact in the Internet era (S. Zhao, 2006). Rather than having to work through separate realms of "online or offline," "virtual or real," or "synchronous or asynchronous," social actors traverse the world as "collaborative spaces" across material and digital realms "while simultaneously interacting with the cultural inscriptions written into the experience" of these intertwining social milieus (Farman, 2013, p. 45). Actions and relations in the "virtual" space are "real" so long as they have actual consequences for and effects upon social agents. Moreover, Internet socialities also resist the rigid classification that previously separated interpersonal from mass communication, consumers of symbolic content from producers, or private communication from public discourse (Bruns, 2008a; Papacharissi, 2010). Offline personal connections may be maintained as online networks. Private and personal relations may facilitate public and civic participation on the ground. China scholars have shown, for instance, that the cultural practice of *guanxi*, the social networks of personal relations and favours that very much defined traditional Chinese sociality, can reduce barriers to civic participation by diffusing the risks of association and substituting for a public sphere. Pre-existing personal relations can potentially function as a mechanism for coping with the absence of a formal institutional structure of laws and regulations. Consequently, activism in China is often situated in a grey area between state and society where networks take shape from personal and informal interactions between multiple stakeholders acting both offline and online (Sullivan & Xie, 2009).

Internet Events

The sociality of the Internet unfolds in diverse ways through network socio-techno practices embedded in the specifics of the context. A symbolic space is constituted through the cultural process mediated by such sociality. One prominent example of Internet sociality in the

Chinese context has been "Internet events" (Qiu & Chan, 2011). Every year, numerous Internet events capture public attention for their mass participation, spontaneous mobilization, contentious nature, and dynamic processes, as well as their political and cultural consequences (Zhu, Shan, & Hu, 2011; Zhu, Liu, & Shan, 2012; Zhu, Pan, & Chen, 2015 and 2016). Scholars and critics have diligently chronicled and documented many such events over the years. Numerous cases have had significant implications for the expression of public opinion, civic activism, and potential social change in China.

One of the earliest and most publicized Internet events, the Sun Zhigang case, may serve as a good starting point for further discussion. Sun, a new university graduate from a rural area, was detained by police and later beaten to death in a detention centre for rural migrants in Guangzhou in 2003. The news of Sun's death quickly captured national attention as it spread via the Internet. The enormous response to the case made it one of the most memorable social events of the year.

A seemingly contingent rupture on the surface, the Sun Zhigang case was embedded in several densely intertwined and rapidly changing structural relations and institutional forces in Chinese society. First and foremost, the case implicated the deeply entrenched urban-rural divide in Chinese society (Y. Zhao, 2008). This schism was intensified when the economic reforms that began in the late 1970s had more or less relaxed the previously state-enforced restriction on the mobility of rural populations to the cities. Several highly developed urban areas in China had seen a growing number of rural migrants driven by an increasingly unsustainable agricultural sector and greater economic opportunities in the cities (Y. Zhao, 2008). However, rural migrants remained subject to various restrictions in terms of their employment and mobility in the cities. They were required, for instance, to obtain and carry a temporary work permit and a temporary residence permit. Failing to do so, as in Sun's case, subjected them to fines and detention.

Second, Sun's case exposed a growing bureaucratic crisis in state law enforcement (Y. Zhao, 2008). Faced with reduced state subsidies, the police departments relied on collecting fines from detainees to sustain the operations of city detention centres. Subsequently, due to the expanding scope of retention and shortage of personnel, detention centres were often staffed with temporary hires with little training and few qualifications. These developments all left shortfalls within which police brutality could mushroom.

Third, the changing political economic structure in the media market also played a crucial role in elevating the visibility of the Sun Zhigang case (Y. Zhao, 2008). As a result of the ongoing media commercialization that introduced market forces into the originally highly centralized media system operating on government subsidies, popular commercial newspapers flourished (see chapter 2). The story of Sun was first publicized by *Southern Metropolitan News* (*SMN*), at the time a new commercial paper trying to distinguish itself in the increasingly competitive market by cultivating an accessible tabloid style, publishing muckraking investigative stories, and adopting a liberal orientation. Attracting many liberal intellectuals to pen in-depth social commentaries, the paper was poised as an opinion leader in the Chinese commercial media sector (Y. Zhao, 2008). Also relevant was *SMN*'s status as a subsidiary affiliated with the party organ of the Guangdong provincial party committee, which was administratively superior to the party-state authorities in Guangzhou city, where the case occurred. The segmented political and media administrative regime created room for *SMN* to carry out its muckraking mission without fear of restriction by local authorities.

Finally, the case erupted at a critical moment for the central government's response. Mid-March 2003 witnessed the election of a new central administration at the conclusion of China's Tenth National People's Congress, signifying "the first smooth and orderly transition of power in modern Chinese history" (Tai, 2006, p. 221). In retrospect, Sun's arrest was almost fateful, given the heightened security at this politically sensitive moment. Equally significant was the new Chinese president Hu Jingtao's political stance. Trying to get out of the shadow of his predecessor, Hu was keen to establish his administration as people oriented and one that aligned with ordinary people, the poor, and the underprivileged. In the aftermath of Sun's death, the new leadership abolished the 1982 disciplinary detention regime and replaced it with a sweeping welfare reform program aimed at assisting the urban homeless, ensuring their basic livelihoods (Y. Zhao, 2008). In addition, suspects connected with Sun's death were arrested, and government officials and police officers faced party or administrative discipline for their roles in the case.

Nevertheless, it was the Internet that played the pivotal role in making the Sun Zhigang case a national event. After *SMN* made its report available on the Internet, the story quickly spread online like wildfire, catching national attention and leading to enormous public outrage. Mainstream national media including *People's Daily* and Xinhua News Agency promptly picked up the story and sent their own reporters to Guangzhou to follow up on the case. More importantly, there had been an explosive spontaneous outpouring of opinion in the form of bulletin board system postings, blog entries, news commentaries, open letters, and public protests on the Internet (Tai, 2006). In his detailed account of the case, Tai (2006) rightly suggested that, without the Internet, the scope of Sun's story might have been extremely limited and may perhaps even have remained an obscure local case. Without the timely dissemination of the news to a national audience through the Internet, it would never have mobilized a coalition of national news media, public intellectuals, human rights lawyers, and other activists; nor would tremendous pressure have mounted for a direct response from the central government, were it not for the palpable public outcry from millions of concerned individuals over the Internet. Based on these observations, Tai (2006) – and many other observers – concluded that the case established the Internet as a vehicle for a fledgling civil society to stand against the repressive bureaucratic system in China.

However, critical media scholar Zhao Yuezhi (2008) has pointed out that the struggle in the Sun Zhigang case had a more complicated pattern than can be captured by a simple civil society versus authoritarian state framework. Zhao took issue with the discrepancies between the language of universal rights in civil society and the dominant online discourse that ignored the social-economic rights of migrant workers in the case. Zhao noted that Sun, although born a rural resident, managed to acquire urban citizenship status by becoming a university student. In fact, his university graduate status gained him valuable social capital through his urban social networks, which became crucial in helping his peasant parents get access to media and material resources in their struggle to pursue justice for their son's death. By contrast, Sun's old status as rural migrant, a symbol of weak social groups, became secondary. Indeed, as the investigation of his death progressed, it exposed the fact that forty-six detainees had died in the same detention centre in the last quarter of the previous year without arousing any public notice (Tai, 2006). Using Sun Zhigang's identity as a point of departure, Zhao further argues that the media and Internet "crusade" on his behalf was a crusade for the civil rights of urban citizens, who were afraid that their own individual rights would be threatened by state administrative power (Y. Zhao, 2008, p. 264). It was in this light that public intellectuals' statements such as "Sun Zhigang died for me" make sense (Y. Zhao, 2008, p. 276). Although calls for the repeal of the detention and repatriation regulation occurred within a discourse of civil rights and constitutional governance, they did not critically question China's development path, which had led to the problem in the first place. The fact is that the detention system was created not by "an abstract evil state bent on curtailing the civil rights of every individual, but to protect the socio-economic interests of the urban population against rural migrants, and as part of China's developmental strategy" (Y. Zhao, 2008, p. 264). With the dominant frames centring primarily on the rule of law, arbitrary administrative power, police brutality, and the basic civil rights of individual citizens and supported by a coalition of the online public, activists, civic rights lawyers, and liberal intellectuals, the main discourse did not address migrant workers' economic and social rights, let alone the class interests of migrant workers and their conflicted class relationships within Chinese urban society (Y. Zhao, 2008, p. 264).

Moreover, Zhao linked the discursive rearticulation to the structural composition of Internet users at the time. Although the number of users had increased dramatically from the mid-1990s to the early 2000s and was approaching 70 million people, it remained the case that the online community was still "disproportionately young, male, urban, and college educated" – just like Sun Zhigang (Y. Zhao, 2008, p. 257). On the other hand, the two largest segments of the Chinese population, peasants and workers, made up only a trifling percentage of the Internet constituency. The three largest groups in the online population consisted of students (30.1%), service and office workers (28.1%), and technicians (15.9%); in short, users derived from the middle strata of contemporary Chinese society (CNNIC, 2003).

Thanks to existing accounts (e.g., Tai, 2006; Y. Zhao, 2008), it becomes clear that the Sun Zhigang event took shape at the intersection of the social and symbolic realms. The response to the event may have been the immediate result of mobilization through the Internet, but it was an inevitable consequence of the structural tensions between multiple social institutions. In other words, the driving force of transformative change in this case, as in the case of any other Internet events, was not the Internet per se, but rather the tensions at the manifold and intertwining structural and institutional disjunctures in a rapidly changing society (Sewell, 2005; see also chapter 2 below). Indeed, the Sun case became a critical social event because the symbolic power it mobilized led to changes in the political and bureaucratic structures in the form of state-sanctioned laws and regulations.

However, it was fundamentally a cultural and discursive process that made the case a truly "transformative event," a term historian William Sewell has used to indicate a significant occasion when a consequence of "contradictions between structures ... touches off a chain of occurrences that durably transforms previous structures and practices" (Sewell, 2005, p. 227). Emerging liberal terms such as "citizen," "civil rights," and "rule of law" took on authoritative meanings when these claims were made on behalf of the enormous level of public opinions

made visible by the Internet. In this sense, "events are, literally, significant: they signify something new" (Sewell, 2005, p. 245). One among
several other high-profile events in the same year, the Sun Zhigang case
has led critics to hail the year 2003 as the "Year of Network Opinion"
in China (Tai, 2006), signifying the beginning of the Internet as a formi-
dable symbolic space. Through the discursive practices of an emergent
coalition of liberal participants, what really exists (the massive number
of spontaneous responses mobilized via the Internet) was interpreted
in terms of what is good (the united public's will) and what is possible
(civil society, a new kind of relation between the state and the public in Chinese society) (Sewell, 2005, p. 245). However, the role of migrant workers as a "counter-public" was largely absent in the process
(Y. Zhao, 2008). Such acts of "signification" have the potential power to
reconstruct the very categories through which we understand political
culture and political action. It is the symbolic power to change cultural
structures that makes happenings such as this one truly momentous
events (Sewell, 2005).

Given their arresting frequency, scale, and impact, Internet events
have been an intriguing research subject for scholars of Chinese communication (see, e.g., Miao, 2014; Qiu & Chan, 2011). Yet there has been
little recognition of the inherent paradox in their understanding: on
one hand, each Internet event is a unique episode of ordering symbolic
practices of diverse and intricately related social actors, both individual and institutional. The forms and nature of Internet events change
from one incident to the next, bringing together a mix of agents, relations, logics, time, and space. Consequently, the social patterning of
the symbolic practices of diverse social actors is necessarily nuanced
and complex. Each event is an erupting occasion wherein social actors
creatively interpret and act in mediated situations and contingencies
within which they are presently embedded. On the other hand, Internet
events are also overlapping and mutually influential (Sewell, 2005). As
an unfolding event weaves together multiple and complex social actors
and institutions, it becomes a node entangled in a loosely articulated
network of social structures. In fact, "the sequences of occurrences"
becomes an event only when "a cascading series of developments ...
would potentially affect structural relations among the broad range of
participants" (Sewell, 2005, p. 227). An event exposes multiple structural ruptures in a rapidly changing society. Actions of different social
actors are motivated by social dislocations brought about by mutating
state-society relations, increasing political decentralization, economic
liberation, social stratification, urbanization, and individualization in
Chinese society. More importantly, as this chapter emphasizes, each

Internet event marks a specific way in which different social forces, differentially located in various kinds of political and economic power structures, operate through the discursive sphere enabled by the Internet. The articulation of these power structures in the discursive event is affected by the power dynamics in the discursive sphere itself. The outcome of discursive articulation bears long-term potential to shape the course toward transforming these very structures.

The meaning of any Internet event, however, is underdetermined by the structural positions of participating social actors alone. In fact, Internet events are often occasions for diverse social groups to re-evaluate the cultural content of important social categories such as gender, age, and class, through symbolic activities (Holt, 1997). In light of the indeterminacy and uncertainty of relations in a rapidly changing society, the preferences, interests, and identities of people are as much outcomes as antecedents of public discussion and debates within the discursive event (Fraser, 1990; Sewell, 2005). The recursive presence of particular group identities is often an outcome of this discursive process (Somers, 1994). The significance of Internet events, therefore, is better understood as inscribed in the discursive practices of understanding and representing patterns of relationships by the participants themselves, which continually shift over time and space (Hall, 1992).

Indeed, Internet events are not independent of their communication. Social tensions play out through a discursive process participated in by all the relevant players variously positioned in the newly constituted symbolic space enabled by the Internet. Unlike traditional media events in the mass communication era, when mass media served a structural functional role in society by exerting centralized control over access to public visibility (Dayan & Katz, 1992), Internet events are the product of the spontaneous process of simultaneous symbolic interactions among diverse social actors. The Internet enables a process in which social actors and groups select, combine, and juxtapose symbolic resources, to produce meanings collectively through emotional compulsion, intersubjective understanding, or rational deliberation (Sewell, 2005; Somers, 1992). The very object of the event is constructed by the particular configuration of collective representations in a given social setting (Hall, 1992). The transformative power of Internet events lies in their capacity to affect how public attention and subjectivity is mobilized, organized, and defined. In doing so, Internet socialities create new modes of exercising symbolic power, the ability to mobilize symbolic resources for the formation, interaction, and transformation of the public. In this light, an Internet event is not simply the outcome of existing structures, but is often a means to strive for a new order.

Conclusion

Social change entails bundles of communications. In times of change, social actors' expectations, assumptions, and habits of everyday life are suspended and raised to the level of discourse, where they can be contested (Bourdieu, 1991; Chouliaraki & Fairclough, 1999).

The rise of the Internet in Chinese society has been deeply implicated in the "identity," "relational," and "ideational" dimensions of social change in contemporary China (Fairclough, 1992). As two examples, *shamate* and *diaosi* are among the new social categories that capture the cultural and social ethos of the moment. They exemplify how discursive practices mediated by the Internet affect the ways in which social subjects and identities emerge and social relations and power dynamics are constructed and negotiated in Chinese society.

As a network of communication that mediates social life, the Internet simultaneously shapes and is shaped by new practices of social interaction. On the one hand, Internet-mediated discursive processes are outcomes of struggles among diverse groups of social actors situated in intertwining structural disjunctions in the changing society. On the other hand, fluid and multifaceted Internet socialities not only open up more space for interaction, but also enact new communicative practices and modes of discursive articulation.

Internet events, in particular, have become an important way in which various understandings and representations of Chinese society are communicated, confirmed, and contested through discourses. While generating and circulating an enormous volume of messages in a variety of picto-textual forms enact palpable representations of public opinion, Internet events acquire their meanings in the ongoing struggle of their participants to interpret these messages. The significance of an Internet event, therefore, is neither determined by the pre-existing power structures nor inherent in the event. As the Sun Zhigang case demonstrates, the outcome of the symbolic struggle arose from the complex interplay of the material structure in which the early Chinese Internet population was embedded and the symbolic structure of the contingent discursive process.

"Internet event" itself is a controversial new category. Many other labels have been used to denote large-scale social events mediated by the Internet. They include "new media events" (*xinmeiti shijian*) (Qiu & Chan, 2011), "online mass incidents" (*wangluo qunti shijian*) (Jiang, 2012), "collective actions," "cyberprotests," and "social movements" (Tai, 2006; G. Yang, 2009; Y. Zheng & Wu, 2005). By applying these different labels, critics, scholars, and commentators from various backgrounds choose to emphasize different characteristics of the events such as their mass scales, dynamic processes, spontaneous responses, political and cultural consequences, and/or their contentious nature. These diverse characterizations reflect the different positions and perspectives of the observers and scholars in their efforts to apply relevant frameworks to relate patterns of communication to broader social concerns.

Following the theoretical explication of discursive formation and Internet sociality in this chapter, the next chapter moves to situate the rise of the Internet as symbolic space in the broad structural transformation of the cultural realm in China. Together, these two chapters set the general framework and background for understanding the three empirical cases in the remainder of the book. These cases strive to illustrate the specific dynamics between discursive practices, social structures, and network communication in their respective intuitional contexts.

2

The Rise of the Internet as Symbolic Space

The twists and turns of a rapidly changing society have generated a host of images of the Chinese Internet: "the public sphere" (Lagerkvist, 2005), "pressure cooker" (Hassid, 2012), "online carnivals" (Herold & Marolt, 2011), "digital opium" (Leibold, 2011), "echo chamber," "online vigilantism" (Ong, 2012), "digital Maoism" (F.Y. Wang, 2009), "cyber-ghettos" (Johnson, Bichard, & Zhang, 2009), "the rumor machine" (H. Wang, 2012). The metaphors and labels are legion. As these varied images reveal, the Chinese Internet comprises material patterns of a myriad of symbolic and interactive practices exercised by an expanding group of social actors.

Diverse empirical accounts bear two significant implications for the understanding of the rise of the Internet as symbolic space in China. First, they have rendered inadequate the dichotomy of "democratic liberation" and "authoritarian control" as the master narrative of the Chinese Internet (Yuan, 2014). Instead, they bring forth the complex dynamics of consonance, conflict, and compromise between growing social forces and the Chinese state (C. Huang, 2007; Meng, 2010; Rosen, 2010). In fact, the rise of the Internet as symbolic space has been possible only within the context of "the fundamental reorientation" of both state and society in China (P.C. Huang, 1993). Actively promoted by the post-socialist reform-oriented state, the commercialization of the media and cultural institutions has set a premise for the development of a relatively independent cultural realm operating on mechanisms other than political ideology. Built by the Chinese government as the information backbone for its ambitious post-industrial development drive, the Internet has been subsequently activated as a key venue for the new cultural realm by the booming information and communication industries, thriving media markets, and flourishing popular cultures it has helped catalyse.

Second, the varied images indicate that the Internet has become an important discursive site on which the growing energy of China's pluralizing social forces plays out. Symbolic interplays mediated by the Internet enact multiple orientations of various publics. Driven by different political and economic interests, the competitive symbolic interactions among the actors in diverse social domains constitute different discursive fields where new identities and relations are generated with the potential to alter the existing order of political and economic life.

The debate contesting the role of the Internet in the changing environment of political communication is itself a telling example. Among the various perspectives on the topic is the prominent discourse that the rise of the Internet has revived a growing civil society in China (Tai, 2006; G. Yang, 2009). In this context, civil society mediated by the Internet may be conceived as a field of discursive connections (Calhoun, 1993a). Within this field, there are clusters of communications organized around various issues, ranging from environmental protection to migrant workers' rights. Involved in these different clusters are varied sets of actors, such as public intellectuals, research institutes, human rights lawyers, journalists, foundations, and government agencies. These clusters may then be woven into a wider network of more universal concerns through even looser communications linking organizations, institutions, and activists. Rearticulating the notion of "the public" around the ideas of civic rights and participation instead of class, exploitation, and the masses, the liberal discourses of civil society have mobilized, organized, and oriented numerous incidents of mass participation in discursive events mediated by the Internet. The symbolic struggles have in turn altered the power of social players in political communication in the Chinese context.

This chapter starts by providing a historical account of the structural transformation of the cultural realm in China to set up the background for the understanding of the development of the Internet as cultural space. It goes on to explicate the multifaceted forces that have structured Internet-mediated cultural spaces. Finally, it posits that symbolic practices and cultural processes enacted by the Internet often form a field structure that comprises highly differentiated positions delineated by actors' political, economic, and cultural capitals and their social interests.

The Structural Transformation of the Cultural Realm

The cultural system in China has gone through a historical rearticulation of the confluence of public policies, commercial practices, cultural events, and popular attitudes in the past decades. The waning of the previously totalitarian political ideology created room for new cultural spaces. At the same time, the development of cultural markets and industries stimulated cultural production and consumption. The simultaneous rise of popular culture sustained broad cultural participation. The rise of the Internet came to serve as a new space for cultural participation. These structural transformations opened up opportunities for actors to forge new positions and alliances through symbolic practices. The interlocking communicative and discursive networks of individuals and institutions produce field structures that organize symbolic struggles for a new order.

Up until the late 1970s, the production and dissemination of social discourse was organized within a highly centralized cultural system in socialist China. In this system, news media such as Xinhua News Agency, *People's Daily*, and China Central Television (CCTV) – as well as other cultural institutions, including film, literary associations, performance arts, and education – operated as public service units (PSUs) owned and funded by the government and its branches (Shambaugh, 2007; X. Zhang, 2006). The system followed an explicit "party principle," demanding that cultural PSUs serve as the mouthpieces of the Chinese Communist Party (CCP) to convey official views to the people (Lei, 2011; Y. Zhao, 1998). In addition, the system was purported to follow the "mass line," a party-mandated public interest principle, to represent and serve "the masses" of the Chinese people (Renwick & Cao, 1999; P. Thornton, 2011; Y. Zhao, 1998). In practice, though, the cultural system tended to deviate from the "mass line," generating an outlook biased toward the elite and the bureaucracy at the expense of the people (Townsend, 1967).

This top-down, pedagogic, and hegemonic system supported the omnipresent party-state as the centre of social life. Intellectuals and media professionals were either affiliated with the political mainstream or silenced for their dissenting voices (Goldman, 2005). Alternative structures of cultural resources, such as those generated by grassroots associations or personal networks, were marginal at best (Tu & Du, 1994). Given the political monopoly over the cultural system, official discourses were able to reach the innermost cells of society, contributing to the politicization of society and the erosion of boundaries between public and private lives (Renwick & Cao, 1999).

Despite the state's substantial retreat from the social realm in the post-socialist era, state political discourses still exert significant influence on Chinese society (Cao et al., 2014). As indispensable instruments to manage social change in China, carefully orchestrated official discourses are crucial to channel important aspects of present change as well as future direction. The established discourses of "social stability" and "national revival" as well as emerging themes of "soft power" and "the Chinese dream," for instance, highlighted "a new set of priorities, imperatives and values that valorize growth and stability, harmony and peace, and prosperity and rise" (Cao et al., 2014, p. 7). Moving away from heavy-handed political ideology, however, official discourses have become increasingly "practical, flexible and adaptive" to an expanded and pluralistic space for bottom-up participation (Cao et al., 2014, p. 12; Mertha, 2009; Shirk, 2008, 2011).

Starting in the 1980s and continuing into the 1990s, the cultural system went through significant transformations as China embarked on state-led economic reforms, opening an era of post-socialist development (Chu, 1994; P.S.N. Lee, 1994; C.C. Lee, 2003; Y. Zhao, 1998, Y. Zhao, 2008). In the early stages of this rapid yet incremental reform process, cultural public service units were allowed simultaneously to conduct commercial activities in an ad hoc fashion. Developing revenue-seeking activities without forfeiting state ownership, cultural institutions morphed into a de facto "dual system" (X. Zhang, 2006, p. 304). The 1990s witnessed a deepening "market economy" in China, a move coinciding with the global wave of neoliberal reforms in different parts of the world (Harvey, 2007). It was also a time when the "dual system" of the cultural sector was further "transcended" by market-driven policies, compelling cultural institutions to develop full-scale commercial subsidiaries, although the state remained a source of funding for key cultural PSUs such as party-affiliated news media (Hong, 2014; X. Zhang, 2006, p. 304).

Developing and strengthening cultural industries became a central task in China's economic restructuring scheme in the 2000s when the central government pushed forward to grow a "cultural market economy" (Hong, 2014; J. Wang, 2001). During this period, partially commercialized branches of cultural institutions were further corporatized, with the state's role switching from that of sole owner to that of shareholder. Global and domestic private capital was allowed to enter the fast-growing cultural market. Encouraged by expansionist policies, new commercial cultural enterprises and media outlets proliferated. Various cultural industries, including film and television production, publishing and distribution, performance and entertainment, and digital video and animation, grew rapidly (Hong, 2014; Y. Zhao, 1998). The reforms in the 2000s, however, also saw the revival of cultural public service units (Hong, 2014; Y. Zhao, 2008). Reiterating "socialist core values," the central government increased the state budget for cultural public services, giving priority to rural and other economically deprived areas that were lagging in the market-driven development. Deeply entangled in the dual system of simultaneously sustaining socialist legacies of PSUs and growing profitable cultural industries, the state has had to constantly realign itself in the evolving relationships between the public and corporate sectors (Hong, 2014).

Nevertheless, the reforms significantly decentralized and diversified China's cultural system. An exploding number of media outlets and growing new digital and mobile distribution capacities created immense market demands for content. Concurrently, global and domestic private media companies competed to establish themselves as serious cultural players (Y. Zhao, 2008). Phoenix TV, one of the most popular channels in China, for instance, started as a joint venture between Rupert Murdoch's News Corporations and domestic capital. In the film industry, Hollywood entertainment conglomerates such as Time Warner teamed up with Chinese partners to remould the infrastructure as well as the cultural content of Chinese cinema. Even key state media institutions such as CCTV came to rely on independent producers and freelancers in the cultural market, instead of in-house personnel, for content production. In fact, domestic private capital dominated drama production, the most lucrative sector in Chinese television markets. Posing serious challenges to the state monopoly over cultural production and distribution, an accumulation-oriented categorization of culture as well as semi-autonomous socio-cultural sites for cultural production and expression emerged outside the state. Privately funded movies, television programs, publishing enterprises, non-official newspapers and magazines, and commercial Internet portals and services are among the major contenders for spreading mainstream cultural discourses (Y. Zhao, 2011; X. Zhang, 1998).

Enforcing profit imperatives, the transition toward the market economy significantly reconfigured power dynamics in the cultural sphere. As the market emerged as "an alternative arbiter" of cultural production, the state no longer possessed hegemonic claim over cultural authority (Hong, 2014, p. 613; C.C. Lee, 2000). Growing market competition exerted economic pressure on cultural producers to maintain high market shares. Consequently, cultural products became more dependent on popular appeal, and therefore more oriented toward and responsive to consumers (Y. Zhao, 1998). The characterization of cultural subjects shifted from the generalized political entity of "the people" as "the masters of society" in the socialist cultural system to "the audience" approached as individual consumers in the cultural markets (H. Yu, 2009). While growing financial independence and relative editorial freedom made room for media professionalism to emerge in direct competition with the paradigm of party journalism (Pan & Chan, 2003), highly commercialized cultural enterprises were compelled to conform to consumer tastes and popular sentiments (Tai, 2015).

No longer chained to communist ideology, cultural production and consumption in themselves became important economic activities in China (J. Wang, 2001). Yet that does not mean that economic rationales have completely taken over the new cultural realm. The reformist state remains a powerful player exercising political influence on cultural markets and institutions (Hong, 2014; J. Wang, 2001). While their commercialized subsidiaries are fully geared up to earn market profits, cultural institutions still serve the needs for meaning and mobilization among both the state and the publics. In this light, culture production has come to operate as a dynamic field where cultural practices can generate capital that various players may exchange for political, economic, and other social resources (J. Wang, 2001; Dai, 1999).

Stimulated by the state's economic initiatives to boost market demand, cultural consumption has come to occupy the centre of Chinese social life. Serving as the material base for popular culture, consumption continues to generate spaces for spontaneous and playful life experiences (J. Wang, 2001; Yan, 2002). In these spaces, people are free to renew their lifeworld experiences by developing friendships, kinship, and voluntary social ties. This kind of horizontal sociability differs from the vertical relationship between the state and subject-citizens (Davis, 2000). Socially connected, interest-oriented, and affectively engaged, online communities, for instance, emerged as a prevalent form of sociality (Kong, 2014). Subsequently, voluntary participation has often been taken as a token of liberal expressions of "egalitarian" consumer publics making free choices and pursuing individual desires (Fung, 2009; J. Wang, 2001). Growing out of "pedestrian pursuits of pleasure, distraction, curiosity, community, sociability," popular culture connects with people's affective feelings and beliefs in ways that official political discourses cannot (Jones, 2006, p. 366). In actively engaging with the "encoding" and "decoding" of cultural meaning, ordinary individuals acquire cultural agency in their everyday lives. Diverse forms of cultural expression become an important way to comment and reflect on a rapidly pluralizing society. Flourishing symbolic practices draw on such diverse cultural sources as ancient historical traditions, nascent modernity of the early twentieth-century republican era, the legacies of Maoist socialism, and contemporary global cultural flows (Link et al., 2001). While still shaped by external political and economic forces, cultural life in China has been reconfigured with a widening range of participants (Cao et al., 2014).

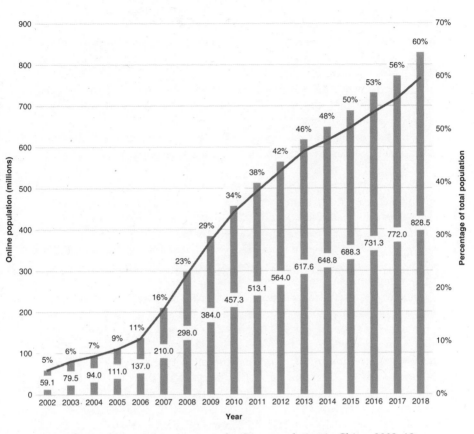

Figure 2.1. Size and percentage of online population in China, 2002–18.
Source: CNNIC (2019)

The Rise of the Internet as Symbolic Space

The Internet in China was born in the midst of social-economic reforms launched in the 1980s, which grew to their full scale in the 1990s
when the country took the decisive turn to establish a market economy.
As of the end of 2018, China's online population has grown to over
829 million, representing 59.6 per cent of the country's total population
(see fig. 2.1). Although great in number, China's online users are still
largely distinct from the Chinese population as a whole. They are relatively young: 53.5 per cent are between the ages of twenty and forty.
In contrast with its early stages, the Internet now connects many more
people with lower levels of education: 63.5 per cent of users have a
junior high or high school education, while 11.5 per cent are college

graduates. Geographically, an enormous digital divide remains. More than 70 per cent of the online population live in urban areas as students (25%), small business owners or self-employed individuals (22.7%), or white-collar workers (11.9%) (CNNIC, 2019).

Although first established at about the same time as in the United States and Europe, the Internet in China had a very different raison d'être (Herold & Marolt, 2011). Before it became a thriving space for information and communication for China's vast populace, it was conceived and built as an information infrastructure for economic development by the Chinese government. In the early 1990s, four major national networks were established, serving as the foundational infrastructure for the country's connection to the world (Shen, 2016). Later, the central government initiated twelve "Golden Projects" to form the technical backbone for various sectors ranging from banking and taxation to security and intergovernmental data exchange (Kluver, 2005; Tai, 2006).

Despite its image as a vehicle to challenge the state's role in the popular "liberation and control" discourse, the Internet in fact owed its existence to the will of the state to strategically boost its developmental capacities, and the Chinese government invested heavily to strengthen its ability to govern. The "Government Online Project," for instance, was launched in 1998 to facilitate the development of online administrative systems among various government agencies. By 2006, all thirty-one provinces, 93 per cent of municipal governments, and 69 per cent of county governments had official portals (M. Jiang, 2015). The effort to develop "e-government" in the 1990s and 2000s has extended well into the social media era. A 2016 directive from the General Office of the State Council required government agents at various levels to incorporate various social media platforms into their efforts, to be more responsive to public opinion (Zhu et al., 2016). Weibo, microblogging services, and WeChat – a cross-platform mobile messaging application – together with various mobile applications have become part of the architecture of public management. By the end of 2018, Chinese government agencies had been opened 17,962 websites, 138,253 Weibo accounts, and many other forms of online platforms (CNNIC, 2019). In addition, all thirty-one provinces as well as 84.7 per cent of provincial and municipal units have WeChat accounts, providing services related to public security, medical care, education, taxation, transportation, weather, tourism, and many other aspects of civic life (M. Jiang, 2015).

Having moved away from the ideological control and mass mobilization of the socialist era, the mode of governance in the post-socialist era is more "administrative and technocratic, and in some fields even consultative" (Heilmann & Perry, 2011, p. 3). Government policymaking processes, for instance, have come to accommodate diverse models involving a slew of non-state actors, including policy researchers, experts, media, stakeholders, and ordinary citizens (S. Wang, 2008). As the party-state's revolutionary legacies wane, efforts to improve administrative efficiency and accountability have become crucial to enhance the regime's performance-based legitimacy. As researchers have noted, China's political elites have become increasingly aware of the importance of incorporating online public opinion into their "strategic calculations" during political processes to generate a new kind of "symbolic legitimacy" (Noesselt, 2014; Y. Zhao, 2012). At various levels of government, the Internet has proven a highly cost-effective tool for providing feedback, channeling grievances, monitoring dissent, and managing public relations (Carnesecca, 2015).

Between the extensive landscape of state infrastructures and the world's largest online population lies a burgeoning commercial space. China's Internet industries have experienced meteoric growth in the past decade. Contrary to the image of a walled-off national "intranet," China's Internet economy is deeply integrated in the world economy in terms of the structure of capital, ownership, and managerial control of its leading corporations (Fuchs, 2016; L. Hong, 2014). Rivaling their counterparts in the United States and elsewhere in terms of revenue, the size of the user base, and stock valuation, Baidu (search engine), Alibaba (e-commerce), Netease (portal), and Shanda (online game) are among the leading players in the market, all of which are publicly traded on overseas stock exchanges (Batjargal, 2007; Jia & Winseck, 2018). They compete for creating and delivering popular online services for fast-expanding markets both home and abroad (see table 2.1). Running on user-generated content, many of these services represent much of what transpires as Web 2.0. Yet these Web 2.0 companies do not function simply as neutral conduits for communication and information. Rather, they are proprietary platforms striving to turn "user participation" into for-profit business (Van Dijck, 2013). For that purpose, their corporate governance structures, technological architecture, and communication protocols devise and encourage particular kinds of sociability and symbolic practices. While this commercial space does leave room for non-market peer-production enterprises, the cultural and social capital amassed are mostly exchanged for economic capital, directly enriching private business interests (Benkler, 2006; Van Dijck, 2013). Table 2.2 lists the most popular social media platforms in China. On these social media platforms, both established and emerging cultural players such as party-affiliated media, commercial media, government agents, private companies, professionals, and individuals vie for public attention.

On top of the interwoven political and economic structures extends a vibrant cultural landscape. If the marketization of cultural institutions

Table 2.1. Most popular types of Internet usage in China (December 2018)

Application	Users (millions)	Percentage of total users
Instant messaging	79.17	95.6%
Search engine	68.13	82.2%
Online news	67.47	81.4%
Online videos	61.20	73.9%
Online shopping	61.01	73.6%
Online payment	60.04	72.5%
Online music	57.56	69.5%
Online games	48.38	58.4%
Online literature	43.20	52.1%
Online banking	41.98	50.7%

Source: CNNIC, 2019

Table 2.2. Most popular social media platforms on the Chinese Internet (as of 2018)

Name	Company	Year established	Number of users (millions)	Main services
WeChat	Tencent	2011	1,100+	Instant messaging (text, video, voice) Group chat Social networking Online shopping, booking & payment
QQ	Tencent	1999	806+	Instant messaging Group chat Games & music Image hosting
Baidu Tieba	Baidu	2003	600+	Online communities Topic discussion boards Commenting
Sina Weibo	Sina	2009	392+	Microblogging Commenting News Video hosting
Douyin	ByteDance	2016	300+	Short video hosting Commenting Tipping

Source: Compiled by the author with data from the corporate websites.

turned the receiving masses into cultural consumers, Web 2.0 provides them a means to become active participants in cultural production (H. Yu, 2009). In their vital entanglement with the lifeworld, online cultural spaces energize spontaneous, heterogeneous, distributed, open-ended symbolic practices (Cao et al., 2014). Discursive struggles over cultural classification and representation now take place in routine interactions of daily life as much as in formal political conducts. In fact, the connection of private life to public and political issues happens more naturally in people's everyday cultural practices than in formal political settings. Take, for example, the popular practice of online parody, or *egao*. Subverting the authoritative meaning in the original message by deconstructing and remixing it online with other readily available multimedia imaginaries, such practices fuse entertainment, political critique, and cultural processes of meaning-making as well as cyber-ritual communication (Meng, 2011; Tang & Yang, 2011).

Extending the scope of the political, the cultural plane has come to serve as an alternative space for social contention (Yuan, 2014). As often as they problematize dominant formulations of key economic and political issues, online discourses are potentially subversive (Cao et al., 2014). Indeed, an unprecedented level of online discourse has promoted a wide range of redistributive and identity claims (G. Yang, 2009; Tai, 2006; Y. Zhao, 2008). Yet the Chinese state should not be seen as the single source of dominance, overshadowing other means of power or forms of oppression in social life (Yuan, 2014). Take the "Human Search Engine," a prominent Internet cultural phenomenon. It is a form of collective Internet vigilantism, which subjects certain individuals to a collective process of identification for the purpose of exposing them to public humiliation or censure. Motivated by popular sentiments, the Human Search Engine often targets economic and cultural elites and contests socio-cultural institutions and practices such as marriage and privacy (Herold & Marolt, 2011). The new feminist movement in China, as another example, extends its public reach through Internet-mediated symbolic activities in efforts to bring about cultural and normative change to patriarchal conventions and practices, rather than only aiming at political and economic policies of the state.

Increasing commercialization is accompanied by popular participation in the cultural realm previously monopolized by state power. While the rise of popular culture may draw public attention to private affairs at the expense of more important issues in social life, it often blurs the boundaries between the public and the private, and between the political and the cultural, by opening up opportunities for previously excluded actors to participate in public communication about a much expanded scope of social issues (Hallin, 2008). In this context, it has become ineffective when conceiving of Chinese communication to assume a monolithic centralized power, "a power that is either in control of everything or in an epic binary battle for democracy and political liberalization" (Cao et al., 2014, p. 3; Xia & Yuan, 2014). Rather, diffuse powers interact to shift political, economic, and cultural relations in various social domains. Consequently, the cultural realm teems with indeterminate processes of interpretation, negotiation, and contestation, which are participated in by diverse players including agents of the state, the market, and the popular culture.

The Internet as symbolic space comprises multiple concurrent sites where actors engage in plural discursive projects. Imbued with struggles, contradictions, and incoherence, the symbolic Internet does not take shape in homogeneity but rather in systematic articulations of difference (Lemke, 2005; H. Yu, 2009). In this context, symbolic practices mediated by the Internet often form a highly porous field structure in shifting processes negotiated by "differentially embedded social actors who mobilize resources through diverse extensive networks of engagement in order to pursue their interests and objectives" (Barnett, 2003, p. 78). Moreover, rather than pre-conceived interests and coherent agendas, such a structure enables emergent ways of relating to each other and evolving orientations toward social life, which are constantly renewed during the very symbolic processes.

The Public Realm and Many Publics

The development of the Internet as symbolic space has often been understood within the rising discourses of civil society and the public sphere in China (Herold, 2008; Rosen, 2010; Tai, 2006; G. Yang, 2003; X. Zhang & Zheng, 2009). These two concepts have frequently been applied to understanding the emergent public realm as a result of social and economic changes in the past decades in China (Calhoun, 1993a; Huang, 1993; Perry, 1994). Whereas the idea of civil society prescribes a self-organizing socio-economic sphere independent of the specific direction of state power, the notion of a public sphere emphasizes the formation of the public out of communicative actions of social actors in the making of such an autonomous society (Calhoun, 1993a; Habermas, 1974). Considered a liberal alternative to the diminishing socialist model of political communication, scholars have frequently applied the public sphere model to comprehend the ideas, practices, and outcomes of symbolic activities mediated by the Internet (Herold & Marolt, 2011; Lagerkvist, 2005). The Internet is characterized as a relatively free space for the dissemination of information and the formation of public opinion, often at the expense of the authoritarian Chinese state. The conceptualization of the Internet in terms of a public sphere codifies symbolic participation as public deliberation and citizen rights vis-à-vis the state. The concept of *wangmin* (netizens), for instance, is often used to describe Chinese online users. The diverse interests and activities mediated through the Internet are subsumed through this term into a unified category and imbued with the values of civic participation and a sense of solidarity (Han, 2018). "Netizens," as a discursive category, has become the online surrogate of "the public," "the abstract counterpart of public authority" in civil society discourse (Habermas, 1991; Rowe, 1990). The invocation of the term often captures the sense that a democratic social order is at stake, therefore legitimizing accompanying discourses.

The changing conception of "the public" is central to understanding questions regarding new patterns of political communication, the reorganization of the public realm, and broader issues of the shifting state-society relationship in China. The development of civil society and a public sphere in the Chinese context has long been contested (Calhoun, 1993a; P.C. Huang, 1993; Wakeman, 1993). Critics argue that the main components of civil society, such as opposition between state and society, the economic foundations of a free market, a strong sense of privacy based on private property, codification of civil rights and freedoms, and principles of sociability and public discourse, are by no means already institutionalized practices, let alone established common goods, in China. Indeed, the development of a public sphere in China is contingent on public debates over these very issues among various social interests (Calhoun, 1993a). In this light, the symbolic struggle surrounding civil society can be conceived as constituting a discursive field, where social players, including the state and various social groups, organize their symbolic practices around the contending values of autonomy and civic participation. In their discursive contestation of the ideas of civil society, players exchange their economic, political, or cultural capital for symbolic power to promote their particular views and strengthen their positions in the field.

More importantly, the emerging public realm may involve different power relations instead of a preordained antagonism between civil society and the state (P.C. Huang, 1993; C. Huang, 2007). In fact, the shape of the public realm is contingent on the interplay of state authorities with a multitude of self-interested actors (L. Zhang & Ong, 2008). At the same time, the singular and universalistic category of "the public" is subject to articulation. Internet events, for instance, produce multiple and diverse representations of "the public" by various social groups in emergent patterns of alliance or rivalry through diverse modes of network communication. Emerging as webs of critical or affective discourse, and cooperative or antagonistic decision-making, the publics created through these processes vary in scope, power, internal structure, and interaction dynamic (Emirbayer & Sheller, 1999). Moreover, as a cultural and political construct, the conceptualization of "the public" as a whole often privileges certain constituent identities over others (Calhoun, 1998b).

The development of discursive fields and the formation of publics are mutually constitutive. On the one hand, various publics are constituted in their attendant discourses in different discursive fields mobilized around certain issues, in a process through which social identities become meaningful and have effects (Gleiss, 2015; Laclau & Mouffe, 2001, p. 966). On the other hand, a field is often where players employ their social and cultural capital to imply, invoke, or represent "the public" for legitimacy. Both the publics and fields are formed "in the interplay of public expansion, contraction, and reaction to new situations." Consequently, they are "ever-changing, emergent, and multiple, since new situations continually elicit new genres of communication, new styles of contestation, new solidarities or enmities, and new settings for interaction" (Emirbayer & Sheller, 1999, p. 164).

Symbolic Power and Symbolic Transactions

In light of the structural diversification of the cultural realm and the pluralization of cultural agents, emergent patterns of symbolic interaction between economic and political actors and various self-organized publics can often be observed in issue-specific discursive fields. A discursive field is where players accrue the capacity to influence social discourses in their interest by successfully valorizing their social resources – political, economic, and cultural capital – in exchange for symbolic power (Bourdieu & Wacquant, 1992). As the defining element of a discursive field, symbolic power at the most general level concerns the capacity to establish – through discursive processes – the practices, cultural categories, and cognitive schemes by which aspects of social life are experienced, understood, and codified (Bourdieu, 1991).

The dynamics of a particular discursive field are affected not simply by how the issue is embedded in existing power relations but also by how symbolic power is constituted through the exchange of different forms of capital in the ongoing struggles in the discursive field. There have been some general trends in how symbolic power is configured in the symbolic spaces mediated by the Chinese Internet. First and foremost, symbolic power is no longer tied solely to political capital, power endowed to actors by political institutions. While monopolizing political capital in many social domains, the Chinese state, for instance, often fails to command enough symbolic power to determine the outcome of its attempts to influence public opinion, which has become more and more important to legitimizing its governance. At the same time, the fast development of a market economy, as well as the advertising, cultural, and Internet industries, has elevated the potency of economic capital. Monetary or financial resources and properties can readily be cashed in for cultural and symbolic capital. More importantly, the state and market forces exert influences on the cultural realm not only from the outside but also from within by way of their discursive agents. It is important, therefore, to examine the contested symbolic interactions between different players and identify the mechanisms that render some of them subordinate to others (Fraser, 1990).

The composition of symbolic power and the transactions involving various capitals are as dynamic as boundaries between these fields are loose on the Chinese Internet. Despite the prevailing image of the Chinese state in the dominant literature on the Chinese Internet as an oppressive power restricting a fledgling "public sphere," the Internet opens up new social and symbolic spaces largely due to the changing role of the state in social life. The boundaries and autonomy of emerging discursive fields are a function of these fields' complex relationship with the political power. Many discursive fields are often constituted in the very struggles of social actors resisting the direct imposition of political power onto the growing public cultural space. Instead of exerting political power from outside by imposing a comprehensive – albeit fragmented and inconsistent – regulatory and censorship regime comprising ideological, institutional, and technical instruments (Yang, 2009), the Chinese state has become more adaptive to strategies of orchestrating or influencing public discourse from within the symbolic spaces mediated by the Internet.

The capacity to elicit, respond to, and direct public opinion has become the integral element of symbolic power for the state. For that reason, the state has been keen to co-opt the Internet into its comprehensive architecture of public administration by establishing a myriad of websites, portals, and social media accounts to disseminate information, provide services, and foster interactions between government and citizens (Jiang, 2015; Zhu et al., 2015 & 2016). These efforts are part of an attempt by political players toward "transforming a complex territory into a readable map" for effective governance (Creemers, 2017, p. 95). P. Thornton (2011) suggests that the evolution of public opinion management is an iterative project to contain the spontaneity of China's citizenry and create a predictable political environment.

These efforts, however, can by no means completely shut down autonomous and spontaneous network communications. Numerous Internet events, for instance, have shown that new forms of political communication have opened up the political field to discursive participation by the publics. Concurrently, the state has to respond to the changing dynamics of the new symbolic spaces. The "fifty-cent army" (*wumao dang*) is a notorious example that attests to the clumsy effort of the state to adapt to its new position. They are a large group of commentators paid by the government to populate online discussions with content supportive of official policies and critical of dissent. The highly derogatory name came from the satirical rumour, as a form of popular resistance, that the government pays them fifty cents for each message posted (Han, 2015).

A more successful example concerns the China Communist Youth League, a revolution-era political organization that has enjoyed renewed popularity among recent generations of Chinese youth, largely due to its adoption of novel popular cultural strategies such as recruiting movie stars for its mobilizing campaigns. Many critics believe that the Youth League has managed to exercise influence on the "little pinks" (*xiao fenhong*), a boisterous group of young nationalists (mainly females) that has recently emerged to turn the Internet into a battleground for mass protests against "unpatriotic" individuals such as separatists from Taiwan (Economist, 2016b). In a recent directive, the Youth League requested that its local agencies make an effort to recruit ten million young people as "cyber civilization volunteers," serving as "good Chinese Netizens" who promote the "voice of good youth" and "spread positive energy" on the Internet (Zhu et al., 2016; Xu & Denyer, 2015). The Youth League is a success story – albeit a contested one – of a political actor who strives to re-energize the social capital of its gigantic nationwide network of millions of Chinese youths with updated cultural strategies for exchange of symbolic power.

Discursive fields are equally permeable to the economic interests of cultural markets and industries. After all, the interfaces of the symbolic spaces are mostly various proprietary media platforms owned and operated by profit-driven commercial corporations (Y. Hong, 2014; G. Yang, 2009). To attract web traffic and boost content popularity, commercial service providers resort to a variety of marketing tactics. "Stir frying" (*chaozuo*) and "pushing hands" (*tuishou*), for example, are commonplace practices to manufacture Internet events by "stirring up" public sensations and pushing them to the front stage of public attention (G. Yang, 2009). The "Internet water army" (*wangluo shuijun*), as another example, is the commercial equivalent of the fifty-cent army. On command of marketing or public relationship companies, paid posters would "flood" the Internet with comments and (dis)information to attract public attention, influence public opinion, or conjure up a fictitious public event. A large percentage of trending topics on Sina Weibo, as a result, are set through the continuous retweets of a small number of fraudulent accounts (Q. Gao et al., 2012). At the same time, movie stars and other celebrities are actively recruited to open up accounts in order to attract their fans to the social media platform. These widespread practices have created an extremely competitive and complex symbolic environment where various players compete to set the public agenda (L.L.Yu et al., 2015).

These examples are among many that demonstrate the new dynamics with which political and commercial players valorize their symbolic power in new symbolic spaces mediated by the Internet. While symbolic power has always been important for both the state and capital to conceal, propagate, and legitimize themselves in order to make themselves fully effective, new complex patterns of collaboration and conflict reveal the new logics of capital exchange. The state strives to gain cultural leadership in order to maintain the current political structure and social cohesion, while at the same time benefiting from the cultural markets it has unleashed (J. Wang, 2001). For these purposes, it often resorts to more effective yet subtler ways of conducting capital transactions for symbolic power. At the same time, the commercial interests look to harness popular cultural consumption for economic gain, which can be exchanged for symbolic power to legitimize further economic profits.

In addition to political and economic capital, cultural capital is another important source of symbolic power. It encompasses various forms of cultural knowledge, competence, or dispositions, such as educational and professional qualifications, linguistic and cultural proficiency, or lifestyles (Bourdieu, 1984). Institutional and individual players from the realms of science, education, and especially the media and journalism possess higher amounts of cultural capital than they do economic and social resources, especially in the professional sector. At the same time, the emerging popular and consumer cultures constitute fields of mass cultural production, where urban middle-class individuals with cultural and economic resources may take an active role in discursive processes. Cultural capital is closely related to social capital, the sum of the resources that can be mobilized among social networks of actors. Social organizations and individuals differ greatly in the size and composition of their social networks mediated by the Internet (Anheier et al., 1995). Social capital can be accumulated through new forms of Internet socialities such as viral, mimetic, and rhizomatic ways of spreading messages.

The terrains of the discursive fields, therefore, are shaped by the distribution of cultural and social resources among their players. Culture in the Chinese context has always privileged and pointed toward elites, except during the brief disruption of Mao's era. Political decentralization, economic liberalization, and popular participation in the reform era have posed significant challenges to traditional cultural elites and left a tremendous gap in the discursive space into which other actors can move (J. Wang, 2001). The Internet embodies discursive processes by which an expanded range of actors compete to fill the gap. Opinion leaders in social media, as an example, come from more diverse backgrounds. On Sina Weibo, for instance, there are 3,300 so-called big Vs (verified accounts) that have more than a million followers (Creemers, 2017). These accounts are held by news media professionals, scholars and researchers, corporate executives and entrepreneurs, government and party officials, writers, activists, lawyers, movie stars, and "grassroots" individuals (Zhu et al., 2015 & 2016). Highly influential in shaping public opinion and information dissemination on important social issues, these opinion leaders are able to convert the political, economic, or cultural capital they have accumulated elsewhere into social and symbolic capital. In contrast with the larger population, most of these opinion leaders belong to well-educated middle-class strata endowed with higher economic and cultural capital to start with (Zhu et al., 2015 & 2016).

The discursive fields mediated by the Internet are often highly hierarchical, because of the unequal distribution of symbolic resources among social groups. While the Internet population rapidly grows in size, the composition of symbolic spaces is reflective of the growing social stratification in China. A large proportion of the Chinese population is still located on the other side of a digital divide, with little or no access to the Internet and other symbolic resources. The vast number of rural peasants and urban laid-off workers has little means to represent themselves in social discourses. Zheng and Pan have shown with a nationally representative sample that the Internet affords more opportunities for the socio-economically advantaged segments of the population (J. Zheng & Pan, 2016). Highlighting inequalities in access to media, cultural studies scholar Sun Wanning acutely observed, "having a voice or having access to means of voice-giving is in reality often contingent on an urban residential status, a good education, sufficient cultural and social capital, or plenty of money – none of which are readily available to the real poor" (Sun, 2012). Similarly, Y. Zhao (2003) points out that, "while the rising business and urban middle classes are increasingly using the media to articulate their interests and shape state policies towards their preferred ends, the rally cries of tens of thousands of Chinese workers and farmers in their struggles for economic and social justice, for example, have simply fallen on deaf ears in the Chinese media system" (p. 63). The Sun Zhigang case introduced in the previous chapter demonstrated the implication of the overrepresentation of the educated middle classes and the underrepresentation of rural populations in early Internet events (Qiu, 2009; Sun, 2012). In this context, "the public," as a discursive construct, often represents only certain constituents while leaving out others.

Moreover, public participation cannot be reduced to a question of inclusion versus exclusion. Actors differ in their capacities to mobilize resources in terms of networks, know-how, techniques, and perceptual and linguistic skills, all of which provide crucial social and cultural capital in the formation of discourse and opinion. Such acquired competence is linked to actors' habitus – deep-seated and socially shaped sentiments, tastes, and perceptions, which manifest structured and unequal social distribution (Bourdieu, 1984; Crossley, 2003). Chinese power elites, for instance, are adroit at integrating various forms of Internet communication into their new public management strategies, ranging from strategically invoking public opinion to manipulating global communication flows, to generate new kinds of symbolic legitimacy (Y. Zhao, 2012). The educated middle strata tend to be more highly disposed toward and better resourced for engagement in public discourse than is the working class. Recent years have seen an increase in the number of high-profile Internet events focusing on civic issues that concern mostly the urban population, ranging from police brutality and the medical system to public safety and education (Zhu et al., 2015 & 2016). The prominence of civic issues over political and economic redistribution attests to the fact that actors richer in symbolic capital can dominate the public agenda.

Yet discursive fields have interstitial momentums. The economic, institutional, and cultural capital that social groups have at their disposal may be drastically transposed in network communication such as in an Internet event. Spontaneous symbolic events may provide mechanisms for social forces to articulate ephemeral yet apparent unity through speech acts at a time when "class consciousness" has not been fully developed by any social strata in contemporary China (Y. Zhao, 2012). The outburst of a pro–civic rights "middle-class consciousness" against arbitrary administrative power in the Sun Zhigang case was one case in point (Y. Zhao, 2008). Moments of structural disjuncture such as this provide underprivileged social groups with opportunities to appropriate available technological and symbolic resources for autonomous communicative action. Through divergent and countervailing networks of communication, social groups may mobilize to act as counter-publics in China's increasingly stratified society (Xing, 2012).

Dynamic symbolic transactions in porous fields are associated with fluidity in the positions and relations of actors in those fields. Reflecting the increasingly differentiated nature of contemporary Chinese society, discursive fields are where the reflexive transformation of identity unfolds. In discursive fields, the players in social action "derive their meaning, identity, and significance from the changing positions they fill within ongoing transactions" (Emirbayer & Sheller, 1999, p. 164). At the same time, the players affect how cultural and symbolic resources are distributed within the field in their struggles to recruit agents, form alliances, and accumulate resources. In this light, it is less useful to draw a dividing line between the players by imposing predetermined categorical definitions, than to describe the state of these struggles and therefore of the frontier delimiting the territory held by the competing agents (Bourdieu, 1990, p. 42; Crossley, 2003). Battles over symbolic power often take the complex form of both conflicts and coalitions between these players (Hesmondhalgh, 2006). Consequently, the "official," "elite," and "popular" realign and regroup in efforts to define discursive framings of key socio-political issues, events, and developments (Bai, 2012; Dai, 1999; J. Wang, 2001). The topography of the field defies conventional binary logics such as the state versus civil society, authorities versus dissenters, or elites versus the grassroots. Instead, the players are defined in "a matter of relationality, of conjunctural shifts and alliances," of making connections with other players and their discursive representations (Emirbayer & Sheller, 1999, p. 164).

Conclusion

The rise of the Internet as symbolic space in China is premised on the political and economic developments in the past few decades. The Internet started with the state's infrastructure drive to network the state-managed economy in the early 1990s (Mueller & Tan, 1997). Later, in the broad context of socio-economic reforms, policymakers liberalized value-added Internet services to domestic and international investors to boost Internet services, applications, and content. The commercial Internet grew rapidly out of the effort of early entrepreneurs who benefited from a market with few vested interests and scant regulatory oversight (Y. Hong & Xu, 2019). Concurrently, the cultural realm has gone through a structural transformation in China. This chapter has sketched some broad trends in the transformation: the deregulation of cultural policies, the decentralization of cultural authority and resources, the privatization of ownership and management of cultural institutions, the development of cultural economies and industries, and the rise of cultural participation and populism (L.L. Chu, 1994; Y. Hong, 2014; C.C. Lee, 2000; J. Wang, 2001; Y. Zhao, 2008).

The development of a cultural economy in post-socialist China has dramatically changed the balance of forces in cultural production and consumption. Now at full throttle, commercial forces have become a competing and consecrating power, which has pulled discursive spaces away from the political and intellectual pole toward the commercial pole (Y. Zhao, 2011). Far beyond simply shaping opinion, commercial incentives promote the formation of consumerist subjects (Benson, 1999; S. Zhao, 1998). No longer commanding the hegemonic power in public communication, the political elites must grapple with the challenges posed by the rise of a cultural economy and a pluralizing array of voices (C. Huang, 2007). As symbolic production and consumption occupy a central place in social life, culture has become the vantage point from which to observe the dynamics among various political and economic interests in contemporary China (J. Wang, 2001; Dai, 1999).

Against this backdrop, discursive fields emerge from two seemingly opposite trends in cultural life in China today. On the one hand, a cultural realm has emerged where productive and consumer activities achieve a certain, always relative, degree of independence from direct and external political and economic constraints. On the other hand, there has been greater interaction between public participation and political and economic forces. While the autonomy of a discursive field is defined by its capacity to resist symbolic violence exercised by dominant politico-economic forces in society, its substance is always delineated by players embedded in concrete political and economic positions.

The importance of the Internet for public expression and participation has turned critical attention back upon the role of discursive practices in social organization and reproduction. In this chapter, the more general question of social change has been conceptualized as changes in relationships between the fields of politics, economics, and discourse, and further analysed in concrete terms using empirical data generated in the course of communication and interaction (Chouliaraki

& Fairclough, 1999; Lemke, 2005). The field framework aims to capture the motion of interlocked trajectories of transition in contemporary cultural life in China. As a structured space of positions, a field is both the means and the outcome of complex power relations among actors differentially equipped with social resources. While differing from other fields that are organized around different pursuits such as money and power, discursive fields intersect with these fields across intricate patterns of capital exchange (Bourdieu, 1991). More specifically, discursive fields affect all other fields through their capacity to define social categories and legitimate symbolic representations, through which social issues are expressed and settled.

Political struggles in contemporary China often hinge on symbolic mobilization and discursive contention in attempts to control shared meanings (e.g. Cao et al., 2014; Liang, 2018). The contemporary Chinese political landscape breeds exuberant discursive sites for contending important issues ranging from neoliberal strategies and revolutionary legacies to elite divisions, central-local dynamics, popular discontents and inspirations, and international geopolitics (Y. Zhao, 2012). Persistent nationalist discourses, for example, have been sustained by a contentious field comprising simultaneously the neo-traditionalist project of reviving Confucian values, a new-left criticism accusing capitalist development of betraying the socialist nationalist cause, and a middle-class sentiment of appealing to individual rights in order to neutralize class conflict (Guo, 2004; Calhoun, 1993d, p. 160). Chapter 4 in this book discusses how network communication has modified the content of contemporary Chinese nationalism.

Similarly, the country's economic activities are affected by the articulation of a complex array of discursive elements. These include concepts such as "growth," "private property," "free market," "consumerism," objects such as products and communication technology, codes and practices such as financial and credit systems, property rights, employment law, and workplace codes, as well as a range of sometimes overlapping subject identities such as capitalist, entrepreneur, consumer, client, worker, and so on, who share particular characteristics such as "self-reliant," "rationally calculating," "competitive," and so on (Dahlberg, 2014, p. 258; Fisher, 2010). In this light, market expansion in China can be understood as the articulation of new identities and practices within capitalist discourse in the changing relations between the state and the market, as well as between production and consumption (for further discussion, see chapter 5).

Multifaceted dynamics of state power and market integration have rendered inadequate the conventional problematization of Chinese communication simply in terms of the tension between an increasingly autonomous civil society and the centralized political control of the one-party state (C. Huang, 2007). Straight binaries such as state versus society, communist authoritarianism versus laissez-faire capitalism, or elite versus popular are dissolving in the divergent trends of the historical transition of China's cultural system (J. Wang, 2001; Dai, 1999). The cultural realm is important in the state's post-socialist developmental strategy both as cultural industries and as public cultural institutions (Y. Hong, 2014). Concurrently, multiple social actors with diverse interests and goals struggle to speak in the name of the public(s) in new symbolic spaces for cultural participation. Some take issues with state decision-making, some focus on justice and fairness in economic affairs, while others challenge conventional structures of "domination, exclusion, and inequality rooted in social institutions, norms, collective identities, and cultural values" in civil society itself (Emirbayer & Sheller, 1999, p. 162).

The complex, dynamic configuration of social and cultural relations, captured through the notion of a field, offers a model that can do justice to the many and diverse modes of cultural participation on the part of a broad range of individuals, institutions, and ideas. The symbolic spaces mediated by the Internet are conducive to the formation of discursive fields, where symbolic power, a meta-capital over the rules of play, is produced and transformed. New forms of symbolic, cultural, and social resources enabled by the Internet significantly affect the processes and outcomes of symbolic interactions. Network communication and Internet sociality mediate not only the forms of contentions around which actors orient their symbolic actions, but also the content of such actions as a certain version of reality constructed through network communication.

The next three chapters provide empirical cases where discursive practices of agents, in extended social interactions mediated by the Internet, have constituted social change in some important realms of social life in contemporary China. The case of network privacy in chapter 3 identifies relevant discourses from diverse domains of privacy practices, relates them to the structural contexts in which they are produced, and pieces together a web of meaning that redefines privacy. The case of cyber-nationalism in chapter 4 and the case of the network market in chapter 5 aim to reconstruct the respective fields of discourses in network communication and analyse the mechanisms and strategies associated with social actors' locations within them.

3

Assembling Network Privacy

"Privacy is dead, get over it!" The notorious proclamation made by Sun Microsystems CEO Scott McNealy two decades ago is often quoted as an ominous announcement of the looming information society, wherein pervasive technologies would inexorably encroach on our privacy. Years later, Yanhong Li, founder and CEO of Baidu, Google's counterpart in China, offered his own remarks on privacy as this now international information paradigm plays out in China. At a high-profile forum on development and the future, Li reportedly said, Chinese people are more open-minded and relatively less sensitive about privacy. If they can trade privacy for convenience, security, or efficiency, in most cases, they will do it (J. Ma, 2018).

Privacy has become one of the defining issues in today's information-saturated society. Both popular and scholarly discourses are imbued with uneasiness over ubiquitous public surveillance and information appropriation due to the advance of new extractive technologies for data collection, storage, analysis, and dissemination by both the government and the private sector (Marx, 2016). The above quotes from the leaders of global information markets have revealed two focuses of the mainstream public debate about privacy: first, the primacy of the informational market paradigm; and second, privacy as a liberal ideal (Cohen, 2012). Within the informational market paradigm, privacy is typically understood as a commodity that can be readily traded off for other benefits such as convenience or efficiency. A pragmatic and rational consumer in the market would consent to the erosion of privacy in exchange for other benefits. This rational instrumental approach has a complex relationship with the longtime Western liberal tradition that defines privacy as an inherent right of self-sufficient and autonomous individuals. These two aspects form the implicit frame of reference in Yanhong Li's comment about privacy in the Chinese context.

Concerns about privacy, however, are not reducible to the need for information control in the market. Nor is the image of a rational consumer vis-à-vis the market or an autonomous individual in liberal ideology adequate to depict the selfhood cultivated in diverse and changing privacy practices across time, space, and cultures. Privacy develops in the dynamic interaction between the always-evolving sense of self and its changing socio-spatial milieus (Cohen, 2001; Kisselburgh, 2008). The deep integration of network and mobile communications into the fabric of daily life interacts with existing psychological, social, and symbolic conventions for practising and understanding privacy (Kasper, 2005; Solove, 2002). In this light, understanding privacy requires that we examine how increasingly networked social spaces affect social circumstances in which self-society relations are redefined by practices of self-identification and association (Cohen, 2012).

Privacy in the Internet era does not mean insulation from society but rather entails new horizons of sociability (Gumpert & Drucker, 1998). Far from a separate and plastic cyberspace, where the real-world constraints of time, space, and body are transcended (Cohen, 2012), the Internet has reconfigured not only the media of communication – the means of information access and dissemination – but also the conditions, constraints, and expectations of social interaction. This chapter examines privacy through the lenses of identity and association in the Internet-mediated lifeworld that is undergoing rapid transformation in the Chinese context. Embedded in the lifeworld, which is open to change, social actors redefine privacy through symbolic practices to negotiate self-identities and boundaries in various social realms of that lifeworld.

This chapter posits that the reformulation of privacy takes place in the dynamics of a discursive field comprising diverse social domains. Privacy takes on new meaning through connections and contrasts with other changing notions and ideas in the lifeworld. This chapter focuses on identifying relevant threads from diverse domains of privacy and provides a useful synthesis by piecing together the web of meaning that redefines privacy. In doing so, it sheds fresh light on the social construction of the cultural contents of privacy in fast-changing Chinese society.

Practices and Values of Privacy in Chinese Society

Although a desire for privacy appears to be universal, the meaning and social customs surrounding it differ notably across socio-historical contexts (Gumpert & Drucker, 1998; B. Moore, 1984; Zarrow, 2002). A society's characterization of privacy says much about both its theoretical and its normative understandings of such fundamental issues as the nature and forms of human existence, the essence of political reality, and the relative importance of the individual versus the collective (Capurro, 2005; Ess, 2005;). Mainstream scholarly discourse on privacy tends to privilege liberal individualistic understandings of these issues, since the conventional concept of privacy has evolved within the sociopolitical values of Western democracies. The evocation of the right to privacy represents a commitment to limited government powers in the interests of individual autonomy and liberty at the socio-political level. Grounded in this broad socio-political framework, privacy is a means for the individual to achieve the ultimate end of self-realization in the private realm (Altman, 1975; Margulis, 2003a, 2003b; Rawlins, 1998; Regan, 1995; Westin, 1967, 2003).

Within this liberal framework, privacy in the online environment has often been defined with reference to problems of information control. And the Internet, a cyberspace free from social constraints, is considered a natural milieu for the autonomous disembodied self with predefined privacy preferences (Cohen, 2012). Such conceptions are inadequate to understand privacy and self-formation in concrete social practices with broad social purposes and implications. Far more than an abstract right of an autonomous self threatened by surveillance technologies, privacy concerns a social subject – one who is always already embedded in a larger society (Cohen, 2012).

The problem of privacy is often subsumed within a broader discussion of the relationship of the private realm to the public realm. Our contemporary preoccupation with privacy, researchers argue, is not simply due to recent technological effects but is also related to a long-term concern about changing public life (Gumpert & Drucker, 1998). Richard Sennett (1976) and Ray Oldenburg (1989), for example, have documented the decline of publicness and the devaluation of obligation. Michael Brill (1989) argues that the deterioration of public life happens not only in physical places but also through channels of communication.

The public/private divide is a cultural historical construct that different societies have construed in different ways (Zarrow, 2002). Cultural and political traditions and realities that delineate public or private spaces and conduct serve as the material conditions of privacy. As these conditions come under pressure, the theoretical and normative roots of privacy shift accordingly. Recent concerns about privacy have arisen in the broad context of contemporary China's rapid social change. The liberation of personal feelings and bodies from political manipulation in the post-socialist era and their recognization as being within the private realm took place simultaneously as economic reforms and market relations redrew the boundaries of individuality (Liu, 2019). The structural change in social relations has brought about the "individualization" of Chinese society – the growing legitimization of the individual in socio-political practices (Yan, 2009). The individual, whose socio-political identity had previously always been prescribed by the social collectives in which they were embedded, has emerged as an independent social category. The lives of Chinese people have been increasingly oriented toward personal well-being and improvement, shedding age-old moral preferences for collective welfare (Yan, 2009). The unprecedented changes in social conditions have created new opportunities for ordinary people to imagine and practise the idea of the private self. Recent empirical studies have shown that the Chinese increasingly prioritize individualist factors when assessing their own happiness and life satisfaction (Steele & Lynch, 2013). And certain elements of individualism are increasingly valued by China's millennial youth (Moore, 2005).

It is also significant to note the rise of the individual in relation to the family and kinship, the two categories that have long culturally defined the Chinese individual. No longer expected simply to perpetuate the family lineage, individuals in contemporary Chinese society instead pursue their interests through the workings of both the family and "practical kinship." Consequently, one's personal network and emotional attachments to kin and friends have become increasingly important in defining individual identity (Yan, 2009).

Privacy as a concept has a unique trajectory in the Chinese context. There is no single Chinese word encompassing all the meanings attached to the English word "privacy." In English, "privacy" contains several layers of meaning, ranging from inner, personal, and family life separate from the public, to individual rights and related concepts (Zarrow, 2002). The indigenous concept of 私 (*si*) in Chinese, representing the ideas of the personal and the self, has undergone a long ideational evolution to shed its negative connotations and acquire legitimacy as a private realm in a collective society. This adaptation of moral values with regard to the private realm in Chinese society reflects the unusual political conditions and increasing tempo of commercialization since the end of the sixteenth century (Zarrow, 2002).

Similarly, recent decades have also witnessed a reorientation of thought about the nature of 公 (*gong*), as in the ideas of the public, the communal, and public space. The rising individuals in Chinese society have been struggling to renew their relationship with new forms of socio-economic institutions, as well as with the party-state, which has played a key role in directing the process of individualization. State-led socio-economic reforms and polices profoundly affect and effectively manage the interplay among the individual, social institutions, and the market. For this reason, the changing relationship between the individual and the party-state in China does not represent a categorical shift toward the same individual-society relationship that exists in the West (Yan, 2010). If the pursuit of individual interests in China drives an increasing awareness of consumer rights and the development of rights-assertion activities, which in turn produce rights-bearing citizens who promote the rule of law in a civil society, the terms through which this change is realized must necessarily adapt to or arise within the context of the country's own socio-political history and reality.

The elusive conceptualization of privacy is also reflected in the difficulty of codifying the concept as an object of legal protection in China. Until recently, there was no specific definition of privacy – or the right to it – stipulated in dedicated legislation in China. The Civil Law, for instance, protects some elements of privacy under the right to reputation (Y. Wu et al., 2011). The rapid development of Internet industries and the information market in recent years has precipitated the need to protect "online privacy," which is premised on maintaining the safety of "personal information" against misuse and exploitation for commercial purposes. The state and governments at various levels have issued numerous laws and regulations aimed to achieve personal information protection as well as market efficiency and state security (J. Xu, 2015; Yang & Xu, 2018). Fragmented and inconsistent, however, the regulation of "online privacy" stipulated by the legal and political institutions has failed to define a clear or coherent meaning or boundary of privacy.

Against such a social-historical backdrop, this chapter grounds the understanding of privacy in a socially constructed self that is rooted in embodied individuals and communities in the everyday world. Conditioned by everyday expectations and experiences, privacy takes shape in a dynamic process of negotiation and reorientation of the shifting self-society boundaries. By adopting this framework, this chapter addresses two major caveats in mainstream research on privacy. First, the focus on the normative dimension of privacy propels researchers to seek the essence of privacy in abstraction, to debate a priori conditions for privacy, and to search for rigid conceptual boundaries at the expense of rich and embedded privacy practices (Solove, 2002). Second, the emphasis on these premises effectively locks the notion of privacy into the particular context of liberal individualism and makes it difficult to understand privacy practices in social environments that did not arise within modern liberal traditions.

Privacy as a Web of Meaning in the Mediated Lifeworld

Situated in broad social technical changes yet unfolding in a most palpable way in everyday life, the reconceptualization of privacy can best be understood through a lifeworld approach. Originated from Husserl and then elaborated in sociology by Schutz (e.g., Schutz & Luckmann 1973), Berger and Luckmann (1966), Habermas (1987), and others, the notion of "lifeworld" refers to a shared universe that is socially and linguistically constituted by people through their everyday communications. Lifeworld is where "communal reality construction gives to shared meanings the character of obvious facts" (Baxter, 1987, p. 55). It comprises an interlocking range of "zones," extending from interpersonal encounters to "vague attitudes, institutions, cultural structures and humanity in general" (Schutz & Luckmann, 1973, p. 61). These zones take shape as the individual comes to know and build meaningful relations with different personal and collective entities inhabiting their social universe. These entities range from family, relatives, and friends to cultural and professional groups, politicians, parties, civic organizations, governments, and nations. The lifeworld approach emphasizes the important role of language in enabling members of a community to exchange ideas and share experiences. Language is both "the basis" and "the instrument" of the collective repertoire of knowledge that constitutes the social world (Berger & Luckmann, 1966, p. 68).

The Internet has proven to be a particularly versatile vehicle for navigating the expansive structure of the lifeworld (Bakardjieva, 2009). The involvement of the online world in the socialization process has contributed to the formation of a new interaction matrix, including lived as well as mediated experiences, for the maintenance of intersubjective reality (Y. Zhao, 2006). In particular, the Internet enables new spatiotemporal zones – the zones of "there and now" and "there and then" – which allow people to experience "intersubjective closeness" that was previously possible only in the "here and now" situation of face-to-face communication (Berger & Luckmann 1966, p. 38). No longer necessarily bounded by propinquity, personal connection and commitment through small groups and other dense or multiplex social networks can now be achieved through mediated communication. Defined by its mode of relating, the outgrowth of lifeworld social interactions facilitated by Internet-mediated social networks may bring different sorts of people into contact with each other and provide bases for them to develop multifaceted relations.

New practices and cultural representations of privacy take place in this mediated lifeworld. Similar lifeworld experiences spread through dense network communication. Multiple exposures in turn enhance the spread of similar ideas and practices (Weng et al., 2014). In this recursive process, a discursive field is formed in cognitive and moral negotiations between different meaning-frames constructed by different communities in the lifeworld.

When people employ the word "privacy" to refer to the expansive range of perceptions, practices, and beliefs, they actively redefine or constitute its discursive content. The new privacy schema contains the sum of interconnected discursive elements representing specific practices, or disruptions of such practices, in the various domains. Privacy, therefore, does not present itself in essence. It can be recognized only through identifying and analysing what Ludwig Wittgenstein called a pattern of family resemblance of practices. As Solove (2002) suggests, "we should act as cartographers, mapping out the terrain of privacy by examining specific problematic situations rather than trying to fit each situation into a rigid predefined category" (p. 1126). The task of conceptualizing privacy, therefore, becomes one of mapping the topography of its discursive network of interrelated symbolic components. Guided by this analytical approach, in this chapter I use semantic network analysis to map the meanings of privacy as formulated through social discourses in Chinese social media.

The venue for this empirical effort is Sina Weibo, one of the largest social media platforms in China. Sina Weibo is a Twitter-like microblogging service provided by the Sina Corporation. Launched in August 2009, Sina Weibo quickly became the most popular social media site in the country. It is reported to have over 300 million registered users and generate about 100 million posts per day. The speed and scale at which information spreads on the Sina Weibo network has made it far less subject to control and censorship by the authorities and a preferred platform for news dissemination and social networking (Magistad, 2012; Qu et al., 2011; Yan, 2011). In this study, the symbolic field formed around discourses and practices of privacy on Weibo is both the context for and the result of privacy's changing meanings and patterns.

Semantic network analysis has its origin in cognitive science literature, which argues that there exists a structural meaning system in human cognition (A.M. Collins & Quillian, 1972). Like most social-scientific approaches, semantic network analysis assumes that meaning is relational. In other words, meanings are not inherent in words; rather, words derive their meaning from the other words with which they appear and interact (DiMaggio et al., 2013). Therefore, to extract meaning from a text, semantics networks map the relationships among words in the text by examining the frequency and distance of word association (co-occurrence). Extending beyond the standard content analysis of texts and frequencies of concepts, such a method reveals the manifest meaning structure of the text and indirectly represents the collective cognitive structure among the text's creators (Danowski, 1993; Doerfel, 1998). Chung and Park (2010) applied semantic network analysis to presidential speeches to understand both the rhetorical styles and the characteristics of presidential administrations' political and social viewpoints. Zywica and Danowski (2008) analysed the semantic networks of open-ended survey responses of two Facebook user groups and found different meanings of their offline and online popularity.

This relational assumption about meaning manifests in semantic network analysis in two ways. First, the network is constructed by identifying terms based on their relations to other terms. A semantic network for privacy, for example, is made up of the words that frequently appear together with the word "privacy" itself. Then all these words, as nodes, are linked together by the frequencies with which each concept co-occurs with the other concepts. Second, the interconnected words and terms constitute the semantic environment in which privacy is instantiated. Network clusters may emerge organically from the larger network. A cluster is a densely connected subset of nodes (words) more related to one another than to other nodes in the network. Network clusters provide a means of operationalizing contextual polysemy, in which privacy takes on different meanings depending upon the context in which it appears. Each cluster can be viewed as a distinct discursive domain for privacy that is embedded in it (DiMaggio et al., 2013). The interlocking range of clusters constitutes a detailed semantic map of the cultural structure underlying privacy practices and discourses.

The data for this study were gathered by doing a search on weibo. com using the keyword 隐私 (*yinsi*, privacy). The resultant 18,000 items were randomly selected among all the postings generated by Sina Weibo users. In the first step of the analysis, both a conceptual and a relational analysis were conducted on the text in order to identify privacy-related concepts and measure the frequencies of the co-occurrences of these concepts.[1] A semantic network was then generated by linking

---

1 Working with Chinese characters posed one of the major challenges to the analysis because most textual analysis tools are designed for English and also because it is sometimes difficult to find a direct English translation for the Chinese words. A meaningful interpretation of the findings depends on the successful tokenization of the Chinese corpus and network construction. For this, ICTCLAS (http://ictclas. org/, ICTCLAS, 2012) was used to select all the nouns, verbs, and adjectives from the cleaned corpus (ICTCLAS, 2012). Prior to analysis, the raw corpus was scrubbed of

these words based on the frequencies of their co-occurrence. The resultant network comprises 385 nodes (words). Next, a cluster analysis was performed.[2] A semantic cluster may reflect a unique dimension of meaning embedded in the concept of privacy. To yield optimal results, the dominant keyword 隐私 (*yinsi*, privacy) was excluded from the cluster analysis and visualization. These clusters are further explained with more detailed examples of the postings following the conventional discourse analysis principles. Finally, the full network and the clusters were visualized in eleven figures.[3] The sizes of the nodes in the figures are proportionate to the percentages of the nodes linked to them. The distance between words reflects the strength the relationship between these concepts – that is, the frequency with which the word pair is linked. Concepts with stronger relationships appear closer together, and concepts with weaker relationships are further apart.

Privacy with Family Resemblance

The semantic network of privacy that emerged from the analysis sheds light on the cognitive and cultural structures underlying the privacy discourses and practices on social media (see figure 3.1 for the full semantic network). The findings show that the privacy schema is constituted by distinct domains, represented by the eleven clusters (ordered by size) discovered in the cluster analysis. These mutually distinct yet organically related semantic clusters effectively identify several important dimensions of the concept of privacy as reflected in social media

---

irrelevant information such as user ID and textual "noise" such as stray punctuation, symbols and affirmative utterances (a, en, o, etc).

The analyses were conducted using WORDij 3.0 (Danowski, 1993, 2012–20), a computer program that combines multiple analytic techniques including content analysis, computational linguistics, and network visualization. Wordij 3.0 has been used in many research projects published in leading journals to perform text mining (e.g., Peng et al., 2012) and semantic network analysis (e.g., Smith & Parrott, 2012; Zywica & Danowski, 2008). In my analysis, I used WORDij's WordLink program to identify concepts that co-occur with the word 隐私 (privacy) more than ten times in the corpus. Co-occurrence of a word pair is defined as the two terms appearing together within a three-word window (see Danowski, 1993).

2 The network was generated with NodeXL (see Smith et al., 2010), an open-source template for Excel. The network data, consisting of a list of concept node pairs and their aggregated frequencies, were first loaded into NodeXL to create the network. Then a cluster analysis was conducted using the Clauset-Newman-Moore algorithm (Clauset et al., 2004).

3 The visualization of the findings was done with Gephi (https://gephi.org/).

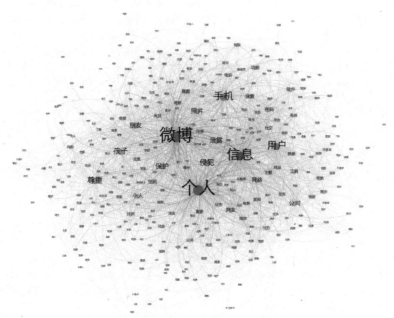

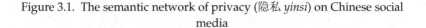

Figure 3.1. The semantic network of privacy (隐私 *yinsi*) on Chinese social
media

discourse. These dimensions delineate the lifeworld domains wherein
the private self interacts with other key actors in contemporary Chinese
society. The thematization of privacy takes shape in the representation
and negotiation of the diverse practices and understandings across
these social domains.

Privacy concerns are most immediate, and thus most palpable, in the
personal realm where the individual conducts daily life in close company
with family and friends. Tensions between boundaries naturally extend
to professional environments as professional relations become disentan-
gled from personal relations. Farther away from the personal realm lie political discourses. Organized around the trope of privacy on social media,
such political discourses often reflect how Chinese individuals envision
their relationships with public institutions and the state. Together, these

domains constitute a lifeworld embodying a logic of understanding that does not fit the abstract liberal theorization of the self or its understanding of the Internet as an isolated cyberspace of information flow. Rather, these discourses and practices provide concrete contexts to evaluate the practical purposes and normative ends of privacy in light of Chinese society's changing traditions and realities. Moreover, the cluster analysis provides clues to understand social media as a socio-technological space where network communication reformulates and accentuates the concerns and conflicts of the lifeworld. In the following sections, the eleven clusters are grouped within three larger domains in which they naturally assemble: the personal, public, and socio-technological.

Privacy as Personal Boundary

Cluster 1 has the largest number of words (see fig. 3.2). In that cluster, the word that co-occurs most frequently with "privacy" (*yinsi*) is "the individual" (*geren*). Respect for "individual privacy" (*geren yinsi*) or the lack of "individual privacy" are the two most common themes in the social media discourse. "Privacy" seems to be inherently linked to an acute sense of individuality, which may be evidence of an ongoing process of individualization in the broad context of the economic and cultural changes taking place in contemporary China (Yan, 2009). The relationships between privacy practices and the emerging individual, however, differ from those expressed from the classical liberal perspective, which prescribes privacy as a means for the individual to achieve the ultimate end of self-identity and self-realization. In this framework, liberal selfhood is believed to be developed through purposive, often solitary activities, such as self-expression and secluded contemplation (Cohen, 2012). Social relationships, on the other hand, are deemed either voluntary or barriers to individual independence (Altman, 1975; Margulis, 2003b; Rawlins, 1998; Westin, 1967). In contrast, the new sense of individuality in the Chinese social media engages in constant dialogue with a network of relations. As evident in the findings, the notion of individual privacy frequently arises in interpersonal relationships, as in the following example:

> Please respect our individual privacy, if you dare to eavesdrop on my phone conversations again, I'll never tell you who called and what it's about again ...

In fact, the overwhelming majority of the words in cluster 1 describe various social roles such as Mom (*mama*), children (*haizi*), wife (*laopo*),

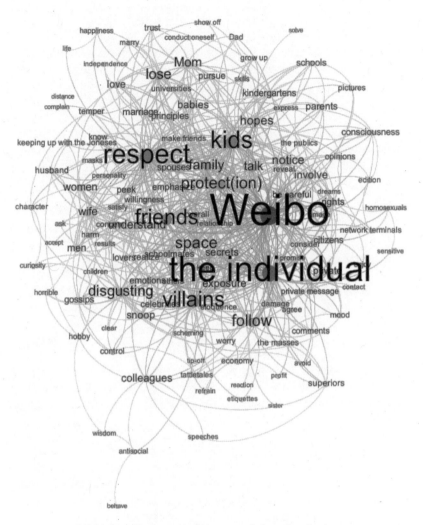

Figure 3.2. Cluster 1 in the personal domain of privacy

husband (*zhangfu*), and superiors (*shangsi*), and social relationships such as friends (*pengyou*) and colleagues (*tongshi*). The rest include organically related concepts that describe social settings, such as family (*jiating*) and marriage (*hunyin*); awareness, emotions, and actions with regard to privacy, such as respect (*zunzhong*), lose (*shiqu*), disgusting (*taoyan*), and villains (*xiaoren*); as well as associated themes and subject content, including hopes (*xiwang*), happiness (*kuaile*), and growing up (*chengzhang*). This group of concepts essentially depicts a personal realm for the notion of privacy.

The networks of relationships within which individuals are born and acculturated are critical constituents of evolving subjectivity (Cohen, 2012). The word "privacy" takes on diverse and particular meanings when it is talked about in relation to parents, siblings, friends, significant others, colleagues, and schoolmates, instead of presumed associations created by voluntary choice. Interpersonal boundaries of various sorts function to enable differential control over flows of information and affiliation (Cohen, 2012). In the following posting, for instance, privacy is understood as secrets keeping a woman from getting close to her romantic partner.

> You don't let me touch your cellphone saying that I need to respect your privacy. I don't understand: if you don't have anything to hide from me why can't I take a look at it? You can inspect my phone however you want because I love you so much that everything I have is open to you. The fact that you keep me away from your phone only makes me feel that you are keeping secrets from me ...

In a sense, the concept of privacy provides an opportunity for people to think about their personal boundaries and make sense of the evolving social norms that regulate personal relationships. Many examples on Chinese social media show that privacy takes form in a changing lifeworld inhabited by embodied subjects struggling to adapt.

> A personal space is needed even when with the best friend. Privacy not only won't estrange feelings but also allows us to establish the sense of safety and trust.

> Violate your privacy, meddle with your friends, ... make you so tired, I feel sorry about it. But don't you think love is selfish? ... Don't you think we need to sacrifice for love, don't make me feel that your schoolmates and friends are more important than me! I do care!

Boundaries and boundedness are as important to the development of subjectivity as are care and affiliation (Cohen, 2012). Cluster 8 (fig. 3.3), which is considerably smaller that cluster 1, seems to indicate that family affairs (*jiashi*) may lead to the negative emotion of fear (*haipa*) if members hold viewpoints (*guandian*) that neglect (*hulue*) or pry (*datan*) into privacy instead of being considerate (*titie*) toward each other.

considerate

neglect

fear

care

viewpoints

family affairs

pry

Figure 3.3. Cluster 8 in the personal domain of privacy

Concerns about privacy are often discussed in relation to social roles and the obligations prescribed to those roles. Thus, the emerging individuality that privacy cultivates still must negotiate with existing cultural conventions and institutions. For instance, a mother's responsibility trumps the sense of privacy over her body, an idea forcefully expressed in the following posting:

> The so-called privacy of a female's body is nonsense: when feeding a baby, a woman's breast is not just for display but a practical tool!

Lastly, privacy is very much a gendered topic on Sina Weibo. The following is one of many different versions of a typical friendly reminder to women who are susceptible to the pitfalls of unwise relational moves, of which privacy is one:

> It's silly for a woman to ... pry into a man's privacy like a spy.

But apparently men are equally subject to judgment when it comes to privacy:

> So fragile as to reply on the privacy settings to shut off comments, are you still a man?

These examples demonstrate that, rather than serving the purpose of one's self-contained, abstract, and chosen identity, ideas of privacy often are expressed in lifeworld terms that are relational, embodied, gendered, and role-oriented. Instead of the autonomous and solitary, individuals and communities are situated in concrete patterns of everyday practice. Privacy on social media, as mediated lifeworld, draws as much on role defining as on emerging individuality, as often on obligations as on rights, as much on emotion as on information, and as much on interpersonal border control as on relationship maintenance. Mediating social interaction both physically and conceptually, privacy provides not only a mechanism for embodied practices of boundary management to operate but also a conceptual vehicle for people to contemplate and formulate relational norms, as the following posts suggest:

> If a guy would: 1. Tell you his QQ [a popular Chinese IM platform] password. 2. Tell you his bankcard password ... 4. Allow you to check his cell phone anytime ... Then, marry him!

> Many people show their understanding and sympathy for you only to pry into your privacy. This common sense should be remembered all the time to protect yourself.

Our understandings of selfhood may constitute a coherent system that responds dynamically to practical circumstances (Cohen, 2012). Yet, as a contested concept reflecting much tension in the changing habits and routines in the personal realm, the privacy regime is necessarily fragmented with limited coherence. The following, for instance, is an opposing comment in immediate response to the previous one about marriage:

> Everyone needs freedom, privacy, character and temperament. Point 1, 2, 4 ... are rather perverse ...

Detached from its liberal roots, the rationale of privacy protection in Chinese society is often presented as an instrumental good rather than an intrinsic value (Lü, 2005; J. Xu, 2015). Sina Weibo offers ample evidence that privacy is indeed often linked to practical concerns in the lifeworld. For instance, it is part of the material condition for information safety and parental responsibility:

> It's common on Weibo that proud parents use their children's pictures as their profile pictures, mention their children's names, and the names of their kindergartens and schools, expose their neighbourhoods in pictures ... Hope parents realize these are all children's important privacy, think twice before you post on Weibo.

Yet at same time, some communities have come to embrace privacy as an intrinsic imperative and relate it to other fundamental moral values such as dignity and respect.

> An important criterion to judge if one is a person of virtue or vice is to see if she is interested in other peoples' privacy ...

> Three kinds of wealth in one's life: 1. health, 2. privacy, 3. freedom.

Privacy operates as a mechanism by which a person regulates accessibility to others. Personal space and territorial behaviour are among the principal regulatory mechanisms in this process (Cohen, 2012). The three nodes in cluster 10 – rooms (*fangjian*), glass (*boli*), and intimate (*qinmi*) – capture the socio-spatial aspect of privacy. Lastly, cluster 11 contains two nodes – angry (*shengqi*) and sad (*shangxin*) – that denote the socio-emotions associated with relational management (fig. 3.4).

Privacy in Public Domains

The findings of the network analysis show that similar patterns extend from the personal out to other, broader domains. Words making up cluster 3 (fig. 3.5 and cluster 4 fig. 3.6) seem to describe socio-professional environments of the privacy concept. We can see words such as students (*xuesheng*) and teachers (*laoshi*) paired with words such as classrooms (*jiaoshi*) and dormitories (*sushe*). Boss (*laoban*) and customers (*kehu*) appear with offices (*bangongshi*). Civil servants (*gongwuyuan*) and officials (*guanyuan*) are close to governments (*zhengfu*). Venereal disease (*xingbing*) is linked with hospitals (*yiyuan*). Cluster 9 (fig. 3.7)) is apparently derived from public responses to the scandal (*chouwen*)

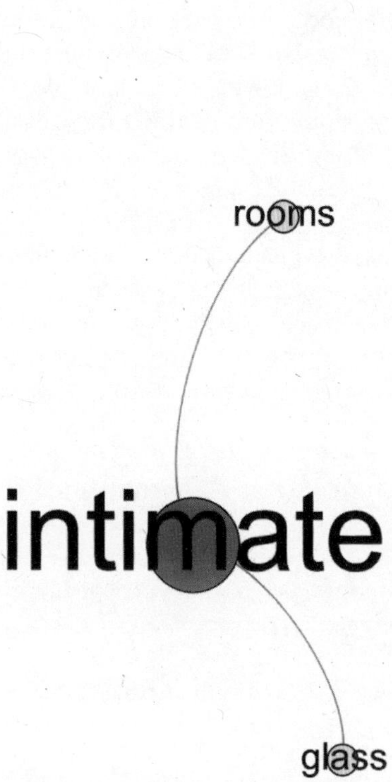

Figure 3.4. Clusters 10 (left) and 11 (right) in the personal domain of privacy

of one (or more) fame-hungry actress (*nvxing*) in entertainment programs (*jiemu*).

Practices of privacy are situated in multiple social milieus as people socialize in various, often overlapping, milieus and institutions defined by different norms of identity performance and relational obligation (Cohen, 2012). Different institutions, such as the hospital or the classroom, figure differently in relation to both subjectivity and privacy. In rapidly changing Chinese society, social relations in various social institutions, such as employee-employer, citizen-government, and consumer-market relations, have become ever more complex. The dynamics of social interactions and emerging norms are often reflected in privacy concerns:

Marriage and family are beyond the authority of an employer. An employer's interference is an immoral and illegal infringement of employees' privacy.

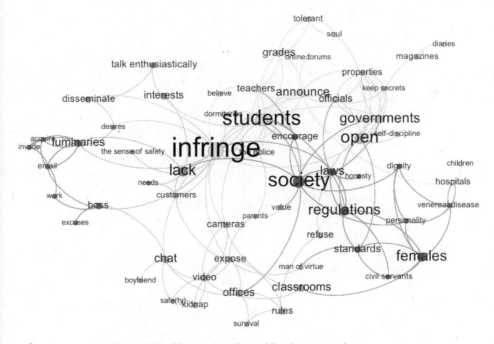

Figure 3.5. Cluster 3 in the public domains of privacy

XX hospital ignores patients' right to privacy by leaving patients' medical records open for unauthorized access by anyone ...

A sense of distinction between the self, the private (*si*), and the public (*gong*) arises when people pay more attention to the boundaries between impersonal professional environments and the personal realm. Nevertheless, such a distinction is still nebulous and subject to discussion, as exemplified in the following much-reposted posting:

[Ten pieces of wisdom at the workplace] 1. Don't be antisocial, have harmonious interpersonal relations. 2. Don't confide to colleagues. 3. Don't handle personal things during business hours. 4. Don't gossip about colleagues ... 5. Don't reveal privacy at will ...

As China is well on its way to becoming a more open, modern, and highly mobile society, there have been rising concerns about how the

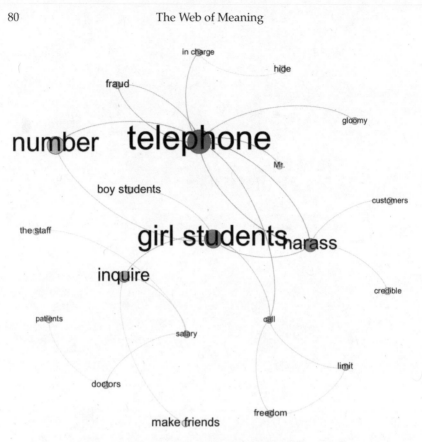

Figure 3.6. Cluster 4 in the public domains of privacy

long tradition of personal trust adapts to increasing interaction among unrelated individuals. In response to new types of social interaction, the following post laments the loss of strong emotional interpersonal attachments to the ills of urbanity:

> This city is big enough to tolerate all your eccentricities and habits. People are busy with their own lives, taking indifference as a respect for privacy. People always say it's fine, nothing serious, alright OK, So do you. People come to you to confide their grievances, and leave you to go on with their lives afterwards, you don't care much about it either because you only pretend to listen. The world is so big but we are so lonely!

The semantic analysis shows that, beyond entangled webs of personal relationships, privacy still belongs to more general and abstract

Figure 3.7. Cluster 9 in the public domains of privacy

"others" (*bieren, taren, duifang, renjia*). Between understandings of privacy in the contexts of particular personal relationships and a general sense of privacy for all, there are a wide range of different privacy practices with both positive and negative connotations: see (*kan*), spread (*chuanbo*), touch on (*chuji*), discuss (*yilun*), leak (*xielu*), disclose (*toulu*), share (*fenxiang*), gossip (*bagua*), infringe (*chufan*), invade (*qinfan*), dig (*wa*), pry (*kuitan*), expose (*jielu, baolu*), publicize (*xuanyang*), and lose (*nongdiu*). Some are positive – care (*zhuzhong*), respect (*zunzhong*), preserve (*baoliu*), protect (*baohu*), guarantee (*baozhang*) – the rest are neutral, such as self-express (*shai*), or new, such as forward (*zhuanzai*), a novel ICT-enabled action. Exemplifying Wittgenstein's family of meanings, these clusters of action words constitute an impressive display not only of the broad set of connotations the concept of privacy entails, but also of the nuanced understandings of privacy practices embedded in an expanded scope of social relationships.

Farther into the public domain, privacy is discussed in terms of law, regulation, policy, and social order, as evident in words such as police (*jingcha*) and society (*shehui*), as well as standards (*biaozhun*), values (*jiazhi*), rules (*faze*), and laws (*falv*). The thematic words of this socio-professional sphere seem to be infringement (*qinfan*), survival (*sheng-cun*), safety (*anquan*) and dignity (*zunyan*). In the same vein, cluster 6 (fig. 3.8) discusses legal consequences with nodes such as police (*jingcha*), police station (*jingchajv*), fines (*fakuan*), and detention (*jvliu*). Cluster 7 (fig. 3.9) touches on even broader political concepts, such as the state (*guojia*), human rights (*renquan*), the people (*renmin*), and top secrets (*jimi*). These two clusters represent the public and political spheres in which privacy is experienced and understood.

There is ample evidence on Weibo that people have begun to talk about privacy as a kind of right (*yinsiquan*). However, the use of the word "rights" does not necessarily indicate a liberal legal notion that conceptualizes privacy as a corollary to self-ownership and ownership of private property (Cohen, 2012, ch 6, p. 2) The reference to rights is often a form of emphasis when applied to networks of relations for Chinese social media users.

> Do I have the right to privacy or not! I can't eviscerate myself to show you everything even in the name of the greatest love!

Privacy is deemed a human right in liberal frameworks, which are premised on the primacy of the private individual and their separation from – or even opposition to – the state and other forms of social power. Emphasizing the choice and control of the autonomous individual, this perspective sees important threats to privacy arising from organization-individual relationships (Margulis, 2003a; Regan, 1995; Westin, 2003). Yet, in the Chinese context, the right to privacy is often understood and grounded in particular personal experience – for instance, as a consumer in the market – and the belief that the government has the responsibility to make public policies protecting this right.

> Car insurance is expiring. Have been bombarded by text messages and phone calls from many insurance companies for almost a month. I don't check such texts or answer such calls anymore. There have been numerous public discussions about personal information being profited from and appropriated. When will the government issue laws to protect citizens' basic right to privacy? My request is not too demanding, living on this land, I need to feel a sense of safety.

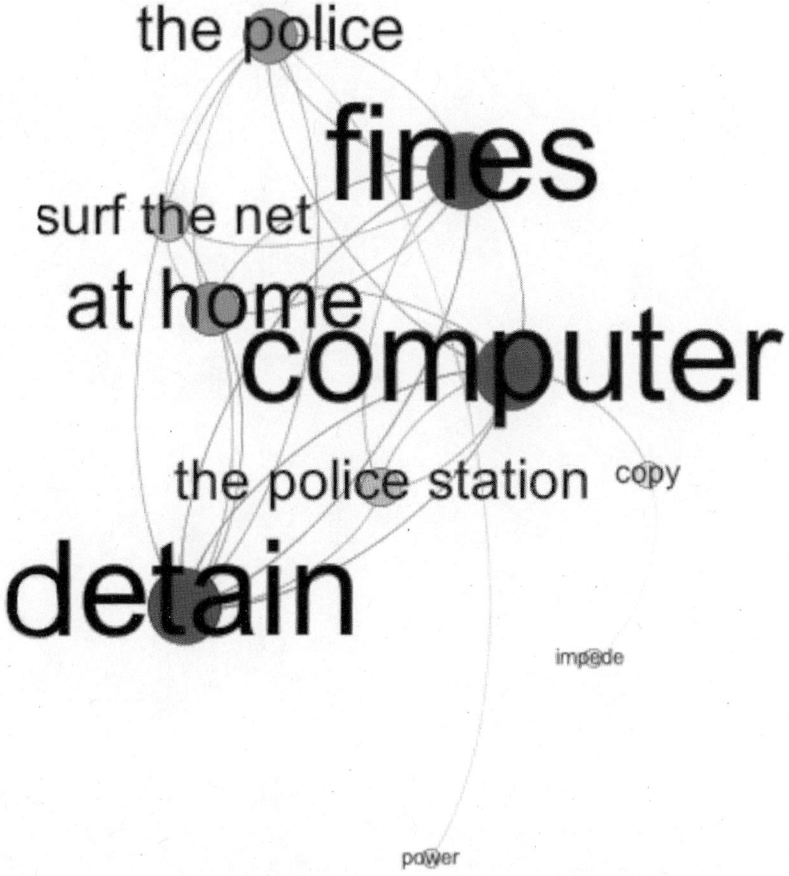

the police

fines

surf the net

at home

computer

the police station   copy

detain

impede

power

Figure 3.8. Cluster 6 in the public domains of privacy

Resistant to the abstractions in most rights theories, privacy is firmly grounded in social contexts and places that give it meaning (Cohen, 2012). In fact, the notion of liberal rights has become an important part of the political discourse on privacy coming from an increasingly individualized, urban, young, and relatively better-educated "middle social stratum" that populates Chinese social media (CNNIC, 2010; P.C. Huang, 2009). This middle stratum shows much enthusiasm for following what are democratic ideas to re-imagine and reorganize political life for the public good:

residence

guarantee

commerce

the state top secrets

the people

human rights

global

Figure 3.9. Cluster 7 in the public domains of privacy

... In the U.S., it is ok to keep a secret of one's property but that of government officials must be open to public scrutiny; in the U.S., the right to privacy is guaranteed for everyone but government officials.

Comment No. 2 on [the pending regulation that requires real names for user registration on online forums and Weibo]: I support real name registration for the purpose of cracking down on online rumors and crimes, but the premises for that are 1, the ability of websites to protect users' privacy; 2, if the government can tolerate reasonable criticisms; 3, if online criticisms and disclosures are protected from retribution. Under the current circumstances, these premises are non-existent.

Privacy in Socio-Technological Domains

Last, but certainly not least, there is ample evidence that heightened privacy concerns grow out of the imbrication between network technologies and daily life. Cluster 2, the second-largest of the eleven clusters, teems with words about information, technology, and diverse subjects and practices in relationship to them (see fig. 3.10). The nodes such as user (*yonghu*), website (*wangye*), software (*ruanjian*), cellphone (*shouji*), network (*wangluo*), and download (*xiazai*) carry the technological dimension of the privacy concept. Obviously, privacy concerns are accentuated by the ease of information dissemination enabled by digital media technologies. This informational and technological aspect intersects with both social and institutional practices. For instance, journalism and the media are represented in such words as the media (*meiti*), news (*xinwen*), report (*baodao*), and reporters (*jizhe*). Similarly, cluster 5 (fig. 3.11) sheds light on a specific concern about how technology is applied in daily life, namely, the ease of shooting (*paizhao, paishe*), displaying (*zhanshi*), forwarding (*zhuanfa*), and deleting (*shanchu*) photos (*zhaopian*) and records (*jilu*). In addition, words in the cluster such as strangers (*moshengren*), familiar (*shuxi*), and city (*chengshi*) depict the larger social context within which technology operates.

Further analysis indicates that the socio-technological space of the Internet has three interlinked effects on privacy practices – informational, social-spatial, and symbolic. First and foremost, the information exchanged through social networks constitutes individuals and communities as "transparent objects of others' knowledge." Network spaces legitimize and reward practices of self-exposure and peer exposure, which "operate as both spectacle and discipline" (Cohen, 2012, ch. 6, p. 7). Concerns about privacy reveal our constant struggles to manage the degrees of disclosure and informational representations enabled by network media to fit existing and emerging social norms (Palen & Dourish, 2003).

Heightened concerns over privacy in contemporary society are often attributed to the development of an information society, where uncontrolled flows of personal information on open networks threaten individual autonomy and self-determination (Cohen, 2012). The semantic clusters emerging from my analysis provide hints about information society not as a vacuum space but as a place where the networks of social relationships are mediated through technological boundaries and boundedness. By enabling control over flows of information and forms of affiliation and accessibility to others, these socio-technological networks function to enact "personal spaces" for regulating social relationships within which individuals develop (Cohen, 2012).

The socio-technological domains identified in the semantic network analysis demonstrate that the emerging socio-technological

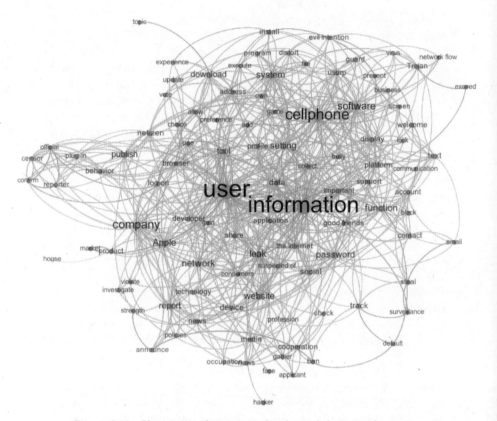

Figure 3.10. Cluster 2 in the socio-technological domain of privacy

environment has brought about a range of new privacy-regulating
behaviours. Mediated social networks as socio-technological artifacts
take shape simultaneously with other new conventions in making contemporary Chinese society. By reordering the spaces of everyday life in
ways that both channel embodied practices and contest unexpected behaviour, they often lead to the steady decline of clearly situated actions
and thereby create urgency for new understandings (Palen & Dourish,
2003). A new privacy concept, accordingly, is constituted in personal
boundary-management practices that respond dynamically to changing circumstances (Cohen, 2012).

> ... mortgages take away the future, marriages take away passion, the mar-
> ket takes away the bottom line, Weibo takes away privacy.

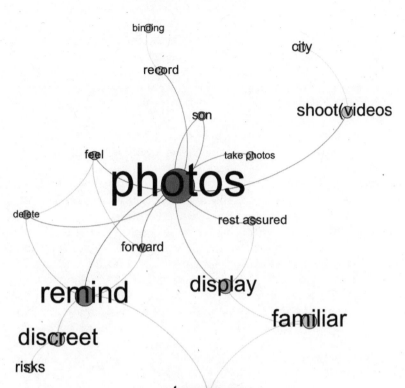

Figure 3.11. Cluster 5 in the socio-technological domain of privacy

Weibo is the easiest way to pry into privacy.

... things that are made public on Weibo cannot be called privacy, can only be called personal things ...

The nature and function of social media as socio-technological spaces become implicated in the debates over what constitutes "private" and "public" at a time when the two axes of the lifeworld are undergoing radical transformation in contemporary China. The following two examples, for instance, instantiate the notion of "public privacy," which occurs when individuals express themselves openly in an anonymous environment – in this case, an anonymous virtual environment (Westin, 1967, pp. 31–2). However, people may have different understandings of the character of such an environment. While some mean to make aspects of their private lives public, others deem such a virtual environment to be an extension of the private realm.

> I don't have any schoolmates on Weibo, all my grievances are to myself, therefore I have my privacy.

> I'm lucky that no one from my family knows my Weibo ID ... It would be really awkward if they snoop on my privacy. Really awkward.

In the interstices of the informational and material architectures of social life, privacy operates as the means for boundary management in the service of always-emergent subjectivity (Cohen, 2012, ch. 6, p. 18). Capurro (2005, p. 40) argues that when "our being-in-the-world-with-others is basically a being-in-the-networked-world," the very nature of autonomy and individuality seems to evolve into, paradoxically, a networked individuality. Confusions voiced on Sina Weibo seem to reflect the complexity Chinese individuals face in response to both the cultural self as a network of relations and the new technologically enabled networks of connections. The resulting norms of communication and interaction redefine the capacity of the Internet to function as contexts within which the self is developed and identity performed (Cohen, 2012).

Lastly, the Internet provides network symbolic spaces for the reformulation of privacy. Privacy discussions, as this chapter has demonstrated, unfold at the intricate intersection between network discursive process and lifeworld experiences. Privacy discourses originate from the comments made and shared in the familiarity and multiplexity of networks of personal relationships. Addressing various issues in diverse social domains, these discourses constitute a field where ideas of privacy are formed and changed, not just reflected. This process is one of meaning, through which the stock of knowledge about privacy may be produced through debate and reflection on everyday practices. In the context of quickly transforming Chinese society, however, the communal understanding of the practices and norms of privacy is often challenged by the lack of a common stock of knowledge and the breakdown of consensus in the cultural sphere.

At the same time, differentially embedded actors are grounded in communities of varying strength, which offer them varying social, economic, and cultural resources for participation in the discursive process. In this sense, symbolic practices may also establish and reinforce frames of relevance for constructing meaningful boundaries of

communities, regulating their memberships, and thereby securing solidarity (Couldry & Hepp, 2018). Consequently, symbolic processes are
imbued with conflicts and negotiations.

Conclusion

Broad structural changes have unleashed aspirations and experiences
of the increasingly autonomous individual and provided contexts for
imagining and practising new types of social relations in contemporary Chinese society. Expanding market relations, rapid urbanization,
growing information industries, and emerging social spaces that are
increasingly networked are all part of the contemporary environment
that is nourishing and reframing people's practices and understandings of privacy in China. The mainstream approach to privacy, however, is often premised on the conception of self as derived from liberal
political theory. Under this framework, selfhood is defined as essentially autonomous and self-contained, independent of cultural context.
Accordingly, privacy exists only to protect self-contained individuals
from negative technological effects (Cohen, 2012). The abstract notion
of selfhood and rights without context does not provide an adequate
baseline for understanding privacy in the Chinese context. Moving
away from this essentialist conception of privacy, this chapter decou-
pled the understanding of privacy from prevalent liberal individualist
premises and situated it within the complex self-society relationship.

Premised on the emergent, relational development of the individual in a rapidly changing society, the conception of privacy involves
a parallel process of reorienting the self and reimagining an integrated
lifeworld extending from interpersonal relations to those of the professional, the political, and the institutional. Rooted in diverse social
institutions and domains such as family, work, the market, and the
state, all with their own organizing principle and related routines and
rituals, concerns about privacy reveal our constant efforts to manage
the boundaries between these different domains of action and degrees
of disclosure (Cohen, 2012; Palen & Dourish, 2003). The empirical analysis in this chapter has shown that the notion of privacy has penetrated
deeply into the personal realm in Chinese society. On the one hand, privacy has been integrated into practices and norms around social roles
and personal relationships. The choice between disclosure and privacy
reveals expectations and strengthens or weakens trust in personal
relationships. On the other hand, the notion of privacy brings about
ideas and practices that stir changes in the personal realm. Spouses
and friends must struggle with the heightened sense of individual

independence embedded in the concept, as much as women and men have to face new behavioural stereotypes in the name of privacy. The role-oriented and gendered discourse on privacy reflects the intensified conflicts between rights and obligations, disclosure and distance, and dependence and independence in the personal and other closely linked socio-cultural realms. Moreover, privacy is understood in the Chinese context for both its intrinsic values and instrumental purposes. The dignity of the self and the safety of the family are the two forces driving the increasing consciousness of the privacy concept.

More importantly, the sense of self is experienced in new forms of sociality in the emerging new contexts of social and public realms, while concerns for privacy embody patterns of social interaction in these new contexts. People express in privacy concerns their experiences with others in professional settings and in the contemporary socio-spatial environment of heightened mobility. Privacy is embraced as a form of legal rights for consumers in the market. Privacy consciousness also applies to the political arena, both reflecting and affecting power relationships among the government, officials, and ordinary citizens.

Privacy is a sweeping term encompassing everything from the quest for personal dignity and safety to the growing sense of political participation in contemporary China. It carries fresh perspectives for understanding the relationships between self and others, the individual and collectives, and private and public, as well as spatial boundaries in broader contemporary Chinese society. Reflecting a time when the demarcation of the public and private is being reconstructed, privacy is subject to re-evaluation as "a common value shared by individuals, a public value significant to the political system, or as an individual liberty" (Gumpert & Drucker, 1998, p. 410). The analysis in this chapter reveals growing sensitivity to state surveillance and the intrusion of commercial interests. We see emerging lifeworld discourses organized around a free-standing right-to-informational-privacy theme (Westin, 2003). The notion of privacy is also connected with the exercise of responsible citizenship. Yet discussion of privacy in the individual-state relationship must be situated within the long Chinese political tradition where the state is bestowed with both moral and absolute authority, while the individual relies on the state for protection and well-being (Yan, 2009).

The urgent sense of privacy originates from our interactions with and within the contemporary information-rich environment. Regarded as a vast web of free-flowing information without geographic borders, the Internet has become a major source of privacy concerns. Privacy protection is a necessary means to safeguard our right to control our own information. Privacy in the network information society, however, cannot be understood in purely informational terms. Information on the Internet affects people living in the real world in ways that bear the imprint of political and institutional influences (Cohen, 2012).

Capable of facilitating communication around a variety of styles and topics, the Internet may enact different relational contexts when its network structure intersects with the social world in different ways. Often Internet-mediated communications take place among people related to each other indirectly – through formal organizations rather than direct personal contacts. Comprising sites of impersonal anonymity, such network social spaces reproduce structures of complex association in the system, such as the market, bureaucracy, or professionalization (Calhoun, 1998a; Habermas, 1987). In addition, the Internet is changing social interactions in the lifeworld, where the reality of everyday life used to be organized around the "here and now" of the individuals who interacted with each other in face-to-face situations.

The concept of privacy serves as an interpretive device for exploring the lifeworld implications of the socio-technological spaces enabled by social media such as Sina Weibo. By tapping into the rich discourses on Sina Weibo, this chapter has explored the meaning of privacy through related terminological dimensions of particular privacy practices, especially instances of disruption and conflict in privacy practices. The conception of privacy is rooted in the everyday practices of situated, embodied individuals and communities. Far from simply a technical conduit, the socio-technological space exemplified by Sina Weibo operates along informational, as well as social spatial, dimensions of the lifeworld. It is a place where privacy is displayed, practised, and contested. The discourses on privacy not only reflect, but also constitute changes in, people's lifeworld in light of an information-rich network environment that affects the collective understanding of selfhood by changing the relationship between self and society.

4

Articulating Cyber-nationalism

The mid-2010s have witnessed the global rise of nationalism. Following the Brexit referendum in the United Kingdom and Donald Trump's ascent to presidency in the United States, right-leaning nationalist parties have sought paths to political power throughout Europe. Their political programs often ride on growing populist sentiments, especially of those who perceive themselves as being excluded from economic growth under global capitalism, which, in the past decades, has benefited the economic and cultural elites disproportionately. It's worth noting that social media played a crucial role in facilitating the populist construction of national interest and sovereignty. Bypassing the "biased" mainstream media, political leaders and nationalist propogandists have been keen to reach out to increasingly disenchanted social groups on Facebook and Twitter, changing how politics is conducted and posing challenges to the public sphere ideal (Groshek & Koc-Michalska, 2017; Ott, 2017).

Long before Trump pledged to "Make America Great Again," Chinese leaders vowed to lead a "great rejuvenation of the Chinese nation" (Z. Wang, 2014). In fact, nationalism has long been a prominent political ideology and practice in contemporary China. Critics have argued that its persistence was due mainly to the demise of the revolutionary ideology of the ruling Chinese Communist Party (CCP), which left a "vacuum in commitment to public goals" in Chinese society (Guo, 2004; Unger, 1996, p. xi). The party-state therefore had to renew patriotism as the basis for legitimizing its rule (S. Zhao, 1997, 1998). Yet contemporary Chinese nationalism manifests itself as more than a political project of the authoritarian state. It is also a result of cultural construction, "a cognitive, affective, and discursive category deployed in daily practice" by increasingly autonomous and differentiated social forces striving for their own expressions of national consciousness (Bonikowski, 2016, p. 427). Indeed, the historical and ideological notions of Chinese nationalism have been challenged as the growing market economy and mass culture flourish within the domain of everyday life, adding essential variations to nationalist discourses in today's China (X. Zhang, 1998). Moreover, the Internet, poised to challenge the state's monopoly over symbolic spaces, has served as a new public arena where nationalism is expressed, contested, and redefined (Cairns & Carlson, 2016; Hyun & Kim, 2015; M. Jiang, 2012). Having developed its own characteristics in the expanding online space, "cyber-nationalism" is both an extension and a variation of existing nationalist currencies (X. Wu, 2007).

Understanding Chinese nationalism may shed light on how this local variant is affected by factors common to similar episodes in other countries around the globe. This chapter aims to decode the multifaceted content of contemporary Chinese nationalism by examining an explosive nationalist event over the Diaoyu Islands that erupted in mid-2012, a recent episode of a long historical territorial conflict with Japan. Situating cyber-nationalism in a historical account, this chapter provides an in-depth analysis of social media discourses around this dispute. It reveals that Chinese nationalism is far more than simply a state-manufactured doctrine for political legitimacy. Just like nationalist currents elsewhere, contemporary Chinese nationalism is intimately tied to the collective aspirations of various social groups for their own political and cultural representations of national identity both within and beyond their changing society. As a politically relevant cultural construct, the nation is articulated through people's experiences of their changing socio-economic positions. Rather than being constituted by a single category of homogeneous individuals, the nation is a complex web of relationships among diverse groups. Instead of representing "a united people striving together for China's modernization" under the leadership of the state (Pan, 2010, p. 519), nationalist expressions nowadays reflect various societal constituencies responding differently to "the development of the market and the influx of discursive resources that had come with market expansion" in contemporary China (Townsend, 1996, p. 22).

Cyber-nationalism in China

The evolution of cyber-nationalism has been concurrent with the development of the Internet as a symbolic space in China (X. Wu, 2007; J. Wu et al., 2019). Since its inception in the mid-1990s, the Internet has hosted waves of nationalist ideologies and practices with its rich symbolic resources and diverse online communities. Among the earliest nationalist voices were those of college students, both at home and abroad. Critical of the weak official stance in a series of high-profile international events, such as the anti-Chinese riot in Indonesia in 1998 and the bombing of the Chinese Embassy in Belgrade by NATO in 1999, these young and educated early adopters of the Internet passionately debated international policies and relations, expressing earnest yearnings for a strong nation. As the Internet further expanded, self-organized populist online communities, such as Strengthening the Nation Forum, the Iron and Blood Community, and the Patriotic Alliance, became the main venues where nationalist views gained wider reach beyond elite and intellectual circles. Contrary to the criticism that these nationalist currents were mostly the result of government manipulation, early cyber-nationalist groups were often highly critical of official policies and strongly motivated to engage in social intervention and civic participation. Instead of irrational and incited emotions, passionate debates often took place among those "informed nationalists," who had systematic worldviews as a result of their access to and experiences with the outside world (Wu et al., 2019; Y. Zhou, 2006, p. 208).

As the Internet further expands into social life, newer generations of the Internet population grew up in Internet cultures brewed in the accelerated development of a market economy and the upsurge of commercial culture. They became the main force in a new wave of nationalist events such as the worldwide rally protesting the sabotage of the Olympic torch relay by Tibetan separatists and a series of related boycotts against foreign businesses in 2008. While having inherited the critical realism of the previous generation, these new patriots were keen to express their national identities through popular and consumer cultural symbols (Wu et al., 2019).

A recent episode of cyber-nationalism, the case of the Diba expedition in early 2016,[1] has demonstrated new trends of cultural participation on the Chinese Internet (H. Liu, 2019). During this highly publicized event, a massive group of boisterous millennials, mostly female, bombarded the Taiwanese leader Tsai Ing-wen's Facebook page and the websites of some Taiwanese newspapers with playful and humorous emoji packs in response to Taiwan's separatist stance. Immersed in digital cultures of online gaming, fandom communities, and social media, these digital natives equipped themselves with virtual private networks (VPNs) to cross the Mainland firewall, organized themselves into teams with various coordinated tasks through Baidu forums, QQ groups, and Weibo postings, and broadcast their activities live online during the event.

---

1 A popular user-founded online forum on Baidu. It was dedicated to a Chinese soccer player. It is where the term *diaosi* originated (see chapter 1).

What further distinguished this newer generation of nationalists, comprising mostly what critics call "little pinks," from their antagonistic, hawkish, and often patriarchal counterparts from previous generations was the playful integration of online subcultures and consumer cultures into their political participation (Z. Wang, 2019). Their characteristic expressions are versed in digital literacy, which has been cultivated by commercial logics and global cultural flows (Wu et al., 2019; G. Yang, 2019). Quotidian, social, and entertainment-oriented, their expression of national identity has become a natural extension of their emergent urban subjectivity. More than simply venues, tools, or resources, the fluid and decentralized network of the Internet mediated simultaneous action and intensive interaction on a mass scale, infusing the symbolic process with a burst of energy of identification. Thus, the Internet has become both the form and content of such a process.

The development of cyber-nationalism results from the co-evolvement of nationalism and mediated symbolic space in contemporary Chinese society. It defies the simplistic dichotomies such as the official versus the popular, political manipulation versus cultural identification, and the emotional versus the rational, which have infested existing understandings of Chinese nationalism. Above all, it challenges the traditional assumption that Chinese nationalism is characterized by a unified identity shared by all social groups in spite of their diverse political, economic, and/or cultural positions. Indeed, the complexity of China's cyber-nationalism lies in the fact that different generations of nationalist subjects, historical memories, and life experiences co-exist in fast-growing pervasive cultural spaces mediated by the Internet. They develop different features while interacting with each other in intricate ways in the fluid process of nationalist articulation (Wu et al., 2019).

This chapter attempts to decode the content of Chinese cyber-nationalism through the case of the anti-Japanese movement in 2012, a recent episode in the dispute over the Diaoyu Islands.[2] The discourses that emerged during this massive event not only made claims to national sovereignty but also articulated new expressions of Chinese nationalism through cultural expression, political participation, and social interaction. Constituting a symbolic field in the event, the discourses reflected various schools of thought emerging in recent years,

---

2 Known as the Senkaku Islands in Japan, the Diaoyu Islands are eight small islets, 6.3 square kilometres in total area. They are located about 200 nautical miles east of China, 120 nautical miles northeast of Taiwan, and 200 miles southwest of the Okinawa Islands of Japan.

as diverse social groups reformulated their cultural identities and political principles in relation to their changing economic positions on the
local and global stages (Townsend, 1996; Unger, 1996).

This chapter discusses major themes of these discourses, which are
identified with a topic model built with one hundred thousand postings
on Sina Weibo, a major social media outlet during the event. The themes
are broken into eleven topical groups. The groups and their keywords
are shown in table 4.1 in the appendix at the end of this chapter, which
also includes information on methodology. Three broad themes emerged
from further analysis. The first highlights national imagination in mediated symbolic processes in cyberspace. Such national imagination takes
place through concrete symbolic practices of online communities. The
second theme opens up the discussion of nationalism to the consequences
of the rapid socio-economic transformation China has sustained in the
past few decades. It takes notice of the distrust and cynicism that online
users hold with respect to the Chinese state for its inadequate responses
to the dispute and, more importantly, for the repercussions of many of its
neoliberal policies in recent decades. This theme also highlights the dis-
parity and conflict found in the nationalist expressions of different social
groups. The third theme discusses the implications of observed cyber-nationalism in the context of globalization. These three thematic categories
are explained and instantiated with exemplary Weibo postings.

Nationalism as Cultural Identification

The century-old dispute between China and Japan over the Diaoyu Islands in the East China Sea was rekindled when news of an attempt by
the Japanese government to "nationalize" the islands started to circu-
late in July 2012.[3] Extensive media coverage of the issue incited strong
responses from China in the following few months. While the Chinese
government quickly denounced the attempt and refuted Japan's territorial claim to the islands, street protests broke out in numerous cities
across China, creating the largest wave of anti-Japanese demonstrations
since Sino-Japanese relations were normalized in 1972 (Wasserstrom,
2012; Wallace & Weiss, 2015). Fervent nationalist sentiments also surged
online. Incensed reactions to the news took the Internet by storm.

Massive online participation made the dispute an Internet event, de-
noting a period of heightened national self-awareness. An enormous
number of comments were generated on the subject, bringing to light

---

3 The islands are currently "owned" by a private owner in Japan.

latent tensions that predate the event. Cyberspace, especially social media, operated as an important symbolic field where various groups of participants congregated, communicated, and contested. Spreading and condensing through online social networks, a cacophony of voices about national identity, state sovereignty, and international relations were codified into nationalist discourses. These discourses responded to, buffered, and sometimes drove the direction of action on the street.

Sina Weibo pulsated with vivid expressions about the nation during the event. A hashtag circulating widely on Weibo – "The Diaoyu Islands belong to China!" – not only indicated people's passionate participation in the ongoing event but also organized real-time diverse activities into an unfolding collective event. The indivisibility of territory, for most people, was the fundamental indicator of national sovereignty – the notion of the nation as an integral unit as well as an autonomous state. Many comments therefore were adversarial toward the perceived senseless and aggressive violation of the nation's integrity by Japan. Some voiced a demand for tougher actions, including military operations or even an outright war against Japan. Delineating self and other, inside and outside, these comments reinforced a nationalist structure of feelings, providing strong emotional resources for identity and a sense of belonging:

The Diaoyu Islands are the sacred land of China's, will never allow the Japanese to occupy Chinese territory!

Diaoyu Islands belong to us! Look at those unruly gangsters, trampling on our land, so blatantly smug.

People in my online groups are all talking about the current affairs, especially about the Diaoyu Islands, war on the seas, and official pronouncements. High tides of patriotism are spreading. Diaoyu Islands belong to China!

While often embodied in its own sovereign state (Calhoun, 1997), the nation as a community is imagined (Anderson, 2006). Such imagination is sustained and reproduced in everyday life experiences. The Chinese people's sense of their nation, however, had long leaned toward an impersonal and abstract view, due to the exclusive power of the state to conduct national affairs (X. Zhang, 1998). In contrast, cyber-nationalism develops new ways of performing national identity, mediated by the Internet (Z. Wang, 2019). Social media, exemplified by Sina Weibo in this case, provided a means for ordinary people to express their personal engagements with the nation:

Today in a taxi, I chatted with the driver, who's from Liaoning, about the recent development of the Diaoyu Islands. He was extremely upset and emotional about it. When getting off, I was asked if I could get reimbursed on the taxi fare, if not, he wouldn't charge me!

I found clothes with a Diaoyu Islands theme when shopping at Taobao, didn't hesitate to buy it, to show my patriotism, I will post a snapshot when it's shipped to me.

Recommend a song to everyone, by a much admired musician named Li Quan "She is at 26° N," also known as "the Diaoyu Islands." Eh, you will know the rest after hearing it.

It is worth noting that users directed a great many harsh criticisms at the Chinese government on Weibo. Given concerns about social stability and international relations, Beijing had acted cautiously to avoid escalating the confrontation during the event (Gries et al., 2016). Yet, many people considered the diplomatic efforts of the government soft, ineffective, and lacking resolution and force for that reason. This observation confirmed a similar finding by Cairns and Carlson in their study of more than 40,000 influential bloggers on Weibo during the 2012 crisis, which noted the broad level of anti-government sentiment (Cairns & Carlson, 2016).

How generous of the Chinese government: offering the Japanese imperial army the Diaoyu Islands with both hands. Don't blame Japan for calling us coward!

If our leaders were [tough] like the Russian President Putin, would it still be like this today? Our government is no better than that of late Qing Dynasty. The Japanese made arrests in our territorial waters but we didn't respond. Someone sold out our country.

The government's stance toward the Diaoyu Islands differs greatly from that of the people. All I can think is what Xunzi[4] once said, water can overturn the boat as well as carry it.

Although the territorial dispute placed state sovereignty at centre stage, popular expressions of nationalism did not appear to acknowledge an exclusive role by the state in articulating national identity. In

---

4 A third-century BC Confucian philosopher.

addition to disapproval of the government's inadequate measures, there was an emerging sense of popular sovereignty in the form of grassroots agency and pluralism. Activists landing on the Diaoyu Islands were hailed on Weibo as national heroes. More importantly, people were capable not only of distinguishing the nation from the state but also of asserting nuanced understandings of national loyalty and support.

Hongkongers succeeded in landing on the Diaoyu Islands, glorious victory on 8.15! #Defend Diaoyu islands# Hail the 14 heroes!

Kai Fung No. 2 from Hong Kong has successfully landed on the Diaoyu Islands to make territorial claims, but protecting the islands should be the responsibility of the state and government. Now the grassroots took the initiative, it's high time for the government to take further measures.

Zeng Jiancheng, who once burned a national flag, has this time erected the Flag onto the Diaoyu Islands, many people do not understand it. In fact, this is precisely the standard behaviour of a citizen in a democratic society. It confronts internal power and pleads on behalf of the people. Resist external enemies and sacrifice for the country. Imagine, how can someone who is a submissive bootlicker of government officials possibly confront foreign enemies?

All official and grassroots actions about the Diaoyu Islands that took place in the past few days are just like a series of popular lessons on politics. All kinds of thoughts have collided, rhetorics flooded, smells reeked, some of which were rational and others ignorant. What was alerted against emerged, fantasized about happened, glamorized debunked, condemned revealed. The past few days were wonderful, painful, making people calm, reflective, only those who look for answers truly love China!

At the same time, the popular nationalist discourses on Weibo selectively engaged with historical memories of China. For example, China's long history of cultural, ethnic, and political integration contributed to the meanings attributed to the "nation" by the Chinese people (Dirlik, 1996; Y. Zhao, 2010). Among the many reposted comments was a remark made by a legendary general during the Han Dynasty (BC 204–220 AD), an era from which China inherited much of its character and self-identity. "Whoever dares to offend the mighty Han Empire, no matter how far he lives, will be executed," it says, invoking the image of a nation in its prime with much pride and determination (X. Wu, 2007). Another widely circulated posting reads "The Diaoyu islands may belong to Japan but Japan belongs to China!" This seemingly blatant display of cultural arrogance was premised on the historical experience of the two countries, for, until the mid-nineteenth century, Japan was a "conservative, inward-looking tributary state," and therefore much inferior to the Chinese Empire (Tok, 2010, p.18).

Historical memories have always been an essential element in defining the national community in China. Yet history is never a given fact, but rather is continually disputed and reconstructed (Calhoun, 1993a). The shape of historical discourse is the outcome of a power play to define what becomes acknowledged and validated, along with determining who reaps benefit from a given narrative (Renwick & Cao, 1999). Both the Chinese state and various dominant social groups selectively appropriate cultural traditions in discourse to serve as cultural underpinnings of their own political or economic projects (Y. Zhao, 2010). State-sanctioned patriotism, for instance, highlights China's past glory in the pre-modern era, its suffering under foreign aggressors during the "century of humiliation," and its subsequent rise under the leadership of the CCP (Cairns & Carlson, 2016). Such politically legitimizing discourses instill people with patriotic sentiment through education and propaganda (Schneider & Hwang, 2014). This in turn places structural constraints on the people's perception of national identity, creating a relatively unified nationalist community (Tok, 2010).

While historical discourse about the nation is often written according to the interests of the ruling elites, new symbolic venues such as Sina Weibo offer the opportunity for ordinary people to interact with historical content by adopting or rejecting conventional narratives and common sentimental tendencies in that content (Schneider & Hwang, 2014). Repeated invocations of historical memories surrounding China's experience with sovereignty, especially past military clashes with Japan, were topics prevalent on Sina Weibo during the Diaoyu Islands event. Such memories, however, did not simply apply a structural constraint that would demand uniform emotions and actions from people. Instead, the discursive practices placed historical descriptions within the contemporary context, thereby lending history its force with "immediacy, circumstances and practical projects" (Calhoun, 1993d, p. 15).

> #Defend the Diaoyu Islands# August 15 in history, it is a memory of a nation's victory 67 years ago, it is also about the rise of a nation after its failure. The day in this month is about Chinese people alright, in fact, people from Hong Kong, China's Special Administrative Region, all 14 of them driving an iron boat named Qifeng II, besieged by nine or ten Japanese ships, it is about seven brave men who landed on the islands to claim the Chinese territory [and] were arrested by 50 Japanese guards of the islands.

[Re Let Japan Respect China Let Us Honor History] When the 40th anniversary of the establishment of diplomatic relations between China and Japan and the 81st anniversary of the 918 Incident[5] intersected at this juncture, it is hard to talk about friendship only anger and resentment. The Diaoyu Islands dispute will surely become a new starting point for re-examining the Sino-Japanese relation. Reality requires that Japan's respect for China is re-established. 918 is a history of shame. But history is the best teacher. To win the respect of others starts with our respect for history.

These comments seem to confirm that the "century of humiliation" represents neither simply a device created to support state propaganda nor a factual past with insidious influence on the present. Rather, the notion is a constantly reconstructed discourse about the nation's past that lies at the centre of the evolving meaning of "being Chinese" (Renwick & Cao, 1999).

While the 2012 Diaoyu Islands dispute was perceived by many as an occasion for reinforcing the unifying ideology of national sovereignty, the popular sentiments expressed in social media discourses manifested much more diverse tendencies. Situated in growing mass culture and pluralistic everyday life, the discourses did not tie national consciousness to any sole ideological structure – the official project of "the Chinese dream" of national rejuvenation or traditional historical narratives of national sovereignty – but instead embodied a heterogeneous cultural domain consisting of affective identification, personal forms of interaction, and ritualized symbolic practices (Bonikowski, 2016). In contrast to the traditional media propaganda of official nationalism, this nationalism from the bottom up, as mediated by social media, functions as "a set of intersubjective meanings and affective orientations that give people a sense of self and guide their social interactions and political choices" (Bonikowski, 2016, p. 428). Moreover, the populist impulse of cyber-nationalism did not necessarily represent an organic sense of national unity. Indeed, as my analysis would further illustrate, the category of nation and the phenomenon of nationalism was brought into play by the apparent disjunction between people and state.

Nationalism as a Consequence of Neoliberal Development and Subgroup Identification

Amid the energetic, plural, and populist expressions of national interest in the unfolding events of the Diaoyu Islands dispute, jarring voices of dissonance, cynicism, and dissent were hard to ignore. Much discord

5 The Japanese invasion of China, on 18 September 1932.

was expressed as grievances against the side effects of a fast-growing economy in the past few decades, mainly a result of a wide range of neoliberal policies to integrate into global capitalist developments – from the privatization of state-owned enterprises to the dependence on international trade and foreign investment (Harvey, 2007; Y. Zhao, 2008). Agonized by rapidly rising inflation, inequality, corruption, and insecurity, the online populace took the chance to express dissatisfaction in a mix of economic complaints and moral condemnation of social injustice and political corruption, as well as emotional laments over the loss of tradition and order, directed toward the party and state bureaucracies, nouveaux riches, and other social elites. A similar "subnational pattern" was also detected in Wallace and Weiss's 2015 study of the event.

Online users' experiences with rampant government corruption and deteriorating food safety, environments, and city infrastructures gave them little confidence in the government's handling of the Diaoyu Islands dispute. For many, the feeling of injustice and distrust seemed to act as a fundamental brake on their patriotic emotions:

Can you protect your house from being torn down by force?[6] Can you save your job? Can you protect yourself from being run over by a car driven by Li Gang's son?[7] If not, how can you protect the Diaoyu islands?

Classic ways to lose your life in China: eating toxic food, falling from a broken bridge, burned on a defective bus, and drowned in a flood caused by rain. The rest of us could all die from the anger over the Diaoyu Islands dispute![8]

Experts claim that the task of China's national rejuvenation has been completed 62%. The number looks pretty, a golden ratio indeed. In West Han dynasty, during Emperor Wu's times, invaders were punished no matter how far they came from. In Tang and Song dynasties, goods were abundant and people were wealthy, numerous foreign countries sent ambassadors

---

6 The user was referring to the numerous incidents where housing developers, often backed by local authorities, evicted home-owners by brutal force. Many people lost their lives in these events.

7 The drunk driver, Li Qiming, ran over two pedestrians. Convinced his father's position would help him, he shouted "My dad is Li Gang!" to the security guards trying to detain him on the scene. This well-publicized incident provoked strong public outcry over Li's blatant sense of privilege for being related to someone in power. "Li Gang" has since become a symbol of social injustice caused by abuse of power.

8 This user was referencing several recent fatal incidents that had aroused great public concern over public safety issues and that were often due to administrative negligence and official malfeasance.

to pay tribute. Nowadays? The Huangyan Island and Diaoyu Islands are still in dispute, low salaries, high living expenses, poor benefits, polluted environment, low level of happiness, poisonous baby formula and medicines everywhere. Where does the rejuvenation come from?

Some people are concerned about the Nanjing massacre, I support them, but I am more concerned about the Anti-Rightist movement, Cultural Revolution and the Great Famine; Some people are concerned about the Diaoyu Islands, I support them, but I am more concerned with demolitions by force, interceptions of people's letters of complaints (to the government), and cooking oil made of waste. Some criticize all sorts of social problems in the U.S., I support them, but I am more concerned about China's own problems. When it comes to diplomacy and territory, it is the government's responsibility. I praise the government if it does a good job, scold it if not; it is not, however, my responsibility to share its job. I care more about myself and my own business.

It is apparently from such postings that everyday life has come to occupy the cultural centre in nationalist expressions. Grand narratives of history and ideology are understood and evaluated in the context of plural, specific, concrete details of daily life. The CCP's claims to nationalist legitimacy as well as the nature of the political community are contested against real-life appeal. In the vernacular of such expression, for instance, city inspectors – employees of the official agency installed in cities across China to tackle local low-level crime – have become a symbol of abusive administrative power in China's fast-expanding urbanization process. They have been repeatedly criticized for using unjust or excessive force directed at defenceless residents. City inspectors, naturally, were among the popular targets of online cynicism during the Diaoyu Islands event:

We could solve China's territorial issues simply by setting up city inspector bureaus in Sansha, the Diaoyu Islands, and Taiwan. It is that simple ... Whoever is armed with city inspectors controls the world!

When it comes to land use, the party has always dealt with us little guys by tabling the dispute and siding with developers. Now in the dispute over the Diaoyu Islands, the party was shocked to realize that it had become the little guy itself; Japan was tabling the dispute and going right ahead with the development ... Summon the city inspectors to destroy Japan by force.

Moreover, lifeworld concerns seemed to have given rise to a new perception and a new experience of the nation beyond the political realm – socio-economic relations have became a source of meaning that gives form and voice to the nation (X. Zhang, 1998). As the event further unfolded, debates about possible future actions became a focus on Weibo. Among a stock of protest techniques such as petitioning, marching, and occupation, economic boycott emerged as the preferred tactic for many online users. For them, the boycott was the most effective means through which to retaliate and punish Japan because it could severely damage the country's economy, which had become ever more dependent on China's consumer market.

> Diaoyu Islands belong to China! Let us all unite to boycott Japanese goods, even if there are no rewards, this is your obligation! Fellow citizens, remember the shame of history. Repost!!

> Boycott Japanese goods, defend Diaoyu Islands, destroy Japan by making it suffer economically ... What a creative war, it requires we all stand together, but many don't think this way, don't think it's helpful.

> Experts say boycotting Japanese goods is irrational and doesn't help with the Diaoyu Islands. But it goes without saying that Japan has huge market shares in China's electronics market. Take a look at our surroundings, everyone or every family owns one or two Japanese products. So from now on, discipline ourselves, boycott Japanese goods to hit their economy hard. Don't forget our nation's past humiliations and defend our dignity!

These voices were quickly met with forceful counter-arguments. Some pointed out that, since China's economy was deeply intertwined with Japan's, the rejection of Japanese commodities would also hurt China's economic development.

> When our Chinese compatriots landed on the Diaoyu Islands, the Japanese arrested them, declaring to deport them by force. When some Japanese landed on the Diaoyu Islands, we Chinese smashed our fellow citizens' cars, claiming to boycott Japanese goods. Does such a foolish nation really exist in the world? We need to note a difference when boycotting. Boycotting products of Sino-Japan joint ventures is helping the Japanese party to hurt the Chinese manufacturer's profits and Chinese employees. In an era of global economy, many goods are the products of multinational cooperation!

> #Diaoyu islands belong to China# Patriotism is admirable, but I support rational patriotism. Chinese businesses should stand on their own feet, it's much more important than boycotting Japanese goods.

In their 2016 study of the same case, Cairns and Carlson also noted the choice of economic boycott as the preferred means of action by online users. They concluded that the online forum was not as "monopolized by angry youth" as critics claimed because the more "level-headed commentaries" of anti-boycott voices eclipsed the more "virulent sentiments" of those advocating boycotts (Cairns & Carlson, 2016, p. 24). Similarly, in an account of a previous anti-Japanese movement in 2005, Liu also observed diverse positions taken by online users on the issue of economic boycott. He took it as evidence of online publics' deliberative capacities for a democratic process (Liu, 2010). In contrast, I argue in this chapter that economic boycott emerged as a preferred tactic largely because of the structural characteristics of online users, who were better educated and more affluent than the general population. Their socio-economic position explained their familiarity with and knowledge of the workings of the political economy of globalization. In this sense, economic boycott, one possibility among many historically and culturally variable techniques, was presupposed by the emerging socio-economic habitus, the collective disposition, of the mainstream Chinese online population.

In contrast, "others" were more inclined toward high-risk activities. During the 2012 event, numerous protests and demonstrations took place on the street. According to one source, a total of 320 protests took place across China in September, with 128 city-wide demonstrations on 18 September alone (Wallace & Weiss, 2015). In several cities, demonstrations became violent before authorities could intervene. Protesters set fire to a Panasonic factory and destroyed a Toyota dealership in Qingdao (Wallace & Weiss, 2015). In Xi'an, an owner of a Japanese car was fatally wounded by protesters (Hollihan, 2014).

Many of the demonstrators on the streets were unemployed workers, displaced farmers, and migrants, representing a different social stratum than that of the online participants. Laid-off workers participated in demonstrations in Hunan province. Protesters in Shenzhen stormed government offices to demand unpaid wages. Observers of the 2012 event argued that the protests offered an opportunity for these disadvantaged citizens to express their frustration in a country where avenues for political mobilization are limited (Wallace & Weiss, 2015). Official reports also seemed to confirm that the violent eruption of grievances was in part driven by "livelihood concerns" of "underclass people against the polarization between the rich and the poor" (Zhu et al., 2012).

Online public opinion took a sharp turn when news and witness accounts about the violent street protests broke out on Weibo. Immediately, a chorus of voices surfaced to condemn the direction of the protests. The call for "rational patriotism" soon followed. Violence was criticized for being "irrational" because it destroys the "private proper-ties" of our own "citizens." In order to contain chaos and restore order, "true patriots," the online discourse advocated, need to be rational and non-violent. Having to strike a compromise with altruistic patriotism, the discourse of rational patriotism appeared to be driven by an iden-tity that was based on support of private property protection. In other words, the general subject of patriotism had to be reconciled with pri-vate ownership. Again, such a discourse reflected both the material po-sition of an emerging social stratum as conscious property owners and sensitive consumers, and their subjective disposition in contemporary Chinese society. It's worth noting that the discourse of rational patri-otism was in accordance with the official voice at the same time. *Peo-ple's Daily* and Xinhua News Agency, together with many government Weibo accounts, all took pains to propagate the notion of "rational pa-triots" as law-abiding citizens while urging local governments to take measures to control the situation (Zhu et al., 2012). This discourse indi-cated a departure from "patriotism" as official nationalism encouraged by the party-state, which requires unconditional loyalty, commitment, and a readiness for self-sacrifice of all members of the nation.

> People have been so excited about expressing our strong patriotism be-cause of the Diaoyu Islands. It is great. But today I saw the gathering, slo-gan, and demonstration in front of Heiwado [a Japanese store in Changsha, China]. It only hurts our people more if we vent our anger by boycotting Japanese goods and smashing Chinese stores carrying Japanese goods. Maybe we need to be more sober. Why is it that what we wake up to is only a slogan or a gesture in our excitement since the beginning of the incident?

> I promise that: before we take back the Diaoyu Islands, I boycott all Japa-nese products. From now on, I won't travel to Japan; won't buy Japanese books or music albums; won't eat Japanese food. Say "No" to all things related to Japan until Japan behaves itself. Furthermore, I promise that: I won't sabotage or vandalize any Japanese products owned by my com-patriots. I won't break their cameras, won't smash Japanese cars on the street, or burn Japanese comic books ... We have the obligation to boycott but not the right to damage.

> When it comes to defending the Diaoyu Islands and boycotting Japanese goods, we appeal to rationality! No violence! To defend our home country, defend every inch of our land, please start with loving your compatriots, respecting everyone's rights!

The notion of nationalism implies that the nationalist identity takes precedence over all other forms of identity, including those of community, class, political preference, and ethnic allegiance (Calhoun, 1993b). In the case of the Diaoyu Islands, nationalist identity – which itself spawned participation in the unfolding event in the first place – was superseded by a subnational identity emerging among those participating in the events. The mainstream online users occupied what Huang has called a "middle social stratum" in the rapidly stratified Chinese society (P.C. Huang, 2009).[9] Situated between the ruling classes and their social-elite allies, on the one hand, and underclasses of the economically and socially deprived, on the other, this broad middle stratum is subject to the volatility brought about by the country's ongoing market reforms in employment, housing, and health care, and its members face a precarious socio-economic future. They are vulnerable to the drawbacks of the party-state's authoritarian regime, such as corruption, ineffective public services, and arbitrary government administrative power. Most of them, therefore, are sensitive to social justice and motivated to speak on behalf of less privileged social groups (Y. Zhao, 2008). This structural feature may motivate them to participate in proto-civic and proto-democratic political activities. At the same time, however, members of the emerging middle stratum are also striving to come to terms with their own socio-economic identities. How this middle stratum, congregating online, acted and reacted during the Diaoyu Islands dispute reflected both this objective socio-economic structure and the subjective consciousness this stratum has of its position.

The findings in the case of the 2012 anti-Japanese movement suggest that, instead of a static object with a single shared meaning, the nation is a site of active contestations between communities with different socio-economic positions and value systems. In his recent comments on rising nationalism in Western Europe and the United States, sociologist Bart Bonikowski (2016) pointed out that similar political and economic conflicts were at the heart of the recent resurgence of nationalist sentiments. In the United States, the claims of grassroots conservative movements and right-wing politicians have resonated most strongly with economically insecure and racially prejudiced working-class white men. In Western Europe, by contrast, the working and lower-middle classes, who have benefited the least from European integration, have

---

9 This "middle social stratum" in the Chinese context differs from the conventional concept of "middle class," the latter being the majority groups mediating between the traditional poles of capital and labour in a developed capitalist society.

been the most susceptible to anti-immigration and anti–free trade rhetoric (Bonikowski, 2016, p. 434). All these cases seem to indicate that, far from diminishing amid the increasing global interconnectedness, the instrumental and emotional power of nationalism is gaining strength in response to the challenges of globalization.

Nationalism in Globalization

While concerns about inequality, dislocation, and job loss resulting from global capitalist development are behind the recent rise of nationalist politics (Pazzanese, 2017), globalization has long been considered a force that threatens the foundations of national identity. Facilitated in part by the rapid development of network media, increasing global interconnections are believed to have diminished the conceptual and institutional underpinnings of the nation-state (Castells, 2011; Skey, 2009). Following this line of argument, globalization and nationalism are fundamentally opposed to one another and therefore destined for a relationship of resistance and confrontation rather than a mutually beneficial co-existence (Arnason, 1990; Giddens, 1994b; Roudometof, 2014).

Taken as a long-term historical process, however, globalization involves the very emergence of the nation as a cultural and institutional form (Giddens, 1994b; Roudometof, 2014). In fact, the historical emergence and articulation of China as a modern nation-state was intricately related to the processes of globalization. The Chinese nation had long existed in an abstract Chinese world order, which placed its culture at the centre of a universe that extended as far as did its cultural influence (Tok, 2010). The notion of sovereignty, when tied to a claim over territory, had little meaning to most Chinese until the mid-nineteenth century. China's development into a modern sovereign state took place to a large extent through the Chinese people's collective historical experiences of international relationships (Tok, 2010). Among such relationships, the ones with Japan, the United States, and Taiwan have been the most prominent sources for understanding issues regarding sovereignty, nationalism, and the aspirations of the Chinese nation-state. With their different yet intertwining roles, both historically and in the present, China, Taiwan, Japan, and the United States formed, as the event unfolded, a circle of references for national identification (X. Zhang, 1998).

The persisting Diaoyu Islands dispute between China and Japan has to do with historical animosities arising from Japan's belligerent past but also with the competition between the two countries for energy and marine resources in the US-led postwar Asian economic system (Koo,

2009). Informed by the geopolitics in the region, a "new, interest-driven, game-playing paradigm" emerged to shape Chinese people's perceptions of their position therein, as exemplified in the following posts (Y. Zhou, 2006, p. 212).

> Why fight for Diaoyu Islands. It matters in terms of not only our national sentiments, but also our core strategic interests as well as of preserving the fruits of World War II victory. In recent years, Japan has readjusted its military strategy, shifting from being defensive to being more aggressive. The focus of its defence has shifted from the north to the southwest, mainly to China. It also upgraded its SDF [Japanese Armed Forces] to a self-defence force, seriously violating the post–World War II restriction on the country, even the development of weapons of mass destruction. Their national sentiment also took a sharp right turn. So ...

> Gradually China and Japan will find the conflict over the Diaoyu Islands is different from the simple territorial dispute between Japan and South Korea over the Dokdo Islands, it "sours" as it goes on, the strategic ambitions and perplexities of the two countries, and the uncertainty of changing power dynamics in the western Pacific, these big issues will fill up the glass of the Diaoyu Islands. For China, the Diaoyu Islands are no longer a simple territorial dispute. Many of China's key strategic goals and relations are gradually tied to these islands.

Similarly, "the Taiwan issue" embodies both historical experiences and contemporary aspirations for the Chinese people: China's past humiliations during the colonial period, hatred toward Japan during the invasion of Manchuria and the Second World War, unsettling anti-Americanism, and the country's strategic ascendance as a blue-water superpower (X. Wu, 2007). Many mainland online users perceived Taiwan's official response to Japan's sovereign claim over the Diaoyu Islands as firm and courageous. This moment of international relations crisis seemed to have enabled a temporary show of unity in the Chinese nation across the strait. Consequently, this perception seemed to have led mainland patriots toward – as Tok had observed a few years earlier – "a form of new optimism and loud confidence over domestic sovereignty issues" (Tok, 2010, p. 29).

> Today in history: on 15 August 1945, Japan announced to the world its unconditional surrender. On this memorable day, we should remind our future generations to remember the horrendous crimes Japan committed against Chinese people. Now our motherland is rising. We would never

again allow Japan to play gangsters on our territory. Let's fight against imperialist invasion, defend our sovereignty, and protect world peace! Meanwhile, support activities to stand up for the Diaoyu Islands from across the Taiwan Strait and Hong Kong!

People landing on the Diaoyu Islands carried both the Five-Starred Red Flag and Blue Sky, White Sun and a Wholly Red Earth [the national flag of the Republic of China]. It's in today's headline news.

Finally, the United States has always had a shadowy existence in the psyches of the Chinese people because the Americans have long had a strong interest and prominent presence in the Asia-Pacific region. Its close alliance with Japan, involvement in Taiwan, and military partnerships with other Asian countries that have territorial disputes with China have all made the Chinese people believe that the United States is the real power behind Japan, which threatens Chinese sovereignty (Tok, 2010). Moreover, as China's influence continues to grow, its relationship with the United States has become crucial in defining its role in the region as well as on the global stage. In fact, the earliest episodes of cyber-nationalism were mostly direct responses to some high-profile international incidents involving perceived US infringements on Chinese national sovereignty. Salient examples include the bombing of the Chinese Embassy in Belgrade by NATO forces during the Kosovo war in 1999 and the mid-air collision between a Chinese fighter jet and a US intelligence aircraft over the South China Sea in 2001 (T. Zhang, 2013). The shift in political and economic power has led to the perception that the global clout of the United States is eroding, a perception that has underpinned Trump's nationalist approach. The global power shifts have inspired China's ambitions to revive the national and cultural greatness that was eclipsed during the age of Western imperialism. The following posts exemplied the popular setiments in this regard.

Although the Americans "bought" Japan as their own puppet, when put on the table between China and the U.S., it's played by both parties. If Japan is willing to be the puppet to help the U.S. trick China, China's counter-measures then become the game of hitting a dog in front of its master. Beijing and Washington have the tacit understanding that they are playing against each other using Japan as the excuse.

Since Japan started the Diaoyu Islands dispute, it has become clear that the U.S. and Japan were in this together. They were determined to start a war against China, because the first chain of islands is dissolving, and it seems to Japan that China doesn't want to sacrifice development for the incident over several tiny islands.

On 31 August, the famous Chinese entrepreneur and philanthropist Chen Guangbiao published a half-page advertisement in both Chinese and English in the New York Times to declare to the world that "Diaoyu islands belong to China." Sources say that Chen is negotiating with the Japanese media to publish the same advertisement. Comments?

On the economic front, the integration of the Chinese economy with the global market has had multiple effects on Chinese social life. On the one hand, it has exposed the Chinese market in the realm of daily life to global capital, cultures, and ideologies. On the other hand, China's massive penetration by the world market has enabled Chinese consumers to encounter a world of difference, often delineated in terms of nation-state borders. In this world, Chinese are reminded of their fatalistic location in and belonging to a particular community identified by geography, economy, language, politics, a common history, and culture (X. Zhang, 1998, p. 112). The cyber-nationalist discourses in 2012 took place at a cultural juncture between the rapid development of materialism and commercialization of society. The unfolding events generated a process of collective identification by which self-identity and relations with others were constituted through nationalist discourses.

The map service on iPhone5 sold in the Japanese market lists the Diaoyu Islands as part of Okinawa http:t.cn/zlw6B4Q (repost from @ Headline News) Apparently, Apple prioritizes the Japanese market, China's mainland market, for Apple, can be ignored.

Just heard online that the map service in Apple's iPhone5 lists China's Diaoyu Islands as Japan's, while Nokia's map always marks it as China's, Apple's fans in China, you should think twice, do not accidentally become a traitor ~ ~ at a sensitive time, I would rather not have a mobile phone than have this one. So now, we must boycott not only Japanese goods, but also America's Apple.

In this light, contrary to the speculation of the decline of the nation-state in the age of globalization, the more informed the Chinese become, some argue, the more nationalist they may be. "Globalization and nation identity should not be conceived of in binary terms but as two inextricably linked processes. As global cultural flows become more extensive, they [may] facilitate the expansion of national identities and also provide cultural resources which can be domesticated, enfolded within popular and everyday national cultures" (Skey, 2009, p. 338).

Conclusion

Chinese cyber-nationalism, as demonstrated in the 2012 Diaoyu Islands event, comprises wide-ranging public opinions, diverse popular imaginations, and varied efforts at political participation. The 2012 online nationalist currents did not embody a unified ideology or understanding among all participants about the nation's past and present. Instead, they shed light on the country's increasingly differentiated and autonomous social forces, who are eager to express their own understanding of national identity and state legitimacy.

The integration of the Internet into social life has direct bearings on the expressions and implications of Chinese nationalism. As notions of the nation are contested online through popular discourse, the discursive space for national imaginings has grown broader and more complex than that sanctioned by the state. The national self now may be constructed and expressed by ordinary people with differential information access and fragmented social networks. Amid the bustle of consumerism, mass culture, and secular nationalist sentiment, these new social spaces facilitate the reimagination of nationalism in a socioeconomic context (X. Zhang, 1998). Through a culturalist interpretation of nationhood, this chapter has identified multiple sources of Chinese cyber-nationalism, ranging from state sovereignty and boundaries, historical memories, cultural identities, and socio-economic interests to the geopolitical and economic order. Its conception is informed by China's historical experiences of sovereignty as well as by people's experiences of the country's contemporary socio-economic transition in the global context.

The case of Chinese cyber-nationalism bears significant implications for understanding the recent reassertion of nationalism worldwide. Popular nationalist expressions not only add essential variations to the traditional top-down nationalist discourse, but also have changed the rules for describing and analysing contemporary economics, politics, and culture in the fast-changing world (Kaldor, 2004; X. Zhang, 1998). Neither simply a result of state manipulation, nor strictly a democratic movement in civil society, cyber-nationalism effectively remakes an everyday sphere wherein cultural self-identification and political imagination of a new community takes place. Rather than dominated by elite or official discourses, the Internet – and social media in particular – offer a venue within which popular voices may rise. Instead of a coherent ideology, the nation is, in heterogeneous vernacular conception, "a prism through which the social world of the collective self and its relationships with others is viewed, framed, and acted upon" (Pan, 2010, p. 522).

The 2012 Diaoyu Islands dispute also presents a good opportunity to understand the interaction between nationalism and digital space. In both popular and scholarly discourses, nationalism is treated as exclusive while cyberspace is seen as all-embracing (X. Wu, 2007). With its diffuse global network, the Internet is the poster child for the era of liberalization and globalization. "Disembedding" people from the local to form a "global village" or "global civil society" (Anheier et al., 2005), the Internet represents a cosmopolitan ideal advocating for the freedom of all people regardless of their national identities. Scholars seem eager to predict that increased prevalence of information and communication technologies will phase out traditional notions of physical nation-states, suggesting a declining role for the nation-state and nationalism (Negroponte, 1995). Yet the dual rise of nationalism and the Internet subjects the very content of Chinese nationalism to redefinition. Challenging the common understanding of nationalism as unifying, passive, and exclusive, this chapter has argued that the discourse and politics of cyber-nationalism are generative of social change, with important implications for such fundamental processes as class formation, cultural identification, and geopolitical globalization.

As perhaps the most important version of identity politics, nationalism calls up profound aspects of human identity in contemporary societies (Calhoun, 1993b). Instead of diminishing the role of the nation, the experience of globalization provides opportunities for people to rethink their conceptual categories of belonging. This chapter has highlighted the significance of nationalism for establishing both personal and collective identities that help people locate themselves in the world (Calhoun, 1997). As social constituencies respond differently to the tremendous changes, differing levels of identification and categorization might operate in national identification (Guo, 2004). Some people may take their everyday identity for granted or reject the framework altogether; still others are passionate and primed for mobilization. This chapter has provided a case to expound on how people strive to shape their cultural identities in the context of the political status quo, as well as on how different social interests hegemonize nationalistic discourse about historical memories and perceptions of contemporary realities (X. Zhang, 1998). It also confirmed the observation elsewhere that those segments of the population that are acutely threatened by rapid cultural and economic change are most receptive to nationalist political manipulation.

Admittedly, the Weibo data for this study did not include user de-
mographic information. Therefore, there was no direct evidence to
conclude that the authors of these postings had all the socio-economic
features of a middle class. And, in any case, the definition and implications of China's rising middle class has been a contested issue among
social researchers. However, social identity is "no more than a relatively stable construction in an ongoing process of social activity" (Calhoun, 1991). In this sense, class is a "happening" rather than a matter
of socio-economic structure. In Bourdieu's term, identity is a matter of
habitus, an intersubjective process that grants people a practical social
sensibility of how to act (Bourdieu, 1984). Along this line of argument,
the postings may be seen as signs of the emerging consciousness of a
social class in the making. In other words, the analysis has illustrated
a collective identification process without assuming a priori the existence of a well-defined middle class. Nor has the analysis taken these
postings as expressions of their objective interests derived from their
socio-economic standing in contemporary Chinese society.

CHAPTER APPENDIX

Methodology, Topic Groups, and Keywords from Sina Weibo Postings on the Diaoyu Islands Dispute

The Diaoyu Islands commanded the attention of the Weibo sphere, eclipsing all other trending topics at the time (Weibo trending topics, http://data.weibo.com/report/report?order=all-all-all-2012-sj). For this study, 100,000 postings on Sina Weibo were randomly selected from the 48,283,104 generated during the event from July to October 2012. The data for the current study were collected via a keyword search on Weibo. com for postings containing the word *diaoyudao* (the Diaoyu Islands). Textual noise such as punctuation, symbols, or affirmative utterances were removed from the corpus prior to subsequent analyses. Then NLPIR was used for word tokenization, a process by which the texts in the corpus were parsed into meaningful linguistic units.

Topic modelling was also used to analyse conventional texts such as scientific abstracts (Griffiths & Steyvers, 2004) and newspaper archives (DiMaggio et al., 2013; Wei & Croft, 2006). More recently, various versions of such models have been successfully applied to studying user-generated texts in social media (Chang et al., 2009; McCallum et al., 2007; Ramage et al., 2010). For instance, Weng et al. (2010) utilized such a model to explore Twitter users' interests. Ramage et al. (2010) employed this method to categorize Twitter postings according to their substance, style, status, and social characteristics. Moreover, similar models have also been effectively applied to Chinese texts generated on social media platforms such as Twitter (Zhao et al., 2011; L. Hong & Davison, 2010; Ritter et al., 2010).

The specific model used for the analysis was a Labelled LDA (Latent Dirichlet Allocation) topic model. Unlike other topic models, a Labelled LDA topic model can categorize Weibo postings according to learned latent meanings in addition to literal meanings of the corpus. To do so, labelled LDA employs a supervised topic model that first identifies the statistical relationship between a sample text's underlying topics and correspondent tags to describe such topics, and then classifies the whole corpus based on this statistical relationship.

Two steps were involved in building the topic model for our analysis. First a latent content analysis was performed on two thousand postings randomly selected from the corpus. Each posting was read carefully and marked with tags indicating the main topics embedded in the posting. A total of eleven sets of topic tags were created based on the content analysis of these postings. Postings with multiple meanings were marked with multiple tags. This supervised step – that is, the content analysis based on the researchers' reading of the sample postings – enable the injection of meanings embedded in the postings into the computer-generated algorithms at the next step, and therefore helped improve the quality of meaning identification and classification of the topic model.

Second, we fed the computer program with tagged postings from the first step and had it generate a set of probability rules based on the inferred relationship between the tags and the postings. This way our Labelled LDA model was trained to automatically assign the remaining postings to the eleven sets of tags from the first step to form eleven topic groups. Last, the Labelled LDA model summarized the most frequent words from each topic group.

Based on a careful reading of the keywords, the eleven topical groups are further interpreted (see table 4.1). To the extent that these keywords overlap with the topic tags generated by the researchers in the previous latent content analysis, they provide both evidenc of validity for the analysis and hints for further interpretations of the postings. It is worth noting that these keywords were grouped together because they appeared frequently in the postings grouped based on their latent meanings. Therefore, seemingly unrelated words may be categorized into the same group.

Table 4.1. Topic groups and keywords from Sina Weibo postings on the Diaoyu Islands dispute .

Topic group 1: Indicates strong adversarial sentiments and inclination in favour of military acts against Japan. The most indicative words of this group are: war (*zhanzheng*), to start a war (*kaizhan*), Japan Self-Defense Forces (*ziweidui*), Japs (*guizi*), military (*junshi*), the Liberation Army (*jiefangjun*), to control (*kongzhi*), hawkish (*qiangying*), the navy (*haijun*), to bully (*qifu*), aircraft carriers (*hangmu*), and the bottom line (*dixian*).

Topic group 2: Contains news reports narrating Japan's actions and positions in the unfolding events and analyses of effects of Japan's actions in relation to other territorial issues in East Asia. The most indicative words of this group are: to purchase (*goumai*), to nationalize (*guoyou*), protests (*kangyi*), reports (*baodao*), to oppose (*fandui*), the dispute (*zhengduan*), illegal (*feifa*), the prime minister (*shouxiang*), the foreign affairs department (*waijiaobu*), the rightists (*youyi*), South Korea (*hanguo*), Liuqiu (*ryukyu liuqu*), and Tokyo (*dongjingdu*).

Topic group 3: Related to historical memories of the Chinese people stirred up by the current territorial dispute. The keywords include: history (*lishi*), national humiliation (*guochi*), the Mukden Incident (*jiuyiba*), invasion (*qinlue/qinzhan*), the anti-Japanese war (*kangri*), the Chinese nation (*zhonghua, zhonghuaminzu*), to defend (*baowei*), to belong to (*shuyu*), Northeast China (*dongbei*), peace (*heping*), the Second World War (*erzhan*), to commemorate (*jinian*), to surrender (*touxiang*), the anniversary (*zhounian*), and dignity (*zunyan*).

Topic group 4: Concerns the roles, real and imagined, the United States played in the unfolding events in the Asia-Pacific region. The thematic words include: the United States (*meiguo*), the dispute (*zhengduan*), war (*zhanzheng*), aircraft carriers (*hangmu*), international (*guoji*), military (*junshi*), the advertisement (*guanggao*), the *New York Times* (*niuyueshibao*), politics (*zhengzhi*), behind the scene (*beihou*), South China Sea (*nanhai*), East China Sea (*donghai*), Treaty of Mutual Cooperation and Security (*anbao*), military drills (*yanxi*), currencies (*huobi*), the US military forces (*meijun*), Okinawa island (*chongsheng*), statements (*shengming*), conflicts (*chongtu*), to provoke (*tiaoqi*), Asia (*yazhou*), and strategies (*zhanlue*).

Topic group 5: Contains postings depicting various grassroots responses to the unfolding events. This topic group had these keywords: online videos (*shipin*), the people (*renmin*), speeches (*yanjiang*), RMB (*renminbi*), hopes (*xiwang*), to organize (*faqi*), netizens (*wangyou*), to defend (*baowei*), to vote (*toupiao*), to support (*zhichi*), the motherland (*zuguo*), raising the flag (*shengqi*), ceremonies (*yishi*), to donate (*juankuan*), students (*zhongxiaoxue*), and actions (*xingdong*).

Topic group 6: Focuses on the news coverage of and responses to Hong Kong activists' landing on the Diaoyu Islands and their capture, and later release, by the Japanese authorities. The main words in the postings are: Hong Kong (*xianggang*), success (*chenggong*), heroic (*weiwu*), to land on (*denglu/dengshang*), ownership (*suoyou*), illegal (*feifa*), to declare (*xuanshi*), Kai Fung No. 2 (*qifeng*), the sons and daughters of the Chinese nation (*zhonghuaernv*), Beijing (*Beijing*), the Five-Starred Red Flag (*wuxinghongqi*), to pledge (*xuanshi*), to arrest (*daibu*), the mainland (*dalu*), security guards (*baoan*), control (*kongzhi*), warriors (*yongshi*), missiles (*daodan*), ships (*chuanzhi*), heroes (*yingxiong*), action (*xingdong*), safety (*anquan*), to negotiate (*jiaoshe*), consequences (*houguo*), to announce (*xuanbu*), to return (*fanhui*), international (*guoji*), and global (*quanqiu*).

Topic group 7: Demonstrates the strong will expressed by Weibo users to defend the sovereignty of the Chinese nation. The words most frequently appearing in the postings are: nation states (*guojia*), islands (*daoyu*), the world (*shijie*), to defend (*hanwei*), inherent territory (*guyou lingtu*), subsidiary (*fushu*), invasion (*qinfan*), actions (*xingdong*), territorial waters (*linghai*), our country (*woguo*), resolute (*jianjue*), to protect (*weihu*), statements (*shengming*), baseline (*jixian*), developments (*fazhan*), voice (*shengyin*), power (*liliang*), peace (*heping*), stances (*lichang*), sacred (*shensheng*), the United Nations (*lianheguo*), integrity (*wanzheng*), anger (*fennu*), to own (*yongyou*), to negotiate (*tanpan*), measures (*cuoshi*), cohesion (*ningju*), the People's Republic of China (*zhonghuarenmingongheguo*), disputes (*zhengyi*), dignity (*zunyan*), since time immemorial (*ziguyilai*), the Philippines (*feilvbin*), every inch of the land (*cuntu*), to clarify (*mingque*), necessary (*biyao*), and to represent (*daibiao*).

Topic group 8: Expresses the grievances over the injustice and corruption the online stratum had to deal with in their daily life. Such grievances led to cynicism toward and distrust of the Chinese government's handling of the dispute over the Diaoyu Islands. The postings in this group include the following words: protests (*kangyi*), the events (*shijian*), city inspectors (*chengguan*), news (*xinwen*), the people (*laobaixing*), the public (*minzhong*), to despise (*bishi*), the police (*jingcha*), to condemn (*qianze*), to reclaim (*shoufu*), the Japs (*guizi*), to protect (*baohu*), to care for (*guanxin*), the motherland (*zuguo*), Nansha (*nansha*), domestic (*guonei*), to solve (*jiejue*), foreign (*duiwai*), and to retain (*baozhu*).

Table 4.1. *(continued)*

Topic group 9: Focuses on the official responses and diplomatic efforts of the Chinese government. The words in this group include: the China sea (*zhongguohai*), to cruise (*xunhang*), on the sea (*haishang*), security guards (*baoan*), fishing boats (*yuchuan*), to arrive (*dida*), news reports (*baodao*), to protect legal rights (*weiquan*), the administration of fishery (*yuzheng*), law enforcement (*zhifa*), territorial waters (*linghai*), the Ministry of Foreign Affairs (*waijiaobu*), the formations (of warships) (*biandui*), warships (*junjian*), to patrol (*xunluo*), weather forecast (*tianqiyubao*), official business (*gongwu*), the sea (*haiyang*), sea miles (*haili*), ships (*chuanzhi*), to discover (*faxian*), the navy (*haijun*), islands (*daoyu*), the spokesman (*fayanren*), fishing (*zuoye*), warnings (*jinggao*), responses (*huiying*), the East China Sea (*donghai*), to demand (*yaoqiu*), sailing (*hangxing*), directions (*fangxiang*), and airplanes (*feiji*).

Topic group 10: Describes Taiwan's position and responses to the dispute. The main words are: Taiwan (*Taiwan*), fishing boats (*yuchuan*), the police (*jingcha*), sea miles (*haili*), Ma Ying-jeou (*mayingjiu*), the mainland (*dalu*), fishermen (*yumin*), security guards (*baoan*), warships (*jianting*), to declare (*xuanshi*), to land on (*dengshang*), congress members (*yiyuan*), to enter (*jinru*), heading to (*qianwang*), both sides on the Taiwan strait (*liangan*), properties (*caichan*), the distance (*juli*), the Japanese side (*rifang*), to intercept (*lanjie*), ships (*chuanzhi*), confrontation (*duizhi*), to unite (*lianhe*), heroic (*weiwu*), state-owned (*guoyou*), safety (*anquan*), to reclaim (*shoufu*), Okinawa (*chongshengxian*), warships (*junjian*), and cooperation (*hezuo*).

Topic group 11: Comprises postings concerning the protests and boycott of Japanese and American products by Chinese Weibo users. These words include: Japanese products (*rihuo*), to boycott (*dizhi*), compatriots (*tongbao*), cellphones (*shouji*), rational (*lixing/lizhi*), incidents (*shijian*), solidarity (*tuanjie*), to refuse (*jujue*), to use (*shiyong*), the world (*shijie*), economy (*jingji*), to harm (*shanghai*), to purchase (*goumai*), to defend (*baowei*), vandalism (*dazaqiang*), caution (*zhuyi*), domestic (*guonei*), determination (*jianjue*), the United States (*meiguo*), traitors (*maiguozei*), promises (*chengnuo*), the markets (*shichang*), friends (*pengyou*), Nokia (*nuojiya*), cars (*qiche*), fellow countrymen (*guoren*), enterprises (*qiye*), the people (*renmin*), emotions (*qingxu*), and violence (*baoli*).

5

Constructing the Network Market

On 19 September 2014, the New York Stock Exchange saw its largest initial public offering (IPO) in history. With a market value measured at US $231 billion at closing time – bigger than Amazon and eBay combined – Alibaba became one of the world's largest e-commerce corporations. A commercial empire built upon a powerful network, Alibaba exemplifies the perfect combination of two extraordinary developments in China in recent decades: market economy and network technology. Infusing macroeconomic policies, business strategies, and consumer practices with technical infrastructures, Alibaba's success story unfolds at the conjunction of changing relations between state policies and market practices, between production and consumption, and between the local and global markets in the Chinese context. Featuring centrally in the story, the Internet is not only celebrated as a central technical infrastructure for developing a new "network economy," but also serves as a discursive resource for contesting market development in post-socialist China.

The growth of e-commerce in China implies the workings of two intersecting yet distinct fields. First, it involves an economic field of position composed of all types of market roles, including, for instance, Alibaba sellers, buyers, service providers, and other related parties. This field is where the usual behaviour expected in markets takes place: price matches supply with demand in a game where sellers seek maximum profit, while buyers seek the highest utility. The economic field of position is further imbricated with actors in the larger economic context: the state, capital, and labour, whose relations are increasingly subject to market influence in China. The establishment of e-commerce as the newest mode of "network economy" not only entailed changes to the key elements of the market, but also led to a new constellation of power between the central social actors.

In tandem with this economic field of position, this chapter identifies a second intersecting discursive field of "position-taking" in the development of the network market in China. This field is crystallized around several key transformative sites at the intersection of network technologies and the market economy: the network market, the world of production and work, and the consumer and consumption, all of which are going through rapid and simultaneous change (cf. Fisher, 2010). Growing out of the situated interplays between these sub-areas of the market, these sites become places where actors define their self-understandings and interrelations through a discursive process.

Far from being simply a result of technological advancement "plus" market doctrines, the network market of Alibaba is made possible at the point where the two fields intersect. Such a market entails not only business coordination and technological affordances but also new social and political arrangements, leading to ideological transformations and new cultural practices. As Karl Polanyi argued in his seminal analysis of the market, calculative self-interest and profit-maximizing behaviour do not occur simply according to abstract economic conceptions. They are solutions to a compelling real-world problem, which is socially constituted through institutional arrangements and cultural contestations (Polanyi, 1957; Grabher, 2017). In Alibaba's case, the process takes place through digital discourses, which are constituted by actors' understandings of technology and strategic efforts to engineer market relations. Rather than transparent reflections of reality, such discourses articulate particular outlooks on the relationships between network technology and the post-socialist market economy (Fisher, 2010, p. 2).

Centring around network technology as its trope of understanding and presentation, discourses on e-commerce and network economy have played a pivotal role in the recent legitimation and restructuring of China's market economy. By tracing the trajectories of practices, events, and discourses surrounding the "Internet +" policy, entrepreneurship and innovation, and fake goods – three key intersections between the economic and discursive fields – this chapter examines how "global and situated elements, discursive and non-discursive practices, technology and politics, ethics and identity … come together to constitute a context in motion" for the development of network markets in China (L. Zhang & Ong, 2008, p. 9).

As will be illustrated by the case of Alibaba, the ideological function of technology is evident at all levels of the economic field, from personal to supra-national. The state as well as various non-state actors such as corporations, technocratic communities, business associations, the urban middle class, and rural communities all "press their cases," albeit with "uneven levels of planning, organization, and articulation," to forge the discursive space of the network economy (Y. Hong, 2017, p. 12). Discursive articulations precipitated by these actors constitute the outlook of key discursive sites wherein the network market is understood and promoted in the imaginations and practices of these players.

Alibaba: The Bazaar on the Internet

Jack Ma, the company's legendary founder, chose the name Alibaba to bring to mind the magical moment of "open sesame" from the famous folklore. Ma envisioned that his online portal would open a "doorway to fortune" for Chinese manufacturers and merchants trying to reach global buyers. In fact, Alibaba has quickly grown into something much larger than a simple doorway during the past two decades. Under its corporate name, a constellation of subsidiary enterprises have branched out to connect a multitude of sellers, buyers, third-party service providers, strategic alliance partners, and investee companies. Its core commerce includes Taobao, a web portal for consumer-to-consumer (C2C) retail services; and Tmall, a business-to-consumer (B2C) and business-to-business (B2B) retail portal. With some 466 million active buyers by the end of June 2017 and more on its mobile applications, Alibaba currently commands the largest share in the e-commerce market both at home and abroad (Alibaba Group, 2017). In service to its core businesses, Alibaba developed an in-house research institute, a customer services centre, and a retailer recruiting and training establishment, providing such services as Wangwang, an integrated instant messaging (IM) system for buyers and sellers to negotiate product, financial, and logistical details; and an internal search engine powered by its partner Yahoo. In addition, the corporation has expanded further along the e-commerce industry's value chain by developing such key business sectors as Aliyun, a data-centric cloud computing service; Alipay, an online escrow system accounting for roughly half of all online payment transactions in China; and Cainiao, a logistics network. In recent years, the corporation has also entered the lucrative digital media entertainment business and various other emerging technology-driven industries.

In his 2014 open letter to potential investors in preparation for the company's stock market debut, Ma upgraded the corporation's mission from building a "doorway" to an "ecosystem" (Ma, 2014). Building upon its early business mantra, "to make it easy to do business anywhere in the world," Alibaba, Ma states, aims to enable "small enterprises" to "leverage innovation and technology to grow and compete more effectively in the domestic and global economies" (Alibaba Group, 2017). By emphasizing "innovation and technology" – a system comprising the Internet, cloud computing, mobile networks, and big data to manage the flows of logistics, data, and capital – Alibaba highlights the power of its network infrastructure to overcome major practical hindrances to the development of e-commerce in China, ranging from the absence of a nationwide electronic credit payment system to the lack of a reliable and efficient logistics and delivery system and unsatisfactory customer services (Tai, 2006). The innovation and technology discourses characterize Alibaba as "the material expressions" of e-commerce made possible by its advanced technological infrastructure (DeNardis, 2012).

More importantly, Alibaba does not "simply attempt to push the boundaries of technology" but rather to harness the Internet to "create a new business ecosystem" (Alibaba Group, 2017). The notion of "ecosystem" underscores the network market as an autonomous system of seamless communication and exchange of information, products, and services between buyers, sellers, and all other stakeholders. The potentials of technology are deemed the drivers of productivity and efficiency. A "frictionless" market, the culmination of a "network economy," is dependent on the power of technology to channel information flows (Mansell, 2012). The image of a universal and autonomous market, therefore, runs on the organizational and commercial capacities of network technology. At the same time, the "technicalities" of network technology – flexibility, adaptability, decentralization, and self-regulation – work to overcome cultural or geographical barriers while constructing a global market (Fisher, 2010, p. 214). In such a network market, businesses benefit from boosted control over information and logistics, whereas consumers are empowered to overcome restrictions of routine decision-making.

Beneath the veneer of the discourse celebrating the power of network technology lies a particular understanding of the market as a universal, exclusive form of economic arrangement. That is, the market functions as an autonomous, self-subsistent institution, exempt from extra-economic cultural and social factors (Zelizer, 1988). In practice, however, the organization of commercial life never operates neatly according to such neo-classical assumptions (Geertz, 1978; Polanyi, 1957). Although partly autonomous, economic processes are but one category of social relations, interdependent with meaning systems and structures of social relations (Zelizer, 1988).

Dominant discourses about the network economy overlook "the social infrastructure" comprising networks between personal, corporate, state, and supra-national relations (McGuigan & Manzerolle, 2015). On top of the rational calculation of the cost/benefit ratio and the regulation of exchange by the price mechanism, network markets imply a social process in which these actors negotiate the social arrangements of economic transactions and, in doing so, simultaneously formulate their identities and relations in consumption, production, and exchange (Zelizer, 1988). During this process, social actors validate their economic pursuits by discursively invoking existing cultural rules. At the same time, the existing rules are constantly bent and revised in the very process of discursive exchange.

Epitomizing a business model representing seamless integration between technological progress and competitive markets, Alibaba's "friction-free" network market is celebrated as the outcomes of powerful technological infrastructures that facilitate the exchange of information, goods, services, and payments in market transactions with increased effectiveness and at reduced cost. Yet the notion of networks, rooted and constructed in the market paradigm, serves also as the ideological foundation of the new network economy (Fisher, 2010, p. 5). The network economy entails new forms of relationships between actors as well as new institutional infrastructures, such as a legal and regulatory framework, that enable the efficient functioning of the network market (Bakos, 1998). In the following sections, I will trace narratives surrounding Alibaba's network markets to understand transformations in the workings of the network economy.

The Internet +: The Constellation of State and Market

In a speech given at the annual conference of Asia-Pacific Economic Cooperation (APEC) in September 2014, Chinese president Xi Jinping first brought up the term "the new normal" to indicate a stage of "slower, more mature growth" of the Chinese economy (Xinhua News Agency, 2014). In a later meeting on the Chinese economy, Xi stressed the urgency of embarking on "supply-side reforms" to put the economy back on track with "deep structural changes" rather than more short-term stimulus on the demand side. Although Xi did not provide much detail on either of these concepts, the state media, Xinhua News Agency, "neatly tied the two phrases together" in reporting these events: "the supply-side structural reform is the new growth driver under the new normal" (Economist, 2016a). Heralding a renewed effort by Chinese leadership to boost the economy, the terms soon became keywords on the agendas of economic planning meetings. Officials, economists, business academics, and industry practitioners discussed and debated – in numerous news articles and speeches – the actions implied by the emphasis on these terms.

Behind these "slogans in search of content" lay an increasingly open policy process in general (Economist, 2016a). Instead of yielding a regulation or statute in the form of a finished product representing decisions from top officials exclusively, a key national economic policy initiative was launched in the form of public speech and media reporting (Liebman, 2011). Xi's sanction of the terms opened up "spaces" necessary for the concepts to work outside the exclusive institutional apparatus of the state (Mertha, 2009). This episode was only one facet of the recent tendency of the policy process to become more "democratic and scientific." Top-down planning still occurs, but now with the primary aim of staking out a wider strategic vision rather than specifying objectives and methods more narrowly. In this context, policies are increasingly formulated on the basis of inputs from experts in order to achieve a more rational definition of goals and procedures (L. Chen & Naughton, 2016).

Increased consultation in policymaking enables a broader group of actors to participate in the discursive process. Often beginning with a series of high-profile meetings between leading experts and professionals, the consultation process then opens up more broadly, with suggestions solicited at forums and conferences and through the mass media (L. Chen & Naughton, 2016). An even broader group of stakeholders and the public are included when popular support is solicited as a potential source of legitimacy. Consequently, many public policies and laws are now subject to significant debate, "in consultative political institutions such as the National People's Congress" (NPC) or – as often happens – in the media (Liebman, 2011, p. 168). This leaves room for "policy entrepreneurs" – social groups who have become sensitive to their own interests and are keen to invest resources such as time, energy, and money into policymaking processes (Mertha, 2009) – to enter the stage. Needless to say, those rich in political and organizational resources possess the greatest mobilization ability (S. Wang, 2008).

"Supply-side reforms" is one such policy umbrella for important economic initiatives in "the new normal." Under its broad rubric, individual initiatives and policies may be launched without a formal or unified program (Chen & Naughton, 2016, p. 2141). One important cornerstone of this policy-formulation process was laid at China's annual NPC in 2015. In his government work report delivered at the conference, Premier Li Keqiang unveiled "the Internet +" policy, describing in general terms the goal to promote further integration of the Internet with traditional industries to renew economic structures for healthier growth.

According to the policy documents, later posted on the State Council website to follow up with more guidelines, the Internet + required that governments at various levels take measures to facilitate the employment of "mobile Internet, cloud computing, big data and the Internet of Things" to revive manufacturing; to encourage stronger development of e-commerce, industrial networks, and Internet banking; and to help Internet companies become more globally competitive (Xinhua News Agency, 2015a). Innovative information applications, new businesses, original entrepreneurship, and state-of-the-art managerial models were expected to be deployed through implementation of the plan. Under the banner of innovation, the Internet was accorded unprecedented importance as simultaneously "a key economic sector, an indispensable infrastructure, and a pivotal site for catalyzing political-economic transformation" of the Chinese economy (Y. Hong, 2017, p. 9).

Corporate players played a prominent role in this seemingly top-down state-led policy process. The Internet as a fast-growing industry has been propelled mostly by market-driven corporate forces in China (Y. Hong, 2014). As highly motivated policy entrepreneurs, the senior management of leading Internet companies have gained remarkable political influence. Their economic ideas bear considerable weight when the administration paints the Internet industry as "a beacon of hope" for economic restructuring. They are frequently invited to economic round-table discussions and meetings at the State Council. Many have gained membership in the NPC and the People's Political Consultative Conference. In fact, Li Keqiang's "the Internet +" mantra was a direct adoption of the proposal put forward by another high-profile Internet entrepreneur, Ma Huateng, the CEO of Tencent, at the NPC (H. Shen, 2016). The Office of the Central Leading Group for Cyberspace Affairs, a high-level Internet regulation agency, kept the notion on record in the form of a news story posted on its official website, affirming that the concept was pioneered by the Internet industry (Office of the Central Leading Group for Cyberspace Affairs, 2015).

Although it represents the world's second-largest economy, China has long relied on low-end manufacturing and exports for its economic advancement, lacking commanding business models of its own. The burgeoning Internet economy has brought hope for the Chinese government to spur consumption-driven business innovations (Y. Hong, 2014). E-commerce, among other areas, has been promoted by the state and marketing and technocratic communities as a new economic sector that "valorizes" technology, information, and communication (McGuigan & Manzerolle, 2015; Tai, 2006). In the era of "the new normal," e-commerce entrepreneurship is celebrated as a viable model promoted by the Internet + for successful economic restructuring. In this light, the e-commerce giant Alibaba has catered to the state's policy drive for both an innovative network economy and job creation by developing an ecosystem for small businesses and entrepreneurs (Y. Hong, 2014).

The development of the Internet + initiative under the new normal captures "the situated interplay of the state authorities and self-governing practices of economic actors, ... [through] a mobile set of calculative practices" (L. Zhang & Ong, 2008, p. 9). The discursive process is a crucial aspect of such interplay, which further opens up new milieus for articulating diverse political and economic relations in a contingent manner. In the discursive process, actors assemble "objects, situations, and events" to establish a natural, persuasive narrative to define the issue in question. Often pivoting on catchphrases, such narratives take core components and perspectives by which to understand the issue and pack them into "portable" forms to reach out to potential supporters (Mertha, 2009).

Central to the Internet + discourse, technology serves as a legitimizing ideology for economic restructuring and political readjustment for both the state and the Internet industry, against the broad backdrop of post-socialist market transition. The state, sticking to its official rhetoric of a "socialist market economy," extolled the power of networks in the name of social equality and common prosperity. One important potential benefit of the Internet + advocated by the state, for instance, was the prospect of alleviating poverty and reviving the economy in rural China. By promoting technological infrastructures and applications such as the mobile Internet and the smartphone, the policy is expected to help close the digital divide, the most recent form of rural and urban inequality in China (State Council, 2016). E-commerce is called upon as a new model of economic development to raise incomes and create jobs by helping rural farmers and enterprises get their products to urban consumers. Instead of a public and political project, however, such endeavours are expected to be market-dominated processes, relying primarily on private entrepreneurship and market power (State Council, 2016). Initiated in October 2014, Alibaba's Rural Strategy, for instance, planned to invest 10 billion yuan over the next three to five years to build a rural e-commerce service network covering 1,000 counties and 10,000 villages (*qianxian wancun*) in China. "Taobao Villages," where clusters of rural villagers opened retail shops on Taobao (Alibaba's online retail portal), stood out as representing a success story of such efforts. As Alibaba proudly announced on its corporate website, a total of 780 Taobao Villages spanning seventeen provinces and municipalities with more than 200,000 online shops were operating as of 2015 (Alibaba Group, 2016b).

These narratives around e-commerce and the network economy are part of an ideological articulation of the transformation from the socialist to the post-socialist era. The significance assigned to technology by the state and corporate actors has helped legitimize policy to scale back the government's role in economic development and give a freer rein to market forces (Xinhua News Agency, 2015c). While the government promised to continue to "remove roadblocks and pave the way" for entrepreneurship to boost market vitality amid economic slowdown, the information and corporate managers, who have penetrated the culture of policymaking and governance, promoted the elimination of spatial and temporal constraints over markets as the inevitable outcome of network technology (McGuigan & Manzerolle, 2015; Watson et al., 2002).

Gao Hongbing, a vice-president of Alibaba Group, demonstrates this point with vivid examples in an interview:

> The Internet is a typical complex network, an ecosystem … Regulators cannot expect the ecosystem to follow horizontal and vertical structures of a well-organized, prescribed order. An ecosystem is like wild grass, containing great energy beneath the messy surface. The goal of the regulator should not be to mow it into an organized, orderly, neatly looking lawn but to remove detrimental pests. Only this way, wild grass can grow into the trees we expect … Therefore, the future of government governance may be ecological management model. (H. Gao, 2015; Sohu Financial News, 2016)

According to the discourse, as the market becomes integrated into network technology, the technical features of the network render Alibaba's commercial ecosystem "self-sustaining." Power in the network ecosystem, then, is not located within any individual node but operates as distributed power, which is capable of generating organic order to bring about a desired outcome (Fisher, 2010). Taking this logic a step further, individual participants or companies – the nodes embedded in the network – must be flexible and adaptive to the ever-changing topography of the ecosystem. As Jack Ma explained in an interview, "the values of openness, sharing, transparency and accountability are attached to this ecosystem. As long as companies in the ecosystem embrace and adhere to these values, they will succeed" (Netease Financial News, 2013).

The role of digital discourse was paramount in articulating the ideology of transformation, from the time of state socialism to the neoliberalism of the post-socialist era. While the discourse on "industrial technology during socialism was used to legitimize the social compact between capital, labour, and the state, the post-socialist discourse on network technology legitimizes precisely the decomposition of this compact and the constitution of its alternative: privatized relations within the context of a global market" (Fisher, 2010, p. 4). Paralleling the technology discourse that legitimizes the state's withdrawal from the market are the globalization of the economy, the de-hierarchization and decentralization of businesses, and the flexibilization of production and labour processes. Tapping into participatory sentiments of production and consumerism, e-commerce – under the auspices of the Internet + – presents a regulatory regime that has encouraged networked markets to permeate other key transformative sites at the intersection between network technology and the new market economy: the world of work, production, and consumption (Fisher, 2010, p. 5).

Mass Entrepreneurship and Mass Innovation: Production and Consumption

In tandem with the Internet +, the State Council launched another policy initiative to promote "mass entrepreneurship and mass innovation," the "twin engines" of economic growth under the new normal. Li Keqiang sketched out the gist of the policy at the 2015 NPC. Later, the State Council issued more official documents spelling out the general guidelines for improving the environment for entrepreneurship and innovation, pledging itself to increase government investment, lower administrative barriers, improve information infrastructures, and facilitate the establishment of venues for innovation, including university science parks, business incubators, high-tech zones, and experimental regions (Xinhua News Agency, 2016c).

As a champion of both "entrepreneurship" and "innovation," Alibaba was chosen by the government to be among the first seven corporate "demonstration bases" established nationwide. As highlighted on its corporate website, the company states that its "success and rapid growth is built on the spirit of entrepreneurship, innovation" (Alibaba Group, 2016a). Indeed, the growth of Alibaba as a market leader epitomizes the development of e-commerce through entrepreneurial endeavours such as Jack Ma's. As the pioneer of e-commerce, Ma is considered the paragon of a new category of entrepreneurs, who do not simply invent new products for existing markets but devise new markets entailing new modes of production.

Successfully turning "a vision, a group of friends and $60,000" into the world's most valuable Internet company, Ma has become legend in stories told by a chorus of voices in the business and technology world. These stories often attribute Alibaba's success to Ma's personal traits of passion, vision, and courage as an entrepreneur (Tobak, 2014). Such narratives distinguish Ma from the first generation of state entrepreneurs, who were often former bureaucratic managers of state-owned enterprises, and from the collective entrepreneurs, who were a group of energetic non-state actors trailblazing market-oriented practices at the early stage of economic transition from a planned to a market economy (Dickson, 2009; Zapalska & Edwards, 2001). As an individual entrepreneur, Ma embodies the principles of private accumulation and self-interest expressed in profit making and self-promotion.

At the same time, Alibaba's online markets are promoted as an innovative platform for entrepreneurial endeavours of "the masses" – millions of private individuals – and "small and tiny enterprises" (*xiaowei qiye*), the subjects of the State Council's mass entrepreneurship and innovation directive. According to the China E-Commerce Research Center, as of 2014, a total of 7.54 million sellers and retailers operated on Alibaba's retail portals Taobao and Tmall (100EC.CN, 2014). The number of jobs created would be much larger still if those in the logistics, delivery, marketing, IT, and customer service sectors were taken into consideration. Setting up small businesses on Taobao has become an effective way to alleviate the increasing pressure of unemployment in "the new normal" stage of economic development. Moreover, with their low cost and easy access, Alibaba's network markets are inherently inclusive, "empowering the little guys." About half of the online businesses were indeed "small and tiny," with zero employees, less than 30,000 RMB yuan (about US$4,400) in total investment, and in business for less than two years (100EC.CN, 2014).

The e-commerce market has undoubtedly expanded the bandwidth of entrepreneurship. But the expansion is as much cultural as economic. The notion of mass entrepreneurship is premised on individual creativity, authenticity, and autonomy as a private and apolitical project. Entrepreneurial endeavours are embraced as change-creating efforts through which individuals break free from existing constraints within their economic, social, and/or institutional environments for self-actualization and self-authorship (Jennings et al., 2014). It is a common practice for sellers on Taobao to make declarations about their entrepreneurial dreams in their efforts to promote their businesses. Relying as much on individualized stories and communications as on the commercial and organizational potential of network technology, small start-up shops position their efforts within the existing web of meaning. Within such a discursive framework, opening a shop is considered a courageous effort to bootstrap oneself from pre-existing economic or institutional constraints into the pursuit of a dream life, regardless of one's business prospects. Moreover, successful business owners are those who, through "emancipatory entrepreneurship," triumph in achieving their own way in the world, improving social good, or even enacting "brave new worlds" all together (Jennings et al., 2014; Rindova et al., 2009, p. 480).

As "assets to be harnessed into wealth creation," personal characteristics, such as creativity, self-expression, and individual emotions, become "legitimate components" of a new network productive process. Moreover, mass entrepreneurship is made possible only by the ability of networks to "harness the working power of autonomous and dispersed nodes into the productive process" (Fisher, 2010, p. 214). The discourse of innovation presented Alibaba's online market as a network structure made up of the Internet, cloud computing, and big data, and has become the prime venue and key coordinator of production, replacing conventional production sites of stable structures, such as companies or factories. Comprised of homologous nodes, such flat and de-hierarchized networks of production are self-evidently "participatory, inclusive, and democratic, conducive to individual freedom, emancipation, authenticity, self-realization" (Fisher, 2010, p. 7).

Touted as both "a fundamental infrastructure in the e-commerce ecology" and "a marketplace for efficient resource allocation" (Sohu Financial News, 2016), Alibaba's innovative ecosystem is poised to revamp the dynamics of the traditional consumer market, ranging from mechanisms of matching buyer demand with seller supply to the very processes of transaction and logistics. In light of the enormous number of sellers and commodities on its shopping sites, Alibaba's search engine, ranking algorithms, and various management and marketing software have played a determining role in sorting and presenting information about product quality, going prices, and market possibilities. In addition, the company has reshaped the "microstructure" of consumer markets by affecting how buyers and sellers interact and fostering new types of intermediaries (Bakos, 1998). Ali Wangwang, the embedded IM system, for instance, was developed as a real-time communication channel between buyer and seller.

In contrast to the era of mass production – characterized by discrete identities and functional roles, passive and unilateral relationships, and one-way information exchanges between them – the notion of network interactivity enables what may be termed a discourse of "deep engagement" with both production and consumption (Fisher, 2010, p. 7). Indeed, Alibaba's ecosystem targets both sellers and shoppers at the same time. Taobao's C2C business model allows users to choose to participate in transacting as either buyers or sellers. Moreover, the company has invested much energy in developing communities and collaborative networks of sellers and shoppers to engage them in an "immersive" shopping experience (Sun, 2011). Social commerce portals such as Taobao forum (www.taobao.com/forum.php) and group-buying sites such as Juhuasuan (ju.taobao.com) have been set up to facilitate diverse activities including exchanging information about goods and services, reviewing products and sellers, and socializing with other users. In these communities, members are not simply consumers but prosumers who are actively involved not only in marketing, selling, comparing, curating, buying, and sharing products and services, but also in articulating and re-articulating, setting standards for, and negotiating boundaries of their activities (Kozinets, 1999; L. Zhou et al., 2013).

In this context, what "innovation" entails is an ongoing process of structuration between the technological infrastructure and cultural dynamics in the network market (Giddens, 1984). On one hand, an assemblage of articulations based on user-generated product information, including reviews, voting, recommendations, comments, and discussions, stabilizes into an emergent structure of technology use. On the other hand, such a structure of communities and networks encourages cultural consumption, recreation, and creativity, which attaches meanings to consumption situated within everyday practices (Sun, 2011, p. 403). Moreover, the sharing of experiences, problems, and solutions in these milieus makes it easy for Alibaba to collect enormous quantities of information about individual users, which further feeds back into its socio-technological ecosystem.

As a result of this structuration process, new cultural apparatuses and practices are generated, with consequences for the development of the network market. The Singles' Day shopping festival and Taobao's unique transaction language are two prominent examples. On Singles' Day, "11.11," every year, Alibaba launches a large-scale sales event. As the latest numbers indicate, the total gross merchandise volume on 2015's Singles' Day exceeded US $14.3 billion, more than double the US equivalent for Thanksgiving, Black Friday, and Cyber Monday combined. More than just a day of online mega-sales (Lavin, 2016), Singles' Day is also a cultural spectacle. In 2016, for instance, a four-hour nationally televised gala, directed by a Hollywood TV master who had done the Oscars and the Super Bowl, kicked off the festival at midnight. In addition, communication in transactions on Taobao assumes a unique linguistic style, which features unabashedly personal and colloquial lingoes, including phrases such as "Yes, my dearest darling." By borrowing from the private realm, sellers gain the resources to build relationships, trust, reciprocity, and other features of embedded ties

(Carruthers & Uzzi, 2000). Manifest as intertextuality mixing discursive practices from the lifeworld with those of the system world, the fluidity in buyer and seller identities is discursively realized in a shift away from formal business transactions to more interpersonal discourses.

Beneath the veneer of a naturalized yet entrenched process, Alibaba's network markets rely heavily on social re-identification in both the system and the lifeworld. More than a seamless integration with network technology, Alibaba's "new business ecosystem" entails new understandings of the structure, practice, and meaning of the market, modes of production, and the world of work. The discourse of the network economy serves as the ideological base for transforming the traditional identities, relations, and roles of economic actors. Networks become a new productive space defined not by "corporations," "capital," "labour," and so forth, but by the deconstruction of these structures and their reconstruction as entrepreneurs and prosumers – atomistic nodes of production and consumption enabled by the decentralized and interactive network (Fisher, 2010, p. 214). Conventional identities making up the fundamental components of economic activity – production, distribution, and consumption – are blurring. The boundaries between work life and personal life become indistinguishable; workspace and worktime are intermingled with their private, personal counterparts. Work is reconceptualized as a liberating activity of production and consumption, involving "creativity, deep engagement, interactivity, and interpersonal communication" (Fisher, 2010, p. 6). Similarly, the category of worker is substituted for by a new category of the prosumer: an individual and autonomous unit of production, consumption, and entrepreneurship. These new identities, in turn, may profoundly alter how wealth is accumulated and distributed by entailing new modes of exchange, allocation, and valuation (Carruthers & Uzzi, 2000).

Fake Goods: Lifeworld versus System World

Alibaba's discourse of a network market depicts a frictionless, self-regulated global market based on a smooth integration of network technology with consumer markets. However, the global expansion of Alibaba's network market has been far from frictionless. The company has been haunted for years by allegations that its online shopping sites are infested with "fake" goods. The controversy culminated in a lawsuit filed by Gucci, Yves Saint Laurent, and other international brands in 2015, accusing "Alibaba and its 40000 thieves" of being "a giant conduit for counterfeiters" and alleging that the platform "knowingly made it possible to sell fakes" (Ruwitch et al., 2015).

Despite its sheer size, it is not Alibaba, the market, or even China, the world's manufacturer, but the globalizing intellectual property rights (IPR) regime – a relatively recent World Trade Organization (WTO) construct – that provides the criteria for distinguishing between the authentic and the fake, the genuine and the counterfeit (F. Yang, 2015). Within this regime, authentic goods are those represented by brands and logos that indicate truthfully and accurately the authorship and ownership of their corporate producers (Vann, 2006). Upon its accession to the WTO in 2001, China promised to build a more transparent domestic economic structure (Halverson, 2004). It is expected that, as China further integrates into the world market, the country must make significant long-term changes in order for its Internet industries to survive. Online businesses must adopt standardized global business practices, ranging from management and financing to accountability to investors, in the globalized Internet market. Indeed, it is on this platform that, according to Jack Ma, Alibaba's e-commerce ecosystem runs.

Yet, Ma was most defiant in the global dispute over fake goods. In a high-profile interview with Forbes on the subject, Ma was quoted as saying that he "would [rather] lose the case, lose the money" to "gain dignity and respect" for Alibaba and its system, including buyers and sellers (Schuman, 2015). Ma's stance toward intellectual property rights should be considered in context. Since Alibaba's core business is built on providing millions of small entrepreneurs with opportunities and support to start their own businesses, Ma is in a position to feel responsible for all those Taobao sellers, "the little guys," who strive to make a living in often underdeveloped areas of China. "It's not white and black," Ma says. "If you just say, 'Take that down,' it is unfair for that guy [the seller]. We have to also protect these guys, not only the branded businesses. You have to care about all people, their rights" (Schuman, 2015).

Ma's defence brought into the picture the structure, experience, and meaning of both production and consumption in the local market, which IPR's discourse of the standard global market can never eradicate. More importantly, globalized regimes of manufacture, distribution, and consumption paradoxically engender local calculations of value (Kuever, 2014). Consumer practices in local markets may circumvent or subvert mainstream global consumerist schemes such as branding and marketing (Zelizer, 1988). The understandings of "real" and "fake" by Chinese prosumers in their daily consumption practices may not be universally informed by IPR's legal definitions. The legal dispute between Alibaba, a company striving to build a standard market transcending time and space, and IPR and the WTO, the institutional regulative infrastructures governing the global market, must come to terms with millions of local prosumers in China.

Brands encompass both symbolic and material aspects of goods (Kuever, 2014). Symbolically, a brand is expected to relate the commodity to a quality or image in a fixed, direct way (Pang, 2008). While the production of commodities encodes in them complex technological, social, and aesthetic knowledge (Appadurai, 1986), the consumption process allows consumers to experience and express the social world through the symbolic meanings embodied by brands (Holt, 2002). The identity of a brand, therefore, evolves in constant interaction with consumers "through the changing knowledge invested in and extracted from" that brand (Pang, 2008, p. 126). As income inequality increases significantly in China's transition to market economies (Davis, 2005), Chinese people tend to spend more time and energy to improve their social statuses (Walasek & Brown, 2015). Market researchers have observed that Chinese consumers make ample use of brands as carriers of meaning and status symbols in an increasingly stratified consumer society (Kuever, 2014). A counterfeit, in this light, can be regarded as the substitute good of luxury, which provides social meanings such as conformity, face saving, or status seeking. Given that many Chinese consumers knowingly purchase fake products, their demand is one of the driving forces of the grey market (Jiang & Cova, 2012). On a general level, however, the social life of a counterfeit product contains knowledge that seems less controllable and predictable. Consumers purchasing these items have extremely diversified interests and intentions. Nevertheless, by reading them together, consumers demonstrate "a desire and a conscious decision to interpret their own realities and to make sense of the fast-changing world around them" (Pang, 2008, p. 126).

More than status, symbolic value, and social meaning, a brand also serves material functions, such as lowering information costs for consumers by "assuring buyers of the quality and safety of goods, their material content and function, their coverage under warranty, and so on" (Kuever, 2014, p. 174). At the minimum level, the brand is expected to provide stable information regarding the origin of products, materials, and manufacturers. Yet, in the era of globalized production and distribution, brands can no longer be relied upon to communicate such information (Pang, 2008). It has become increasingly difficult to determine a product's or a brand's true country of origin, given such complex global production and distribution schemes as outsourcing and market-specific production (Tian & Dong, 2010).

Having been both the world's largest manufacturer and its largest market in the past few decades, China represents fertile ground for cultivating sophisticated knowledge about global production and circulation for its urban consumers. Anthropologist Erika Kuever (2014) noted, for instance, that in the 1980s and 1990s, when China's export-oriented economy first took off, small *waimao* or "foreign trade" shops existed in many cities across China. Such shops have been selling mainly low-priced goods originally destined for export. Although some such items may have slight flaws, they are still expected to be of better quality than goods meant for domestic consumption. All identifying tags would be removed before these goods were put up for sale. While this may disaffiliate the product from the brand, it does little to delegitimize these products for consumers.

Such historical experience has implications for understanding consumer behaviour in contemporary network markets in China. The same Forbes interview, for instance, told the story of Zhai, a counterfeit goods retailer on Taobao, who operates two Taobao stores selling counterfeit handbags and clothes imitating well-known international brands. Zhai's products come from the very Chinese factories that manufacture the authentic items. Sometimes she got them through backdoor channels from quality-control personnel who would take branded goods off the assembly lines due to minor defects. Other counterfeiters hire workers from the official manufacturer to replicate the real thing using discarded original fabrics, leather, and other raw materials they managed to collect. Sometimes the same manufacturer and factories under contract to produce authentic branded goods would produce extra batches with no labels. Zhai's counterfeits are exact copies of the originals. She sells them at discounted prices and clearly states on her Taobao storefront that they are not official goods (Schuman, 2015).

Zhai's story presents an example of so-called non-deceptive counterfeits – "fakes" that are identical to the legitimate object but that make no claims to authenticity. Chinese consumers have developed a sophisticated vocabulary to describe and evaluate these counterfeits. According to the nature of each product, they are distinguished as *yuandan*, those manufactured with the same design specified in the production order for the originals; *weihuo*, remainders from excess stock; *gendan*, products made with the same materials and designs as the originals but slightly inferior in quality; or *zhuidan*, those made with the same designs but not with materials of the same quality. In social consumption sites such as the Taobao forum, there are many discussions and tips for identifying and purchasing such products. Instead of an "authentic or fake" dichotomy, these notions capture the nuanced distinctions made by Chinese consumers themselves. Shoppers can then assign different values to the goods and make an informed decision based on quality, trustworthiness of the seller, and estimated value. While legal definitions of brand and copyright under IPR do not take into consideration the opinion of any individual buyer, specific knowledge makes all the difference for consumers. The efforts of Chinese consumers can, in this light, be seen as a local process of authentication, with much understanding of its connection to "regimes of value and authenticity elsewhere in the world" (Kuever, 2014, p.185).

In addition to globalized production regimes that have contributed to destabilizing and challenging brands' claims of equivalence across all contexts, local market dynamics also create ample incentives for Chinese consumers to recategorize and recontextualize brands (Kuever, 2014). In navigating the complex, fast-evolving, and multifaceted consumer markets in China nowadays, an ordinary middle-class urbanite may shop in a variety of marketplaces, ranging from foreign or domestic supermarkets and department stores to mom-and-pop shops, sidewalk stalls, village farms, or international chains. This marketplace diversity means that Chinese consumers must constantly evaluate products based on their perceived "truth," evaluated according to function and value instead of simply symbolic aspects (Kuever, 2014). Such practices cannot be contained by the simplistic categories of "authentic" and "fake" dictated by the IPR regime. This situation is both a strategic response to the constant presence of risk due to the lack of legal and regulatory systems (Beck, 1992; Yan, 2012), and the accidental result of learning to navigate diverse marketplaces on a daily basis (Kuever, 2014). Because of low set-up and operation costs, online marketplaces such as Alibaba's Taobao and Tmall attract an enormous number of sellers and host an almost infinite number of commodities. In this light, Alibaba's network markets can be viewed as differentiated and structured spaces of supply and demand, which result from increasingly stratified consumption practices as well as sophisticated and powerful network tools for market segmentation and product differentiation.

The dispute over "counterfeits" in Alibaba's case highlights the effects of the process of globalization on brand "authenticity" and how globalized regimes of manufacturing and distribution produce new calculations of value in the Chinese context (Kuever, 2014). This example accentuates the tension between the profitability of information in the global market and locally embedded lifeworld practices. Patents and copyrights protect the enormous amount of research and development invested in the ever-changing product lines of the established brands, while trademark and trade secret laws guarantee their continued domination. The dominant discursive system of the IPR serves to secure and benefit from the creativity invested in brand-name commodities (Pang,

2008). Yet the brand name is equally affected by the diverse receptions and consumptions of Chinese prosumers. The politics of consumption plays out in everyday practices as prosumers navigate a complex local marketplace, acutely reflecting, in turn, "the ways in which contemporary China is entangled in capitalism" (Pang, 2008, p. 134).

The "consumer revolution" has been a deliberate state policy pursued since the mid-1990s as a strategy to link China's economy with the global market (J. Wang, 2001; Pun, 2003; Yan, 2002). As a result of successful engineering by the post-socialist state, consumer spending has replaced government expenditures to become the biggest driver of economic growth since 2011. E-commerce has become an important retail channel, driving 42 per cent of total consumption growth. At approximately $630 billion in sales in 2015, China's online retail market is the world's largest, nearly 80 per cent bigger than that in the United States (K.W. Wang et al., 2016).

In their efforts to make sense of consumer life in contemporary Chinese society, scholars have debated whether a consumer society in a post-socialist country brings about "the predominance of exploitation and deception, or agency and empowerment" (Davis, 2005, p. 697; Pun, 2003; J. Wang, 2001). Some emphasize "the negative exclusionary and exploitative parameters of the new consumer culture seeing nothing more than a ruse of capitalism or marker of all that is negative about post-socialist city life" (Davis, 2005, p. 692). They believe that consumerism has become a new cultural ideology in Chinese society, silently replacing both Marxist ideology and traditional Chinese values. As an "effective form of capitalist exploitation," it "erodes class consciousness and offers no enchantment, emancipation, or empowerment" (Davis, 2005, p. 696). Far more than simply the "essential twin of production or a neutral information system," consumption is a "new mode of governmentality," one that manipulates and exploits individual desire in the service of domination by capital against the working classes (Pun, 2003, p. 475).

Other scholars approach consumers and the social practices of consumption as "opportunities to identify and understand networks of communication or identity formation" (Davis, 2005, p. 697). Opposing the linear interpretation of subordination and exclusion, this camp emphasizes a consumer culture that "simultaneously incorporates contradictory experiences of emancipation and disempowerment," as often expressed in "individual narratives unfolding against memories of an impoverished personal past during the Mao years" (Davis, 2005, pp. 692 & 709; J. Wang, 2001). In this light, consumption is a process of meaning making rather than a totalizing cultural structure (Zelizer, 1988). Alibaba's case indicates that Chinese consumers may leave their mark on a larger social system through their everyday practices. Such practices serve as interpretable sources for understanding the meaning process of the lifeworld, which "refuses to be shut down by the capitalist discourse, such as that produced by the intellectual property rights regime" (Pang, 2008, p. 117). While such practices may not completely overturn the capitalist order ultimately signified by branding and consumption, the actual social functions and effects of consumption of counterfeits could be considered a kind of "responsible subversion" (Pang, 2008, p. 131).

Conclusion

The development of a network economy in China, as exemplified by Alibaba, takes place as part of ongoing economic restructuring and the deployment of information and communication technology in the process. Far from a natural outcome of applying neutral technological capacities to market mechanisms, however, the development of online markets has been rife with conflicts related to marketization and globalization. Changing structural dynamics of state and market actors in the global context are negotiated and contested in a parallel discursive process. Such a process is organized as a field where various players – including technocratic and business communities, middle-class urbanites and prosumers, and rural villagers and entrepreneurs – with unequal symbolic resources strive to formulate their self-understanding and strategic market positions (Y. Hong, 2017). Consequently, the tensions between socialist ideals and market principles, as well as between globalizing economic drives and lifeworld experiences of local prosumers, constitute the key sites that delineate the discursive field.

Central to China's recent economic restructuring schema, the Internet + as a state policy has elevated the role of the Internet in developing an "innovative" network economy. Premised on the promise of network technology and Internet industries, the development of the network economy is spearheaded as a new economic model. Economic policy processes have become a channel for various players to leverage resources to strategically advance their interests through institutional means. While positioning themselves as instruments for the state's economic restructuring plan, the Internet industries, "with varying degrees of transnational entanglement," have developed their own imperatives, ideologies, and practices (Y. Hong, 2017, p. 12). In the discourse orchestrated by the state in collaboration with these industries, the network market is presented as the natural outcome of a technological process to support smooth communication and transaction of information, products, and services in a marketplace of global scale. Here, the market is implicitly understood as an autonomous and self-efficient system of information and communications, whereas technologies are explicitly promoted as the "drivers" of productivity and efficiency (Mansell, 2012).

Such a discourse of network market masks the complex relationship between technology and the market. On one hand, the notion of network is rooted and constructed within the paradigm of a market structured in a significant part through state policies. On the other hand, the workings of market forces are explained and legitimized by network technology. Alibaba, for instance, relies on keywords underlining the technological features of network, such as complexity, flexibility, interactivity, and decentralization, to present its ecosystem as autonomous and self-sufficient, capable of fostering spontaneous order without needing centralized planning or external governance. Along this logic, as the market is integrated into network technology, it becomes self-regulated and disembedded from social regulation. Subsequently, such a decentralized and autonomous network market requires and enables the network nodes, from individuals to companies to stockholders, to be flexible and adaptive to its fluid environment (Fisher, 2010).

This image of a network market sets the basis for the further articulation of its key elements: network work, network production, and network prosumer (Fisher, 2010). The discourse of mass entrepreneurship, for instance, enables implicit characterization and endorsement of the changing paradigm of production and work, ranging from production forces, processes, and relations to workplaces in the network market (Fisher, 2010). At the same time, the discourse of innovation – promoting digital connectivity that engenders social connectedness and non-market forms of coordination – blurs economic relations with social ones (Grabher, 2017). These disparate themes and their diverse sites are contested and woven together by actors pursuing their respective positions in the discursive field of the network market.

Given its scale and reach, Alibaba's network market is necessarily integrated in the contemporary global political economy. While the structural dynamics of the global market both enable and constrain the practices of Chinese prosumers, the latter ground their consumption practices in their everyday desires and quests for self-definition (Croll, 2006). As demonstrated by the dispute over counterfeits in Alibaba's case, Chinese prosumers constantly redefine and revalue goods with little regard for universalist legal definitions of brand authenticity or "fakeness." While macro forces shape the consumer market and consumer subjects, Chinese prosumers are capable of creating countercurrents through their personal commentary and social discourse (Davis, 2005). "Situated between two contending and yet mutually articulating forces" of state manoeuvring and the global market regime, Chinese prosumers are constantly in search of satisfaction in consumption as well as assurance for their subjective position as consumers and producers (Dirlik 2001, p. 18; H. Yu, 2009, p. 28).

Together these discursive sites piece together "a cognitive map" that helps us navigate the contour of transformations in the development of the market economy in post-socialist China (Fisher, 2010, p. 15). The growth of a network economy required the reorganization of structural relations between society and market, production and consumption, and local and global. For the most part, the dynamics and characteristics of post-socialist economic relations are understood, experienced, and constructed in discursive processes. More than simply descriptions of a contemporary techno-economy, these discourses are central to the constitution of social power relations, institutional arrangements, and the new ways of life arising from the market economy. They are connective tissues between the shift to a post-socialist society and the rise of network technology, between the public productionist world of work and the private consumerist lifeworld (Fisher, 2010).

Just as the market is reduced to an autonomous place, the Internet is often considered neutral, cloaked in the technological discourse of benevolence and progress. In practice, however, "the ideology" of the network – the new egalitarianism through communication – helps legitimize new forms of inequality, segregation, and exclusion in economic processes. Against this backdrop, this chapter has shed light on the social process of marketization in China by relating symbolic practices such as ideology, politics, and culture to forms of organization and systems of authority engendered by such practices (Mattelart & Mattelart, 1998, p. 132).

Conclusion

Taking off at the height of the country's socio-economic reforms in the mid-1990s, the Internet in China has developed alongside the twists and turns of the rapid transformation of contemporary Chinese society. Featured prominently in popular narratives and scholarly discourses, the Internet has been associated with many aspects of social change in China. In the economic realm, as discussed in chapter 5, the Internet is considered a potent infrastructure supporting an information economy, responsible for the newest modes of post-socialist and post-industrial development. On the political front, the Internet is thought to facilitate free speech and grassroots activism in an emerging civil society, at the expense of China's authoritarian regime (Han, 2018; Tai, 2006; Yang, 2009). In this spirit, some believe that the Internet has defined contemporary Chinese experience as much as has the rise of a market economy, as the country continues to quickly become integrated into the global community (R.W. Chu & Cheng; 2011).

Debates about the Internet and social change in China have generated many images of the Chinese Internet. Advocates of civil society argue that free communication and association on the Internet's open network serve as a mobilizing and organizing structure for civic activism. In contrast, the image of the "Great Firewall" reflects the role the Internet plays in enhancing authoritarian control rather than circumventing censorship. Still, the metaphor of the "Great Digital Divide" depicts the unequal adoption of the Internet by different social strata as a manifestation of structural inequality exacerbated by economic privatization in China. Diverse as they are, these images are often premised on a characterization of the Internet as a separate environment "where the real-world constraints of body, space, and time are transcended," or as a flexible, pliable technology that empowers human interaction to serve democratic or market goals (Cohen, 2012, p. 12).

Highlighting the entanglement of the Internet in the cultural processes of social change in contemporary China, the *Web of Meaning* has argued that the Internet is deeply enmeshed in symbolic processes through which social actors struggle to comprehend and contest changing political and economic relations. Far from simply a vacuous space predetermined by the political or economic systems or a neutral technology wielding effects from outside, the Internet mediates complex institutional contexts in which changing identities and relations emerge. By facilitating communicative engagement among an expanding range of social actors, network communication is enrolled into complex power struggles that redefine existing social institutions.

The way in which the Internet becomes imbricated into symbolic processes is complex and dialectic. On the one hand, network communication bears traces of the social structures it expresses. Communicative interactions are social practices that are both enabled and constrained by power relations in various social domains. At the same time, the social logics that underline media practices can bring the Internet's technical capacities into play in unequal and inconsistent ways (Latham & Sassen, 2005). These complex, often inconsistent, symbolic formations may be contingent upon contextual cues enacted by network communication processes particular to the specific social domain. The forms of network communication by which players develop mutual influence are irreducible to existing institutional channels of traditional media and cultural institutions. On the other hand, existing social structures and institutions are subject to change through communicative practices. Relational networks enabled by the Internet reconfigure the means of information access and forms of communication, thereby changing the conditions, constraints, and expectations of social interaction in existing social institutions. By facilitating new ways to organize social life along spatial and temporal dimensions, it has become a vital part of social conditions under which groups vie for cultural and symbolic power to produce new knowledge and social relations (Thompson, 1995; S. Zhao, 2006).

The ensemble of diverse socio-technical practices generated by ordinary users blends versatile communication networks with cultural agency in unexpected ways. These combinations range from the forms of civic and political technology use envisioned by the rationalist and deliberative model of communication to the diverse subjective everyday choices emerging out of the lifeworld (Bakardjieva, 2009). The *Web of Meaning* recognizes both macro-discourses of power and authority and micro-discursive practices by which individuals and groups engage and choose subject positions. The book has highlighted the centrality of discourse to conceive, construct, maintain, and repair social structures, as well as forms of technical mediation that create socio-technological articulations of new institutional contexts. It has striven to show that the mediated social world is constituted by cultural agents' experience and responds to cultural influences at the confluence of both virtual and real social spaces (Farman, 2013). In this world, politics is likely to take place across the boundaries between the institutional core of the system and the outer periphery of various private social spheres (Benson, 2009; Habermas, 1991).

Using three empirical cases, the *Web of Meaning* has examined both lifeworld cultural constructs and political projects of emerging social forces. The case of network privacy has shown that network communication mediates a changing lifeworld where people experience and reflect on existing physical, cognitive, and social mechanisms upon which they draw to understand and practise privacy. The chapter about cyber-nationalism has demonstrated that large-scale national events may turn cyberspace into a discursive field in which social groups with shifting affiliations ponder national identities in relation to their new socio-economic positions. In the case of the network market, the preceding chapter showcased that the Internet, central to post-industrial economic transition, serves not only as an information infrastructure but also a trope of discursive legitimation for existing power players in domestic policy processes and the global regime of capitalist production and consumption. Together these examples weave a multifaceted landscape of social transformation through the socio-technological process of network communication.

Discourses of Social Change

Empirically, the *Web of Meaning* has examined the role of discursive practices mediated by the Internet in the changing institutions of privacy, nationalism, and the market in contemporary China. The book has identified the cultural categories underlying the changing institutional practices and discovered the socio-technological processes that constitute the institutional context. At the same time, it has contemplated the implications of these changes in the global context.

Network Privacy

The rapid and dramatic development of information and communication technologies in contemporary societies has heightened concerns about privacy. Yet it is the entanglement of technology with existing social logic and structures that defines the context for new practices and understandings of privacy. In post-socialist China, depoliticization has liberated a personal realm from the previously totalitarian political control. Decades of economic reform have further created conditions for a private realm within which autonomous individuality may develop. The growing role of the market in regulating social relations, and decentralization of governance, generated a sense of liberation and longing for individual freedom (H. Liu, 2019). Against the background of change in political reality and social organization, privacy is a lens through which we envision individuality in its practical implication for autonomous participants in modern society and understand our dependency on larger social collectives that sustain a certain desirable social order (Kasper, 2005; Reiman, 1976; Solove, 2002).

Despite its prevailing image of being under tight government control, the Chinese Internet embodies a lively social space for the pursuit of private initiatives and expressions. Deeply integrated into everyday life, the Internet makes available diverse forms of communication for people to participate in expanding identity choices and shifting subject positions (Decoteau, 2015; S. Zhao, 2006). It helps enact new discursive repertoires as network communication broadens access to social discourses reflecting on direct experiences of the social world (Bakardjieva, 2009). The Internet has mediated social interactions to create "intermediate areas" that connect the realms of "here and now" and "there and then" to form a new spatiotemporal structure for an individual's lifeworld. One's life reality is no longer confined by physical or geographic proximity, with a sharply defined territorial boundedness and the associated implication of closure (S. Zhao, 2006). More importantly, the Internet weakens the established hierarchy of nested scales that range from the local and regional to the national and global. The result is a reformulation of the lifeworld concept that enables simultaneous interconnection among those previously confined domains (Sassen, 2012).

Privacy manifests as a heterogeneous group of phenomena that people experience and understand in the mediated lifeworld. A network of privacy concepts with family resemblance, identified in chapter 3, shows that privacy practices originate in interlocking zones of lifeworld experience, extending from the most intimate personal experiences to abstract values, institutions, and cultural structures in general (Schutz & Luckmann, 1973). Indeed, privacy is a sweeping concept encompassing everything from the quest for personal dignity and safety to the growing sense of political participation in contemporary China. The notion carries with it fresh perspectives for understanding relationships between self and others, individuals and collectives, and private and public, as well as spatial boundaries in broader contemporary Chinese society. Rather than being premised on the self-sufficient individual who needs protection from socio-technological dynamism, privacy concepts delineate dynamic, emergent subjectivity in relationship with social and technological contexts. The challenge to understand network privacy lies in the dynamics of boundary management at the interstices of informational and social architectures (Cohen, 2012).

Cyber-nationalism

Paradoxically, the rise of nationalism worldwide in recent years is directly related to the shift in global political and economic power dynamics (Castells, 2011; Giddens, 1994b; Rosenberg & Boyle, 2018). A sense that the wealth and global influence of the United States is eroding, for example, underpinned the Trumpian appeal to "make America great again." Similarly, China's fast-rising political and economic clout on the global stage has inspired ambitions to revive its historical status, which had been eclipsed over the past two centuries. At the same time, the development of nationalist political ideologies, economic policies, and cultural identities also represents a direct response to neoliberal trends of globalization that feed into social stratification and cultural prejudice. Many cases have shown that segments of the population who are most receptive to nationalist political appeals are those who are acutely threatened by rapid cultural and economic change (Bonikowski, 2016, p. 434).

In the aftermath of the 2012 Sino-Japanese dispute over the Diaoyu Islands, the prolonged conflicts that emerged in the discursive cyberspace crystallized nationalist sentiment, thereby making nationalism more readily observable. The case demonstrates that nationalism has become intimately tied to Chinese people's aspirations for political and cultural representations of identity both within and beyond their changing society. Heightened national self-awareness brings to the surface latent tensions, both home and abroad. In exuberant online discourses, nationalist imaginations that emerged portrayed China as a rising power in a clash with other major players, namely, Japan, the United States, and Taiwan. At the same time, nationalism also served as a pervasive cognitive and affective orientation that animated everyday politics. The strong sense of distrust and cynicism people held toward the Chinese state reflected its inadequate responses to the dispute and, more importantly, the repercussions of its neoliberalist policies in recent decades. Rather than a coherent ideology, nationalism embodied different meanings that various social groups attached to their national identities, which manifested in their differential actions and reactions to the violent disturbances against private properties during the protests.

The events during the Diaoyu Islands dispute also bore consequences for the balance of state power and civic activism. The impromptu grassroots expression of nationalist demands represented a different form of nationalism than an official patriotism primarily orchestrated by the state (Wallace & Weiss, 2015; Wasserstrom, 2012). The historical and ideological notions of Chinese nationalism are being challenged as the growing market and mass culture flourish within the domain of everyday life, adding essential variations to the nationalist discourse in today's China (X. Zhang, 1998). As increasingly differentiated social forces are striving for their own expressions of national consciousness, such popular sentiments, many observers argue, bear the potential to spawn civic autonomy (Shen & Breslin, 2010; X. Wu, 2007).

Yet the discursive field of nationalism emerging during these events indicated that the nation comprises a highly differentiated web of relationships among diverse people and groups, rather than a single category of essentially homogeneous members (Calhoun, 1997). Articulated with people's experiences of their changing socio-economic positions, the nationalist ideas of autonomy, unity, and identity are essentially contested ways of thinking rather than simply static descriptions of material or cultural conditions (Calhoun, 1993d). The symbolic field that emerged during the movement, therefore, was also a space where participants understood and debated their situation. In such networked communicative interaction, the players discovered common value-orientations among their own social groups and thus gained generalized capacity for action (Baxter, 1987). The event revealed social processes through which groups, especially the so-called middle class in this case, are constituted and sustained through discourses reflecting on a shared collective situation. Yet, far from being a social force with a collective subject with a unifying ideology (Hall, 2005), the constituent social base of the group identified as the Chinese middle class is far from clear. Nor is there adequate evidence to support the ready assumption that middle classes would necessarily initiate political change (Goodman & Chen, 2013).

The Network Market

The development of a network economy combines the summary experiences of two highly significant developments in contemporary China – the transition to a post-socialist economy and the advent of the Internet.

Both technocrats and business communities have touted the Internet as the architecture of digital capitalism that can support an ever-growing range of economic processes, encompassing everything from production and distribution to consumption on a global scale. However, the development of a network economy, as chapter 5 has demonstrated, relies not simply on a digital information infrastructure or automatic market principles; it is premised on the reorganization of social and economic institutions and the readjustment of coordination among the state and various non-state actors such as tech companies and international corporations (Grabher, 2017). This process often requires that relevant actors, "with uneven levels of planning, organization, and articulation, and varying degrees of transnational entanglement," take deliberate efforts to employ performative discourses in national and transnational exchanges of communication (Y. Hong, 2017, p. 12).

By integrating the Internet into the regulative framework, the Chinese state has further embraced market rationality and committed to unleash individual entrepreneurial freedoms and other new sources of private interest. At the same time, non-state actors, including technocratic communities, industry leaders, urban consumers, and rural e-commerce villages, are positioning themselves strategically in the state's efforts supporting post-industrial development (Hong, 2017). As national and transnational players contend and articulate economic interests at the macro level, consumers seek satisfaction and opportunity through their local consumption practices at the micro level (H. Yu, 2009, p. 41).

Meanwhile, discourses about the network market enable power struggles in a complex regime of global corporate governance, coordination, and control (Neilson et al., 2014). Parallel to increasingly globalized production and distribution systems, the discursive field has expanded from the national to the global space. In light of the widespread outsourcing of productive functions and new international divisions of labour, diverse economic actors debate and challenge existing geographical patterns of value creation in the global economy. In this new context, global markets are coordinated and negotiated through active reconstruction of value-added activities by actors embedded in local practices of production and consumption (Neilson et al., 2014).

From the Public Sphere to Discursive Fields

Social change and the role of the Internet as symbolic space in China have often been examined within the master framework of the public sphere (Lagerkvist, 2005). In its ideal form, the public sphere signifies a space where people come together to express their autonomous views for the purpose of influencing socio-political institutions. Often conceived as an information and communication network, the public sphere connects the system world of the state and the market, and the various private realms of the lifeworld (Habermas, 1996, p. 360). The material expression of the public sphere varies, depending on the contemporary social and technological context. Physical space such as coffee shops and private salons were important elements in shaping the development of the bourgeois public sphere in early modern Europe (Habermas, 1991). Later, mass media came to play a crucial role as an intermediary to bring progressive and emancipatory ideas from this outer periphery into the centre.

The rise of the Internet as symbolic space has brought forth discussion of the development of a public sphere in contemporary China. Much research has applied this notion and related concepts of civil society (Tai, 2006; G. Yang, 2009; Han, 2018), citizen/netizen (Lei, 2011), and civil rights (G. Yang, 2003) to characterize symbolic practices in the public space that opened up as a result of changing relations between the state and society in China. The public sphere has become a prominent discursive regime that provides meaning, coherence, and legitimacy to diverse symbolic practices, as well as a powerful imaginary that inspires symbolic action. While this effort is theoretically rooted, the cursory application of these concepts often leads to inadequate understanding of the concrete temporal, spatial, relational, and semantic connections of networked symbolic actions. Many studies focus on reconstructing Internet events through the abstract conceptual filter of citizenship and rights, then rendering them into a general causal model of the inherent antagonism between a fledgling civil society and a monolithic authoritarian party-state in China.

In contrast, the *Web of Meaning* argues that the contemporary public sphere operates as a series of overlapping discursive fields in China. The book has employed the field framework to achieve three purposes. First, the framework provides an analytical strategy for studying the constitutive and transformative power of discursive practices during periods of cultural volatility in the rapidly changing Chinese society. Mediated by network communication, particular fields take shape surrounding the condensation and popularization of specific discursive representations. Communicative practices in discursive fields generate symbolic power and capital in the form of discourse, which is crucial in constituting social relationships, identities, and institutions (Schmidt, 2008). Through the articulation of values and representations, discourse helps formulate lifeworld and system-world orientations. Moreover, the field approach emphasizes "how meaning is produced relationally, both via the play of difference among discourses and among the social agents who produce them" (Benson, 2009). Discursive fields mediated by the Internet are sites for struggles among competing and contradictory representations with potential to change the dominant classifications.

Moreover, the book argues that discursive fields take shape in the particular forms and instances of time-space configurations made possible by the Internet. The Internet enables situated encounters in communicative exchanges between social actors endowed with socially structured resources and competencies. Multifaceted means of network communications, along with the uneven connectedness of groups and communities, lead to differential associations among social actors in diverse social positions. Technological networks condition access to and performance of these positions (Bakardjieva, 2009).

In this context, "the public," the normative subject of public sphere, takes shape in the communication process between interacting players rather than in a priori theoretical assumptions (Emirbayer & Sheller, 1999; Fligstein & McAdam, 2012). The field concept depicts a relational space within which "publics" crystallize around various current topics in numerous and diverse communicative networks (Calhoun, 1993b). In contrast with unified publics in the mass media era, the formation of publics in network communication is more mobile and flexible in its spatial arrangement (H. Yu, 2009). At the same time, diverse goals and interests of plural publics enable the multiplication of subfields and interlocking networks where actors mobilize support and resources to pursue their interests and objectives (Barnett, 2003; Bourdieu, 1991; Ferguson, 1998).

Second, fields are the objects of empirical investigation in the *Web of Meaning*. In this book, I have examined the thematic focuses, internal dynamics, and external relations with broad social contexts of three discursive fields. Each case illustrates the complex process of negotiation and contestation over cultural meanings of the actors, actions, or relations among them in a specific social institution. The book touches on how each field is situated within the prevailing power relations, and how this social location shapes the kinds of themes and approaches that characterize the field.

The case of privacy, examined in chapter 3, demonstrates that the shifting system of meaning grows out of existing social structures of various social domains. The mediated lifeworld is where sets of emergent norms about how to symbolically consecrate the order of privacy originate. The case of nationalism, discussed in chapter 4, sheds light on how the shifting relations between state and non-state actors define the new character of national identity and political institutions. The emergent meanings reflect social actors' sense of their social and economic positions and their understanding of those positions in relation to the state and other social groups. Finally, the network market example in chapter 5 analyses changing relations and identities in organizing economic and market processes and contesting claims defending and justifying those processes. Through the conception of the field, the *Web of Meaning* captures the composite character and cultural power of network discursive processes, which players themselves have in part woven and continue to weave (Chouliaraki & Fairclough, 1999; Crossley, 2001).

Lastly, the field approach enables a form of critique of power relations in discursive processes. A discursive field is defined by the struggle for symbolic power, the power to define social reality according to particular social interests. The notion of the field underscores the nature of social relations as demonstrations of symbolic power rather than mere communication, thereby supplementing questions of meaning with questions of power and value. Symbolic power is capable of shaping the terrain of other fields that constitute society (Bourdieu, 1991). It enables "the processes of legitimation," through which the prevailing structures of advantage and inequality may be presented as natural and inevitable in the attempts of social actors to stabilize fluid – and potentially explosive – social fields in contemporary China (Y. Zhao, 2008, p. 7). Moreover, the field framework links the discourse to the actor's position in the social structure of the field (Bourdieu, 1991). The *Web of Meaning* has focused on both macro discourses of power by institutional players embedded in structural contexts and micro discourses produced by individuals from within their specific life situations and shared subjective experiences (Bakardjieva, 2009, p. 94). In doing so, the book relates larger patterns of hierarchy and domination in social arrangements to patterns of interaction and socially constructed systems of meaning.

Discursive fields enacted through the Internet both reproduce the existing social order and provide interstitial opportunities for change. The field actors classify and construct their understanding of the social world from their particular positions in a hierarchically structured social space (Bourdieu, 1984). They are more likely to develop and maintain social contacts with others who are socially similar to themselves. Such differential association processes contribute to unequally distributed opportunity and resources within the social space (Crossley, 2001). Network communication tends to maintain the uneven connectedness

among networked clusters of actors, thus reproducing existing sociocultural structures (Matei & Ball-Rokeach, 2003). As online social
networks form, they often mirror real-world interpersonal relations
(Hampton et al., 2011). Such mediated interaction becomes integrated
into "habitus" over time. Actors proximate in social space are likely to
develop a similar habitus, which influences concrete interactions and
the development of relationships (Bourdieu, 1984).

  Communicative (re)production, however, can take place only when
it is embedded in patterns of everyday practices and common understandings of what those practices mean to social actors (Bourdieu, 1990;
Giddens, 1984; Sewell, 2005). In rapidly diversifying Chinese society
with a multiplicity of interests along class/social strata, gender, regional, ethnic, and other divisions (Hsing & Lee, 2010; O'Brien, 2008;
Perry & Selden, 2003; Perry, 1994), common understandings can no
longer be assumed in advance, but must be actively sought through
dialogue. Moreover, characterized by flow, fluidity, and mobility, network communication is capable of opening up interstitial spaces for
articulatory struggle that challenges hegemony. Network communicative practices derive meaning from the goals, values, cultures, power
structures, and institutions of users and their environments (Latham
& Sassen, 2005, p. 22). These practices will tend to be developing and
variable in structure and nature, because any social form is subject to
change in pertinent contacts, agents, relations, and logics from one time
or instance to another, across various times and places (Latham & Sassen, 2005). Each Internet event uniquely orders the practices and relations among actors.

  With the field frame, the *Web of Meaning* emphasizes a more pluralistic, open, relational understanding of the contemporary public sphere.
Network communication enables actors in similar social-network positions to formulate collective orientations in pursuit of influence over issues of common concern. At the same time, networks of publics emerge
in the interstitial space between states, economies, and civil societies
as relatively "bounded" and stable complexes of institutions. Despite
the prevailing imagery of representing the dichotomous logics of domination versus resistance, society versus the state, and popular versus
official (H. Yu, 2009), the mediated discursive space in China empowers
working relationships among official, elitist, and popular social actors
by enabling fluid information exchange, political association, and socialization processes.

References

100EC.CN (2014). Jiezhi 2014 nian Taobao Tianmao gongyou 754 wan ge zaixian shangdian. [There were a total of 7,540,000 online shops on Taobao and Tianmao as of 2014.] http://www.100ec.cn/detail--6228137.html

Alibaba Group. (2016a). Company overview. http://www.alibabagroup.com/en/about/overview

Alibaba Group. (2016b, 17 January). An introduction to Taobao Villages. http://www.alizila.com/an-introduction-to-taobao-villages/

Alibaba Group. (2017, 16 September). June quarter 2017 result. http://www.alibabagroup.com/en/ir/presentations/pre170817.pdf

Altman, I. (1975). *The environment and social behavior: Privacy, personal space, territory and crowding.* Brooks/Cole.

Altman, I. (1977). Privacy regulation: Culturally universal or culturally specific? *Journal of Social Issues, 33*(3), 66–84. https://doi.org/10.1111/j.1540-4560.1977.tb01883.x

Anderson, B. (2006). *Imagined communities: Reflections on the origin and spread of nationalism.* Verso Books.

Anheier, H.K., Gerhards, J., & Romo, F.P. (1995). Forms of capital and social structure in cultural fields: Examining Bourdieu's social topography. *American Journal of Sociology, 100*(4), 859–903. https://doi.org/10.1086/230603

Anheier, H.K., Kaldor, M., & Glasius, M. (Eds.). (2005). *Global civil society.* Sage.

Appadurai, A. (1986). Introduction: Commodities and the politics of value. In A. Appadurai (Ed.), *The social life of things: Commodities in cultural perspective* (pp. 3–63). Cambridge University Press.

Arnason, J.P. (1990). Nationalism, globalization and modernity. *Theory, Culture & Society, 7*(2/3), 207–36. https://doi.org/10.1177/026327690007002013

Bai, R. (2012). Cultural mediation and the making of the mainstream in postsocialist China. *Media, Culture & Society, 34*(4), 391–406. https://doi.org/10.1177/0163443711436354

Bakardjieva, M. (2009). Subactivism: Lifeworld and politics in the age of the Internet. *Information Society, 25*, 91–104. https://doi.org/10.1080/01972240802701627

Bakos, Y. (1998). The emerging role of electronic marketplaces on the Internet. *Communications of the ACM, 41*(8), 35–42. https://doi.org/10.1145/280324.280330

Barnett, C. (2003). *Culture and democracy: Media, space, and representation.* Edinburgh University Press.

Batjargal, B. (2007). Internet entrepreneurship: Social capital, human capital, and performance of Internet ventures in China. *Research Policy, 36*(5), 605–18. https://doi.org/10.1016/j.respol.2006.09.029

Baxter, H. (1987). System and life-world in Habermas's theory of communicative action. *Theory and Society, 16*(1), 39–86. https://doi.org/10.1007/BF00162659

Beck, U. (1992). *Risk society: Towards a new modernity.* Sage.

Benkler, Y. (2006). *The wealth of networks: How social production transforms markets and freedom.* Yale University Press.

Bennett, W.L., & Segerberg, A. (2012). The logic of connective action: Digital media and the personalization of contentious politics. *Information, Communication & Society, 15*(5), 739–68. https://doi.org/10.1080/1369118X.2012.670661

Benson, R. (1999). Field theory in comparative context: A new paradigm for media. *Theory and society, 28*(3), 463–98

Benson, R. (2009). Shaping the public sphere: Habermas and beyond. *American Sociologist, 40*(3), 175–97. https://doi.org/10.1007/s12108-009-9071-4

Benson, R., & Neveu, E. (2005). *Bourdieu and the journalistic field.* Polity Press.

Berger, P.L., & Luckmann, T. (1966). The social construction of reality. Anchor.

Bian, Y. (2002). Chinese social stratification and social mobility. *Annual Review of Sociology*, 91–116. https://doi.org/10.1146/annurev.soc.28.110601.140823

Bolter, J.D., & Grusin, R. (2000). *Remediation: Understanding new media.* MIT Press.

Bonikowski, B. (2016). Nationalism in settled times. *Annual Review of Sociology, 42*, 427–49. https://doi.org/10.1146/annurev-soc-081715-074412

Bourdieu, P. (1984). *Distinction: A social critique of the judgment of taste* (R. Nice, Trans.). Harvard University Press.

Bourdieu, P. (1985). The social space and the genesis of groups. *Theory and society, 14*(6), 723–44. https://doi.org/10.1007/BF00174048

Bourdieu, P. (1989). Social space and symbolic power. *Sociological Theory, 7*(1), 14–25.

Bourdieu, P. (1990). *The logic of practice.* Stanford University Press.

Bourdieu, P. (1991). *Language and symbolic power.* Harvard University Press.

Bourdieu, P. (1996). *The rules of art: Genesis and structure of the literary field* (S. Emanuel, Trans.). Stanford University Press.

Bourdieu, P. (1997). *Outline of a theory of practice* (R. Nice, Trans.). Cambridge University Press.

Bourdieu, P. (2005). *The social structures of the economy* (C. Turner, Trans.). Polity Press.

Bourdieu, P., & Wacquant, L.J. (1992). *An invitation to reflexive sociology.* University of Chicago Press.

Brill, M. (1989). Transformation, nostalgia, and illusion in public life and public place. In Irwin Altman and Ervin H. Zube (Eds.), *Public places and spaces* (pp. 7–29). Springer.

Bruns, A. (2008a). *Blogs, Wikipedia, Second Life, and beyond: From production to produsage.* Peter Lang.

Bruns, A. (2008b). The future is user-led: The path towards widespread produsage. In A. Hutchinson (Ed.), *Proceedings of perthDAC 2007: The 7th International Digital Arts and Culture Conference* (pp. 68–77). Curtin University of Technology, Australia.

Cairns, C., & Carlson, A. (2016). Real-world islands in a social media sea: Nationalism and censorship on Weibo during the 2012 Diaoyu/Senkaku Crisis. *China Quarterly, 225,* 23–49. https://doi.org/10.1017/S030574 1015001708

Calhoun, C. (1991). The problem of identity in collective action. In J. Huber (Ed.), *Macro-micro linkages in sociology* (pp. 51–75). Sage.

Calhoun, C. (1992a). The infrastructure of modernity: Indirect social relationships, information technology, and social integration. In H. Haferkamp & N.J. Smelser (Eds.), *Social change and modernity* (pp. 206–37). University of California Press.

Calhoun, C. (1992b). Introduction: Habermas and the public sphere. In C. Calhoun (Ed.), *Habermas and the public sphere: Studies in contemporary German social thought* (pp. 1–50). MIT Press.

Calhoun, C. (1993a). Civil society and the public sphere. *Public Culture, 5,* 267–80. https://doi.org/10.1215/08992363-5-2-267

Calhoun, C. (1993b). *Habitus, field and capital: The question of historical specificity* In C. Calhoun, E. LiPuma, & M. Postone (Eds.), *Bourdieu: Critical perspectives* (pp. 61–88). University of Chicago Press.

Calhoun, C. (1993c). Nationalism and civil society: Democracy, diversity and self-determination. *International Sociology, 8*(4), 387–411. https://doi.org /10.1177/026858093008004001

Calhoun, C. (1993d). *Nationalism and social change.* University of North Carolina Press.

Calhoun, C. (1997). *Nationalism.* University of Minnesota Press.

Calhoun, C. (1998a). Community without propinquity revisited: Communications technology and the transformation of the urban public sphere. *Sociological Inquiry, 68*(3): 373–97. https://doi.org/10.1111/j.1475 -682X.1998.tb00474.x

Calhoun, C. (1998b). *The public good as a social and cultural project* In W. Powell & E.S. Clemens (Eds.). *Private action and the public good* (pp. 20–35). Yale University Press.

Calhoun, C. (2003). Pierre Bourdieu. In G. Ritzer (Ed.), *The Blackwell companion to major contemporary social theorists* (pp. 274–309). Blackwell.

Calhoun, C., LiPuma, E., & Postone, M. (1993). *Bourdieu: Critical perspectives*. University of Chicago Press.

Cao, Q., Tian, H., & Chilton, P. (Eds.). (2014). *Discourse, politics and media in contemporary China*. John Benjamins Publishing.

Capurro, R. (2005). Privacy: An intercultural perspective. *Ethics and Information Technology, 7*(1), 37–47. https://doi.org/10.1007/s10676-005-4407-4

Carnesecca, C. (2015). Voice of the masses: The internet and responsive authoritarianism in China. In H. Kriesi, L. Dong, & D. Kübler (Eds.), *Urban mobilizations and new media in contemporary China* (pp. 117–32). Ashgate.

Carruthers, B.G., & Uzzi, B. (2000). Economic sociology in the new millennium. *Contemporary Sociology, 29*(3), 486–94. https://doi.org /10.2307/2653936

Castells, M. (2011). *The rise of the network society*. John Wiley & Sons.

Chang, J., Boyd-Graber, J., & Blei, D.M. (2009). Connections between the lines: Augmenting social networks with text. *Proceedings of the 15th ACM SIGKDD International Conference on Knowledge Discovery and Data Mining*: 169–78. https://doi.org/10.1145/1557019.1557044

Chen, C. (2015). Setting the press boundaries: The case of the Southern (Nanfang) media group. In G.D. Rawnsley & M.T. Rawnsley (Eds.), *Routledge handbook of Chinese media* (pp. 97–117). Routledge.

Chen, L., & Naughton, B. (2016). An institutionalized policy-making mechanism: China's return to techno-industrial policy. *Research Policy, 45*(10), 2138–52. https://doi.org/10.1016/j.respol.2016.09.014

Chen, S.W. (2014). Baozou manhua (rage comics), Internet humour and everyday life. *Continuum, 28*(5), 690–708. https://doi.org/10.1080/10304312 .2014.941334

Chen, W., & Reese, S.D. (Eds.). (2015). *Networked China: Global dynamics of digital media and civic engagement: New agendas in communication*. Routledge.

Chilton, P., Tian, H., & Wodak, R. (Eds.). (2012). *Discourse and socio-political transformations in contemporary China*. John Benjamins.

Chouliaraki, L., & Fairclough, N. (1999). *Discourse in late modernity* (Vol. 2). Edinburgh University Press.

Chu, L.L. (1994). Continuity and change in China's media reform. *Journal of Communication, 44*(3), 4–21. https://doi.org/10.1111/j.1460-2466.1994 .tb00685.x

Chu, R.W. & Cheng, C. (2011). Cultural convulsions: Examining the Chineseness of cyber China. In D.K. Herold & P. Marolt (Eds.), *Online society in China: Creating, celebrating and instrumentalising the online carnival* (pp. 23–39). Taylor & Francis.

Chung, C.J., & Park, H.W. (2010). Textual analysis of a political message: The inaugural addresses of two Korean presidents. *Social Science Information, 49*(2), 215–39. https://doi.org/10.1177/0539018409359370

Clauset, A., Newman, M., & Moore, C. (2004). Finding community structure in very large networks. *Physical Review E, 70*(6), 066111. https://doi.org /10.1103/PhysRevE.70.066111

CNNIC (China Internet Network Information Center). (2003). Statistical reports on the Internet development in China. http://www.cac.gov.cn/files /pdf/hlwtjbg/hlwlfzzkdctjbg012.pdf

CNNIC (China Internet Network Information Center). (2010). Statistical reports on Internet development in China. http://www.cac.gov.cn/wxb _pdf/0228043.pdf

CNNIC (China Internet Network Information Center). (2017). Statistical reports on the Internet development in China. https://cnnic.com.cn/IDR /ReportDownloads/201706/P020170608523740585924.pdf

CNNIC (China Internet Network Information Center). (2019). Statistical reports on the Internet development in China. http://www.cac.gov.cn/wxb _pdf/0228043.pdf

Cohen, J.E. (2001). Privacy, ideology, and technology: A response to Jeffrey Rosen. *Georgetown Law Journal, 89*, 2029–45. https://search.proquest.com /docview/231417146?pq-origsite=gscholar&fromopenview=true

Cohen, J.E. (2012). *Configuring the networked self: Law, code, and the play of everyday practice*. Yale University Press.

Collins, A.M., & Quillian, M.R. (1972). Experiments on semantic memory and language comprehension. In Gregg, L.W. (Ed.), *Cognition in learning and memory* (pp. 117–38). Wiley.

Collins, P.H. (2015). Intersectionality's definitional dilemmas. *Annual review of sociology, 41*, 1–20. https://doi.org/10.1146/annurev-soc-073014-112142

Couldry, N. (2003). Media meta-capital: Extending the range of Bourdieu's field theory. *Theory and Society, 32*(5–6), 653–77. https://doi.org/10.1023 /B:RYSO.0000004915.37826.5d

Couldry, N., & Hepp, A. (2018). *The mediated construction of reality*. Wiley.

Creemers, R. (2017). Cyber China: Upgrading propaganda, public opinion work and social management for the twenty-first century. *Journal of*

Contemporary China, 26(103), 85–100. https://doi.org/10.1080/10670564.2016
.1206281

Croll, E. (2006). Conjuring goods, identities and cultures. In K. Latham, S.
Thompson, and J. Klein (Eds.), Consuming China: Approaches to cultural
change in contemporary China (pp. 22–41). Routledge.

Crossley, N. (2001). The phenomenological habitus and its construction. *Theory
and society, 30*(1), 81–120. https://doi.org/10.1023/A:1011070710987

Crossley, N. (2003). From reproduction to transformation social movement
fields and the radical habitus. *Theory, Culture & Society, 20*(6), 43–68.
https://doi.org/10.1177/0263276403206003

Crossley, N., & Roberts, J.M. (Eds.). (2004). *After Habermas: New perspectives on
the public sphere.* Blackwell.

Dahlberg, L. (2014). Capitalism as a discursive system? Interrogating discourse
theory's contribution to critical political economy. *Critical Discourse Studies,
11*(3), 257–71. https://doi.org/10.1080/17405904.2014.915384

Dai, J. (1999). *Yinxing shuxie: 90 niandai zhongguo wenhua yanjiu.* [Invisible
writing: Chinese cultural studies in 1990s.] Jiangsu People's Press.

Danowski, J.A. (1993). Network analysis of message content. In G. Barnett, & W.
Richards (Eds.), *Progress in communication sciences XII* (pp. 197–222). Ablex.

Danowski, J.A. (2012–20). WORDij Semantic network tools. http://wordij.net

Danowski, J.A., & Cepela, N. (2010). Automatic mapping of social networks
of actors from text corpora: Time series analysis. In N. Memon, J. Jie Xu,
D.L. Hicks, & H. Chen (Eds.), *Data Mining for Social Network Data,* 31–46.
Springer. https://doi.org/10.1007/978-1-4419-6287-4_3

Davis, D. (2000). *The consumer revolution in urban China.* University of
California Press.

Davis, D. (2005). Urban consumer culture. *China Quarterly, 183,* 692–709.
https://doi.org/10.1017/S0305741005000421

Dayan, D., & Katz, E. (1992). *Media events.* Harvard University Press.

De Boni, M., & Prigmore, M. (2004). A Hegelian basis for privacy as an
economic right. *Contemporary Political Theory, 3*(2), 168–87. https://doi.org
/10.1057/palgrave.cpt.9300107

Decoteau, C.L. (2015). The reflexive habitus: Critical realist and Bourdieusian
social action. *European Journal of Social Theory, 9*(3), 303–21. https://doi.org
/10.1177/1368431015590700

DeNardis, L. (2012). Hidden levers of internet control: An infrastructure-based
theory of internet governance. *Information, Communication & Society, 15*(5),
720–38. https://doi.org/10.1080/1369118X.2012.659199

Dickson, B. (2009). Do good businessmen make good citizens? An emerging
collective identity among China's private entrepreneurs. In M. Goldman &
E.J. Perry (Eds.), *Changing meanings of citizenship in modern China*
(pp. 255–87). Harvard University Press.

DiMaggio, P. (1997). Culture and cognition. *Annual Review of sociology*, *23*(1), 263–87. https://doi.org/10.1146/annurev.soc.23.1.263

DiMaggio, P., Nag, M., & Blei, D. (2013). Exploiting affinities between topic modeling and the sociological perspective on culture: Application to newspaper coverage of US government arts funding. *Poetics*, *41*(6), 570–606. https://doi.org/10.1016/j.poetic.2013.08.004

Ding, S. (2007). Digital diaspora and national image building: A new perspective on Chinese diaspora study in the age of China's rise. *Pacific Affairs*, 627–48. https://doi.org/10.1163/22142312-12340031

Dirlik, A. (1996). Reversals, ironies, hegemonies: Notes on the contemporary historiography of modern China. *Modern China*, *22*(3), 243–84. https://doi.org/10.1177/009770049602200301

Dirlik, A. (2001). Markets, culture, power: The making of a "Second Cultural Revolution" in China. *Asian Studies Review*, *25*(1): 1–33. https://doi.org/10.1080/10357820108713293

Doerfel, M.L. (1998). What constitutes semantic network analysis? A comparison of research and methodologies. *Connections*, *21*, 16–26.

Economist. (2016a, 2 January). Reagan's Chinese echo: The mystery of Xi Jinping's supply-side strategy. http://www.economist.com/news/china/21684804-mystery-xi-jinpings-supply-side-strategy-reagans-chinese-echo

Economist. (2016b, 13 August). The east is pink. Youthful nationalists. As online mobs get rowdier, they also get a label. https://www.economist.com/china/2016/08/13/the-east-is-pink

Emirbayer, M., & Sheller, M. (1999). Publics in history. *Theory and Society*, *28*(1), 143–97. https://doi.org/10.1023/A:1006921411329

Ess, C. (2005). "Lost in translation?": Intercultural dialogues on privacy and information ethics. (Introduction to special issue on privacy and data privacy protection in Asia). *Ethics and Information Technology*, *7*(1), 1–6. https://doi.org/10.1007/s10676-005-0454-0

Fairclough, N. (1992). *Discourse and social change*. Polity Press.

Farman, J. (2013). *Mobile interface theory: Embodied space and locative media*. Routledge.

Feenberg, A., & Bakardjieva, M. (2004). Virtual community: No "killer implication." *New Media & Society*, *6*(1), 37–43. https://doi.org/10.1177/1461444804039904

Feng, M. (2017). *Chinese cyber nationalism: The Diaoyu Islands dispute on Sina Weibo*. (Unpublished doctoral dissertation, the Graduate College of the University of Illinois at Chicago).

Ferguson, P.P. (1998). A cultural field in the making: Gastronomy in 19th-century France. *American Journal of Sociology*, *104*(3), 597–641. https://doi.org/10.1086/210082

Fincher, L.H. (2014). *Leftover women: The resurgence of gender inequality in China.* Zed Books.

Fisher, E. (2010). *Media and new capitalism in the digital age: The spirit of networks.* Palgrave Macmillan.

Fligstein, N., & McAdam, D. (2012). *A theory of fields.* Oxford University Press.

Forst, R. (2001). The rule of reasons: Three models of deliberative democracy. *Ratio Juris, 14*(4), 345–78.

Foucault, M. (1971). Orders of discourse. *Social Science Information, 10*(2), 7–30. https://doi.org/10.1177/053901847101000201

Foucault, M. (1972). *The archaeology of knowledge.* Tavistock Publications.

Foucault, M. (1979). *Discipline and punish: The birth of the prison.* Penguin Books.

Fraser, N. (1990). Rethinking the public sphere: A contribution to the critique of actually existing democracy. *Social Text, 25/26,* 56–80. https://doi.org/10.2307/466240

Fu, K.W., & Chau, M. (2013). Reality check for the Chinese microblog space: A random sampling approach. *PloS One, 8*(3), e58356. https://doi.org/10.1371/journal.pone.0058356

Fuchs, C. (2016). Baidu, Weibo and Renren: The global political economy of social media in China. *Asian Journal of Communication, 26*(1), 14–41. https://doi.org/10.1080/01292986.2015.1041537

Fung, A.Y. (2009). Fandom, youth and consumption in China. *European Journal of Cultural Studies, 12*(3), 285–303. https://doi.org/10.1177/1367549409105365

Gamson, W.A., & Modigliani, A. (1989). Media discourse and public opinion on nuclear power: A constructionist approach. *American Journal of Sociology, 95*(1), 1–37. https://doi.org/10.1086/229213

Gao, H. (2015, 30 March). Alibaba jituan fuzongcai jian yanjiuyuan yuanzhang Gao Hongbing tan "hulianwang." [Vice President and Director of the Research Institute of Alibaba, Gao Hongbing, talks about "the Internet."] http://mp.weixin.qq.com/s?__biz=MjM5NzMxMzQ5NQ==&mid=204985857&idx=6&sn=06becc597c8e52d9ae916498dc3f3ca1&3rd=MzA3MDU4NTYzMw==&scene=6#rd

Gao, Q., Abel, F., Houben, G.J., & Yu, Y. (2012, July). A comparative study of users' microblogging behavior on Sina Weibo and Twitter. In *International Conference on User Modeling, Adaptation, and Personalization* (pp. 88–101). Springer.

Geertz, C. (1978). The bazaar economy: Information and search in peasant marketing. *American Economic Review, 68*(2), 28–32.

Gellner, E. (2006). *Nations and nationalism.* Cornell University Press.

Giddens, A. (1984). *The constitution of society: Outline of the theory of structure.* Berkeley.

Giddens, A. (1991). *Modernity and self-identity: Self and society in the late modern age.* Stanford University Press.

Giddens, A. (1994a). *Beyond left and right: The future of radical politics.* Polity Press.

Giddens, A. (1994b). The nation as power-container. In A.D. Smith & J. Hutchinson (Eds.), *Nationalism: A reader* (pp. 34–5). Oxford University Press.

Giddens, A., & Pierson, C. (1998). *Conversations with Anthony Giddens: Making sense of modernity.* Stanford University Press.

Gisele, S. (2003). The literary field between the state and the market. *Poetics: Journal of Empirical Research on Culture, the Media and the Arts, 31*(5–6), 441–64. https://doi.org/10.1016/j.poetic.2003.09.001

Gleiss, M.S. (2015). Speaking up for the suffering (br)other: Weibo activism, discursive struggles, and minimal politics in China. *Media, Culture & Society, 37*(4), 513–29. https://doi.org/10.1177/0163443714566897

Goldman, M. (2005). *From comrade to citizen: The struggle for political rights in China.* Harvard University Press.

Goodman, D.S., & Chen, M. (Eds.). (2013). *Middle class China: Identity and behaviour.* Edward Elgar Publishing.

Grabher, G. (2017). *Embedding disruption: A Polanyian perspective on the platform economy.* Unpublished manuscript.

Gries, P.H., Steiger, D., & Wang, T. (2016). Popular nationalism and China's Japan policy: The Diaoyu Islands protests, 2012–2013. *Journal of Contemporary China, 25*(98), 264–76. https://doi.org/10.1080/10670564.2015.1075714

Griffiths, T.L. & Steyvers, M. (2004). Finding Scientific Topics. *Proceedings of the National Academy of Sciences of the United States of America* 101, no. Suppl 1: 5228–35. https://doi.org/10.1073/pnas.0307752101

Groshek, J., & Koc-Michalska, K. (2017). Helping populism win? Social media use, filter bubbles, and support for populist presidential candidates in the 2016 US election campaign. *Information, Communication & Society, 20*(9), 1389–407. https://doi.org/10.1080/1369118X.2017.1329334

Gumpert, G., & Drucker, S.J. (1998). The demise of privacy in a private world: From front porches to chat rooms. *Communication Theory, 8*(4), 408–25. https://doi.org/10.1111/j.1468-2885.1998.tb00227.x

Gumpert, G., & Drucker, S.J. (2001). Public boundaries: Privacy and surveillance in a technological world. *Communication Quarterly, 49*, 115–29. https://doi.org/10.1080/01463370109385620

Guo, Y. (2004). *Cultural nationalism in contemporary China.* Routledge.

Habermas, J. (1974). The public sphere: An encyclopedia article. *New German Critique, 3*, 49–55. https://doi.org/10.2307/487737

Habermas, J. (1987). *Lifeworld and system: A critique of functionalist reason. The theory of communicative action*, vol. 2 (T. McCarthy, Trans.). Polity Press.

Habermas, J. (1991). *The structural transformation of the public sphere: An inquiry into a category of bourgeois society.* MIT Press.

Habermas, J. (1996). *Between facts and norms: Contributions to a discourse theory of law and democracy.* MIT Press.

Habermas, J. (2007, 21 May). How to save the quality press? Translation of article in *Süddeutsche Zeitung*, 16 May. http://www.signandsight.com /features/1349.html

Hall, S. (1982). The rediscovery of ideology: Return of the repressed in media studies. In J. Stoley (Ed.). *Cultural theory and popular culture: A reader* (pp. 111–41). Pearson Education.

Hall, S. (1986). On postmodernism and articulation: An interview with Stuart Hall. L. Grossberg (Ed.), *Journal of Communication Inquiry 10*(2), 45–60. https://doi.org/10.1177/019685998601000204

Hall, S. (1992). The question of cultural identity. In S. Hall, D. Held, & A.G. McGrew (Eds.), *Modernity and its futures* (pp. 273–325). Polity Press.

Hall, S. (2001). Foucault: Power, knowledge and discourse. In M. Wetherell, S. Taylor, & S.J. Yates (Eds.), *Discourse theory and practice: A reader* (pp. 72–81). Sage.

Hall, S. (2005). The rediscovery of "ideology": Return of the repressed in media studies. In M. Gurevitch, T. Bennett, J. Curran, & J. Woollacott (Eds.), *Culture, society and the media* (pp. 61–95). Routledge.

Hallin, D.C. (2008). Neoliberalism, social movements and change in media systems in the late twentieth century. In D. Hesmondhalgh & J. Toynbee (Eds.), *The media and social theory* (pp. 43–58). Routledge.

Hallin, D.C., & Mancini, P. (2004). *Comparing media systems: Three models of media and politics*. Cambridge University Press.

Halverson, K. (2004). China's WTO accession: Economic, legal, and political implications. *Boston College International and Comparative Law Review, 27*(2), 319–70.

Hampton, K., Goulet, L., Rainie, L., & Purcell, K. (2011). *Social networking sites and our lives*. Pew Internet & American Life Project. https://wijvan.winkwaves.com/documents/2668/PIP_-_Social_networking_sites_and_our_lives.pdf.

Han, R. (2015). Defending the authoritarian regime online: China's "voluntary fifty-cent army." *China Quarterly, 224*, 1006–25. https://doi.org/10.1017/S0305741015001216

Han, R. (2018). *Contesting cyberspace in China: Online expression and authoritarian resilience*. Columbia University Press.

Harvey, D. (2007). *A brief history of neoliberalism*. Oxford University Press.

Hassid, J. (2012). Safety valve or pressure cooker? Blogs in Chinese political life. *Journal of Communication, 62*(2), 212–30.

He, B. (2006). Western theories of deliberative democracy and the Chinese practice of complex deliberative governance. In E. Leib & B. He (Eds.), *The search for deliberative democracy in China* (pp. 133–48). Palgrave Macmillan.

Heilmann, S., & Perry, E.J. (2011). Embracing uncertainty: Guerrilla policy style and adaptive governance in China. In S. Heilmann & E.J. Perry (Eds.),

Mao's invisible hand: The political foundations of adaptive governance in China (pp. 1–29). Harvard University Asia Center.

Herold, D.K. (2008). Development of a civic society online? Internet vigilantism and state control in Chinese cyberspace. *Asia Journal of Global Studies, 2*(1), 26–37.

Herold, D.K., & Marolt, P. (Eds.). (2011). *Online society in China: Creating, celebrating, and instrumentalising the online carnival.* Taylor & Francis.

Hesmondhalgh, D. (2006). Bourdieu, the media and cultural production. *Media, Culture & Society, 28*(2), 211–31. https://doi.org/10.1177/0163443706061682

Höijer, B. (2011). Social representations theory. *Nordicom Review, 32*(2), 3–16. https://doi.org/10.1515/nor-2017-0109

Hollihan, T. (Ed.). (2014). *The dispute over the Diaoyu/Senkaku Islands: How media narratives shape public opinion and challenge the global order.* Springer.

Holt, D.B. (1997). Poststructuralist lifestyle analysis: Conceptualizing the social patterning of consumption in postmodernity. *Journal of Consumer Research, 23*(4), 326–50. https://doi.org/10.1086/209487

Holt, D.B. (2002). Why do brands cause trouble? A dialectical theory of consumer culture and branding. *Journal of Consumer Research, 29*(1), 70–90. https://doi.org/10.1086/339922

Hong, L., & Davison, B.D. (2010). Empirical study of topic modeling in Twitter. *Proceedings of the First Workshop on Social Media Analytics*: 80–8.

Hong, Y. (2014). Between corporate development and public service: The cultural system reform in the Chinese media sector. *Media, Culture & Society, 36*(5), 610–27. https://doi.org/10.1177/0163443714532978

Hong, Y. (2017). *Networking China: The digital transformation of the Chinese economy.* University of Illinois Press.

Hong, Y., & Xu, J. (2019). Communication, culture, and governance in Asia | Toward fragmented platform governance in China: Through the lens of Alibaba and the legal-judicial system. *International Journal of Communication, 13*, 4642–62.

Hsing, Y. & Lee, C.K. (2010). *Reclaiming Chinese society: The new social activism.* Routledge.

Huang, C. (2007). Editorial: From control to negotiation: Chinese media in the 2000s. *International Communication Gazette, 69*(5), 402–12. https://doi.org/10.1177/1748048507080863

Huang, P.C. (1993). "Public sphere" / "Civil society" in China? The Third Realm between state and society. *Modern China, 19*(2), 216–40. https://doi.org/10.1177/009770049301900207

Huang, P.C. (2009). Zhongguo de xiaozichanjieji he zhongchanjieji: Beilun de shehui xingtai [Petty-bourgeoisie and middle social stratum in China: The paradox of social formation], *Rural China 6*(1), 1–14. https://doi.org/10.1163/22136746-00601001

Huang, R., & Sun, X. (2014). Weibo network, information diffusion and implications for collective action in China. *Information, Communication & Society, 17*(1), 86–104. https://doi.org/10.1080/1369118X.2013.853817

Hyun, K.D., & Kim, J. (2015). The role of new media in sustaining the status quo: Online political expression, nationalism, and system support in China. *Information, Communication & Society, 18*(7), 766–81. https://doi.org/10.1080/1369118X.2014.994543

ICTCLAS. (2012). About ICTCLAS. http://ictclas.org/ictclas_about.html

Jennings, J.E., Jennings, P.D., & Sharifian, M. (2014). Living the dream? Assessing the "entrepreneurship as emancipation" perspective in a developed region. *Entrepreneurship Theory and Practice, 40*(1), 81–110. https://doi.org/10.1111/etap.12106

Jia, L., & Winseck, D. (2018). The political economy of Chinese internet companies: Financialization, concentration, and capitalization. *International Communication Gazette, 80*(1), 30–59. https://doi.org/10.1177/1748048517742783

Jiang, L., & Cova, V. (2012). Love for luxury, preference for counterfeits: A qualitative study in counterfeit luxury consumption in China. *International Journal of Marketing Studies, 4*(6), 1–9. https://doi.org/10.5539/ijms.v4n6p1

Jiang, M. (2012). Chinese internet events. In A. Esarey & R. Kluver (Eds.), *The Internet in China: Online business, information, distribution and social connectivity*. Berkshire Publishing.

Jiang, M. (2015, 4 September). Architecture of social management: From E-gov and Gov Weibo to Gov WeChat. China–US Focus. http://is.gd/2zr8wB

Jiang, Y. (2012). *Cyber-nationalism in China: Challenging Western media portrayals of internet censorship in China*. University of Adelaide Press.

Johnson, T.J., Bichard, S.L., & Zhang, W. (2009). Communication communities or "cyberghettos?": A path analysis model examining factors that explain selective exposure to blogs. *Journal of Computer-Mediated Communication, 15*(1), 60–82.

Jones, J.P. (2006). A cultural approach to the study of mediated citizenship. *Social Semiotics, 16*(2), 365–83. https://doi.org/10.1080/10350330600664912

Kaldor, M. (2004). Nationalism and globalisation. *Nations and Nationalism, 10*(1/2), 161–77. https://doi.org/10.1111/j.1354-5078.2004.00161.x

Kasper, D.V.S. (2005). The evolution (or devolution) of privacy. *Sociological Forum, 20*, 69–92. https://doi.org/10.1007/s11206-005-1898-z

Kisselburgh, L. G. (2008). *The social structure and discursive construction of privacy in sociotechnological realms*. [Unpublished doctoral dissertation]. Purdue University.

Kitchin, R., & Dodge, M. (2011). *Code/space: Software and everyday life*. MIT Press.

Kluver, R. (2005). The architecture of control: A Chinese strategy for e-governance. *Journal of Public Policy, 25*(1), 75–97. https://doi.org/10.1017/S0143814X05000218

Kong, S. (2014). *Popular media, social emotion and public discourse in contemporary China*. Routledge.

Koo, M.G. (2009). The Senkaku/Diaoyu dispute and Sino-Japanese political-economicrelations: Cold politics and hot economics? *Pacific Review, 22*(2), 205–32. https://doi.org/10.1080/09512740902815342

Kozinets, R.V. (1999). E-tribalized marketing? The strategic implications of virtual communities of consumption. *European Management Journal, 17*(3), 252–64. https://doi.org/10.1016/S0263-2373(99)00004-3

Kuever, E. (2014). Mapping the real and the false: Globalization and the brand in contemporary China. In J.W. Schouten, D.M. Martin, & R. Belk (Eds.), *Consumer culture theory* (pp. 173–89). Emerald Group Publishing.

Laclau, E. (2005). *On populist reason*. Verso.

Laclau, E., & Mouffe, C. (2001). *Hegemony and socialist strategy: Towards a radical democratic politics*. Verso.

Lagerkvist, J. (2005). The rise of online public opinion in the People's Republic of China. *China: An International Journal, 3*(1), 119–30. https://doi.org/10.1353/chn.2005.0001

Latham, E.R., & Sassen, S. (2005). Digital formations: Constructing an object of study. In R. Latham & S. Sassen (Eds.), *Digital formations: IT and new architecture in the global realm*. Princeton University Press.

Lavin, F. (2016, 6 November). Alibaba's Singles' Day: What we know about the world's biggest shopping event. *Forbes*. https://www.forbes.com/sites/franklavin/2016/11/06/alibabas-singles-day-what-we-know-about-the-worlds-biggest-shopping-event/#612c31516da7

Lee, C.C. (Ed.). (2000). *Power, money and media: Communication patterns and bureaucratic control in cultural China*. Northwestern University Press.

Lee, C.C. (2003). *Chinese media, global contexts*. Routledge.

Lee, P.S.N. (1994). Mass communication and national development in China: Media roles reconsidered. *Journal of Communication, 44*(3), 22–37. https://doi.org/10.1111/j.1460-2466.1994.tb00686.x

Lei, Y.W. (2011). The political consequences of the rise of the Internet: Political beliefs and practices of Chinese netizens. *Political Communication, 28*(3), 291–322. https://doi.org/10.1080/10584609.2011.572449

Lei, Y.W. (2017). *The contentious public sphere: Law, media, and authoritarian rule in China*. Princeton University Press.

Leibold, J. (2011). Blogging alone: China, the internet, and the democratic illusion? *Journal of Asian Studies, 70*(4), 1023–41. https://doi.org/10.1017/S0021911811001550

Lemke, J.L. (2005). *Textual politics: Discourse and social dynamics*. Taylor & Francis.

Liang, L. (2018). Between emotion, politics and law: Narrative transformation and authoritarian deliberation in a mediated social drama. *China Quarterly*, 1–28. https://doi.org/10.1017/S0305741020000508

Liebman, B. (2011). A return to populist legality? Historical legacies and legal reform. In E. Perry and S. Heilmann (Eds.), *Mao's invisible hand* (pp. 165–200). Harvard University Press.

Lievrouw, L.A. (2004). What's changed about new media? *New Media & Society, 6*(1), 9–15. https://doi.org/10.1177/1461444804039898

Lindtner, S., & Szablewicz, M. (2011). China's many internets: participation and digital game play across a changing technology landscape. In D.K. Herold & P. Marolt (Eds.), *Online society in China: Creating, celebrating, and instrumentalising the online carnival* (pp. 89–105). Routledge.

Link, P., Madsen, R.P., & Pickowicz, P.G. (Eds.). (2001). *Popular China: Unofficial culture in a globalizing society.* Rowman & Littlefield.

Liu, F. (2011). *Urban youth in China: Modernity, the Internet and the self.* Routledge.

Liu, H. (Ed.). (2019). *From cyber-nationalism to fandom nationalism: The case of Diba Expedition in China.* Routledge.

Liu, S. (2010). Networking anti-Japanese protest: Popular sovereignty reasserted since 2005. In S. Shen & S. Breslin (Eds.), *Online Chinese nationalism and China's bilateral relations* (pp. 73–89). Lexington Books.

Liu, S., & Emirbayer, M. (2016). Field and ecology. *Sociological Theory, 34*(1), 62–79. https://doi.org/10.1177/0735275116632556

Liu, X. (2019). *Information fantasies: Precarious mediation in postsocialist China.* University of Minnesota Press.

Lu, R. (2013, 2 December). Vanity fail. Foreign Policy. http://foreignpolicy.com/2013/12/02/vanity-fail/

Lü, Y. (2005). Privacy and data privacy issues in contemporary China. *Ethics and Information Technology, 7,* 7–15. https://doi.org/10.1007/s10676-005-0456-y

Ma, J. (2018, March 26). Yanhong Li: Chinese people is willing to exchange privacy for convenience in most cases. Beijing News. http://www.bjnews.com.cn/finance/2018/03/26/480626.html

Ma, Y.J. (2014, 5 September). As Alibaba's IPO approaches, founder Jack Ma pens letter to potential investors. Forbes. https://www.forbes.com/sites/ryanmac/2014/09/05/as-alibabas-ipo-approaches-founder-jack-ma-pens-letter-to-potential-investors/2/#fe077cc3d1b7

Magistad, M.K. (2012). *How Weibo is changing China.* Yale Global Online. https://yaleglobal.yale.edu/content/how-weibo-changing-china

Mansell, R. (2012). *Imagining the Internet: Communication, innovation, and governance.* Oxford University Press.

Margulis, S. (2003a). On the status and contribution of Westin's and Altman's theories of privacy. *Journal of Social Issues, 59*(2), 411–29. https://doi.org/10.1111/1540-4560.00071

Margulis, S. (2003b). Privacy as a social issue and behavioral concept. *Journal of Social Issues, 59,* 243–61. https://doi.org/10.1111/1540-4560.00063

References 167

Martin, J.L. (2003). What is field theory? *American Journal of Sociology, 109*(1), 1–49. https://doi.org/10.1086/375201

Marx, G.T. (2016). *Windows into the soul: Surveillance and society in an age of high technology.* University of Chicago Press.

Matei, S., & Ball-Rokeach, S. (2003). The Internet in the communication infrastructure of urban residential communities: Macro-or mesolinkage? *Journal of Communication, 53*(4), 642–57. https://doi.org/10.1111/j.1460-2466.2003.tb02915.x

Mattelart, A., & Mattelart, M. (1998). *Theories of communication: A short introduction.* Sage.

Maurer-Fazio, M. (2012). Ethnic discrimination in China's internet job board labor market. *IZA Journal of Migration, 1*(12). https://doi.org/10.1186/2193-9039-1-12

McCallum, A., Wang, X., & Mohanty, N. (2007). *Joint group and topic discovery from relations and text.* Springer.

McGuigan, L., & Manzerolle, V. (2015). "All the world's a shopping cart": Theorizing the political economy of ubiquitous media and markets. *New Media & Society, 17*(11), 1830–48. https://doi.org/10.1177/1461444814535191

McKinsey & Company. (2015). China's iConsumer 2015: A growing appetite for change. http://www.mckinseychina.com/wp-content/uploads/2015/02/China%E2%80%99s-iConsumer-_EN_FNL.pdf

Meng, B. (2010). Moving beyond democratization: A thought piece on the China Internet research agenda. *International Journal of Communication, 4*, 501–8.

Meng, B. (2011). From steamed bun to grass mud horse: E Gao as alternative political discourse on the Chinese Internet. *Global Media and Communication, 7*(1), 33–51. https://doi.org/10.1177/1742766510397938

Mertha, A. (2009). "Fragmented authoritarianism 2.0": Political pluralization in the Chinese policy process. *China Quarterly, 200*, 995–1012. https://doi.org/10.1017/S0305741009990592

Meyrowitz, J. (1986). *No sense of place: The impact of electronic media on social behavior.* Oxford University Press

Miao, W. (2014). Zhongguo wangluo quntixing shijian: Jiyu meiti duoyuan hudong de fenxi lujing. [Internet events in China: A multi-faceted interactive framework of analysis.] *Journalism and Communication Studies, 7*, 49–64.

Miller, D. (1987). *Material culture and mass consumption.* Basil Blackwill.

Moore, B. (1984). *Privacy: Studies in social and cultural history.* M.E. Sharpe.

Moore, R.L. (2005). Generation ku: Individualism and China's millennial youth. *Ethnology*, 357–76. https://doi.org/10.2307/3774095

Moscovici, S. (1984). The phenomenon of social representations. In R.M. Farr & S. Moscovici (Eds.), *Social representations* (pp. 3–69). Cambridge University Press.

Mueller, M.L., & Tan, Z. (1997). *China in the information age: Telecommunications and the dilemmas of reform.* Praeger.

Nathan, A.J., & Shi, T. (1996). Left and right with Chinese characteristics: Issues and alignments in Deng Xiaoping's China. *World Politics, 48*(4), 522–50. https://doi.org/10.1353/wp.1996.0013

Negroponte, N. (1995). *Being digital.* Hodder & Stoughton.

Neilson, J., Pritchard, B., & Yeung, H.W.C. (2014). Global value chains and global production networks in the changing international political economy: An introduction. *Review of International Political Economy, 21*(1), 1–8. https://doi.org/10.1080/09692290.2013.873369

Netease Financial News. (2013, 15 July). Mayun: renhe shangye diguo dou keneng daotai dan shengtai xitong ke buwang. [Ma Yun: It's possible for any commercial empire to fail, but an ecosystem may not.] http://biz.zjol .com.cn/05biz/system/2013/07/16/019470439.shtml

Newhagen, J.E., & Rafaeli, S. (1996). Why communication researchers should study the Internet: A dialogue. *Journal of Computer-Mediated Communication, 1*(4), 4–13. https://doi.org/10.1111/j.1460-2466.1996.tb01458.x

Noesselt, N. (2014). Microblogs and the adaptation of the Chinese Party-State's governance strategy. *Governance, 27*(3), 449–68. https://doi.org /10.1111/gove.12045

O'Brien, K.J. (2008). *Popular protest in China.* Harvard University Press.

Office of the Central Leading Group for Cyberspace Affairs. (2015, 14 August). Ma Huateng: lizu Shenzhen dazao hulianwang shengtailian. [Ma Huateng: Take roots in Shenzhen to create the ecological chain]. http://www.cac.gov .cn/2015-08/14/c_1116260247.htm

Oldenburg, R. (1989). *The great good place: Cafés, coffee shops, community centers, beauty parlors, general stores, bars, hangouts, and how they get you through the day.* Paragon House Publishers.

Ong, R. (2012). Online vigilante justice Chinese style and privacy in China. *Information and Communications Technology Law, 21*(2), 127–45.

Ott, B.L. (2017). The age of Twitter: Donald J. Trump and the politics of debasement. *Critical Studies in Media Communication, 34*(1), 59–68. https:// doi.org/10.1080/15295036.2016.1266686

Palen, L., & Dourish, P. (2003). Unpacking "privacy" for a networked world. *SIGCHI Conference on Human Factors in Computing Systems,* 129–36.

Pan, Z. (2010). Articulation and re-articulation: Agendas for understanding media and communication in China. *International Journal of Communication, 4,* 517–30.

Pan, Z., & Chan, J.M. (2003). Shifting journalistic paradigms: How China's journalists assess "media exemplars." *Communication Research, 30*(6), 649–82. https://doi.org/10.1177/0093650203257843

Pang, L. (2008). "China who makes and fakes": A semiotics of the counterfeit. *Theory, Culture & Society, 25*(6), 117–40. https://doi.org/10.1177 /0263276408095547

Papacharissi, Z. (2010). *A private sphere: Democracy in a digital age*. Polity Press.

Papacharissi, Z. (2015). *Affective publics: Sentiment, technology, and politics*. Oxford University Press.

Pazzanese, C. (2017, 27 February). In Europe, nationalism rising. *Harvard Gazette*. https://news.harvard.edu/gazette/story/2017/02/in-europe-nationalisms-rising/

Peng, T.Q., Zhang, L., Zhong, Z.J., & Zhu, J.J. (2012). Mapping the landscape of Internet studies: Text mining of social science journal articles, 2000–2009. *New Media & Society, 15*(5), 644–64. https://doi.org/10.1177/1461444812462846

Perry, E.J. (1994). Trends in the study of Chinese politics: State-society relations. *China Quarterly, 139*, 704–13. https://doi.org/10.1017/S0305741000043113

Perry, E.J., & Selden, M. (Eds.). (2003). *Chinese society: Change, conflict and resistance*. Routledge.

Pissin, A. (2015). Growing up in mommy's blog. *Asiascape: Digital Asia, 2*(3), 213–37. https://doi.org/10.1163/22142312-12340031

Polanyi, K. (1957). *The great transformation*. Beacon Press.

Poster, M. (1990). *The mode of information: Poststructuralism and social context*. University of Chicago Press.

Postill, J. (2008). Localizing the internet beyond communities and networks. *New Media & Society, 10*(3), 413–31. https://doi.org/10.1177/1461444808089416

Pun, N. (2003). Subsumption or consumption? The phantom of consumer revolution in "globalizing" China. *Cultural Anthropology, 18*(4), 469–92. https://doi.org/10.1525/can.2003.18.4.469

Qiu, J.L. (2009). *Working-class network society: Communication technology and the information have-less in urban China*. MIT Press.

Qiu, J.L. & Chan, T. (Eds.). (2011). *Studies of new media events*. People's Univerity Press.

Qu, Y., Huang, C., Zhang, P., & Zhang, J. (2011, March). Microblogging after a major disaster in China: A case study of the 2010 Yushu earthquake. In *Proceedings of the ACM 2011 conference on Computer supported cooperative work* (pp. 25–34).

Rachels, J. (1975, March). Why privacy is important. *Philosophy & Public Affairs*, 323–33.

Ramage, D., Dumais, S.T., & Liebling, D.J. (2010). Characterizing microblogs with topic models. *Proceeding of the Fourth International International Conference on Weblogs and Social Media*.

Rawlins, W.K. (1998). Theorizing public and private domains and practices of communication: Introductory concerns. *Communication Theory, 8*(4), 369–80. https://doi.org/10.1111/j.1468-2885.1998.tb00225.x

Regan, P.M. (1995). *Legislating privacy: Technology, social values, and public policy.* University of North Carolina Press.

Reiman, J. (1976). Privacy, intimacy, and personhood. *Philosophy & Public Affairs, 6,* 26–44.

Renwick, N., & Cao, Q. (1999). China's political discourse towards the 21st century: Victimhood, identity, and political power. *East Asia, 17*(4), 111–43. https://doi.org/10.1007/s12140-999-0019-7

Rheingold, H. (1993). *The virtual community: Homesteading on the electronic frontier* Addison-Wesley.

Rindova, V., Barry, D., & Ketchen, D.J. (2009). Entrepreneuring as emancipation. *Academy of Management Review, 34*(3), 477–91. https://doi.org/10.5465/amr.2009.40632647

Ritter, A., Cherry, C., & Dolan, B. (2010). Unsupervised modeling of Twitter conversations. In *Human Language Technologies: The 2010 Annual Conference of the North American Chapter of the Association for Computational Linguistics,* 172–80.

Rosen, S. (2010). Is the Internet a positive force in the development of civil society, a public sphere and democratization in China? *International Journal of Communication, 4*(8), 509–16.

Rosenberg, J., & Boyle, C. (2018). Understanding 2016: China, Brexit and Trump in the history of uneven and combined development. *Journal of Historical Sociology, 32*(1), e32–e58. https://doi.org/10.1111/johs.12217

Roudometof, V. (2014). Nationalism, globalization and glocalization. *Thesis Eleven, 122*(1), 18–33. https://doi.org/10.1177/0725513614535700

Rowe, W.T. (1990). The public sphere in modern China. *Modern China, 16*(3), 309–29. https://doi.org/10.1177/009770049001600303

Ruwitch, J., Stempel, J., & Raymond, N. (2015, 9 November). Luxury brands suing Alibaba say mediation looks futile after Ma comments. Reuters. http://www.reuters.com/article/us-alibaba-lawsuit-idUSKCN0SZ0AE20151110

Sassen, S. (2012). Interactions of the technical and the social: Digital formations of the powerful and the powerless. *Information, Communication & Society, 15*(4), 455–78. https://doi.org/10.1080/1369118X.2012.667912

Scambler, G. (Ed.). (2013). *Habermas, critical theory and health.* Routledge.

Schatzki, T.R., Knorr-Cetina, K., & Von Savigny, E. (2001). *The practice turn in contemporary theory.* Psychology Press.

Schmidt, V.A. (2008). Discursive institutionalism: The explanatory power of ideas and discourse. *Annual Review of Political Science, 11,* 303–26. https://doi.org/10.1146/annurev.polisci.11.060606.135342

Schneider, F., & Hwang, Y.J. (2014). China's road to revival. In Q. Cao, H. Tian, & P. Chilton (Eds.), *Discourse, politics and media in contemporary China* (pp. 145–70). John Benjamins Publishing.

Schudson, M. (2005). Autonomy from what? In R. Benson & E. Neveu (Eds.), *Bourdieu and the journalistic field*. Polity Press.

Schuman, M. (2015, 23 November). Why Alibaba's massive counterfeit problem will never be solved. Forbes. https://www.forbes.com/sites/michaelschuman/2015/11/04/alibaba-and-the-40000-thieves/#24e4bae129dc

Schutz, A., & Luckmann, T. (1973). *The structures of the life-world*. Northwestern University Press.

Scott, J. (1998). *Seeing like a state: How certain schemes to improve the human condition have failed*. Yale University Press.

Sennett, R. (1976). *The fall of public man*. Cambridge University Press.

Sewell Jr, W.H. (2005). *Logics of history: Social theory and social transformation*. University of Chicago Press.

Shambaugh, D. (2007). China's propaganda system: Institutions, processes and efficacy. *China Journal, 57*, 25–58. https://doi.org/10.1086/tcj.57.20066240

Shen, H. (2016). China and global internet governance: Toward an alternative analytical framework. *Chinese Journal of Communication, 9*(3), 304–24. https://doi.org/10.1080/17544750.2016.1206028

Shen, X.H.S., & Breslin, S. (2010). *Online Chinese nationalism and China's bilateral relations*. Lexington Books.

Shirk, S.L. (2008). *China: Fragile superpower*. Oxford University Press.

Shirk, S.L. (Ed.). (2011). *Changing media, changing China*. Oxford University Press.

Sjovaag, H. (2013). Journalistic autonomy: Between structure, agency and institution. *Nordicom Review, 34*, 155–67. https://doi.org/10.2478/nor-2013-0111

Skey, M. (2009). The national in everyday life: A critical engagement with Michael Billig's thesis of banal nationalism. *Sociological Review, 57*(2), 331–46. https://doi.org/10.1111/j.1467-954X.2009.01832.x

Slack, J.D. (1996). The theory and method of articulation in cultural studies. In D. Morley & K. Chen (Eds.), *Stuart Hall: Critical dialogues in cultural studies* (pp. 112–27). Routledge.

Smith, M., Ceni, A., Milic-Frayling, N., Shneiderman, B., Mendes Rodrigues, E., Leskovec, J., Dunne, C. (2010). NodeXL: A free and open network overview, discovery and exploration add-in for Excel 2007/2010/2013/2016, from the Social Media Research Foundation. https://www.smrfoundation.org

Smith, R.A., & Parrott, R.L. (2012). Mental representations of HPV in Appalachia: Gender, semantic network analysis, and knowledge gaps. *Journal of Health Psychology, 17*(6), 917–28. https://doi.org/10.1177/1359105311428534

Sohu Financial News (2016, 1 September). Alibaba weishenme chengwei guojia shoupi shuangchuang shifan jidi. [How Alibaba becomes a demonstration base for mass entrepreneurship and innovation]. http://pre.aliresearch.com/Blog/Article/detail/id/21053.html

Solove, D.J. (2002). Conceptualizing privacy. *California Law Review, 90*(4), 1088–154. https://doi.org/10.2307/3481326

Somers, M.R. (1992). Narrativity, narrative identity, and social action: Rethinking English working-class formation. *Social Science History*, *16*(04), 591–630. https://doi.org/10.1017/S0145553200016679

Somers, M.R. (1993). Citizenship and the place of the public sphere: Law, community, and political culture in the transition to democracy. *American Sociological Review*, 587–620. https://doi.org/10.2307/2096277

Somers, M.R. (1994). The narrative constitution of identity: A relational and network approach. *Theory and Society, 23*(5), 605–49. https://doi.org/10.1007/BF00992905

Sparrow, B.H. (1999). *Uncertain guardians: The news media as a political institution.* Johns Hopkins University Press.

Spitulnik, D. (1996). The social circulation of media discourse and the mediation of communities. *Journal of Linguistic Anthropology, 6*(2), 161–87. https://doi.org/10.1525/jlin.1996.6.2.161

State Council. (2016, 8 April). Tuijin "hulianwang+liutong" Li Keqiang yaoqiu pochu sida "pingjing." [Moving forward with "Internet + delivery" Li Keqiang requests to break four major "bottlenecks."] http://www.gov.cn/xinwen/2016-04/08/content_5062517.htm

State Council Information Office of the People's Republic of China. (2010, 8 June). The Internet in China. http://www.china.org.cn/government/whitepaper/node_7093508.htm

Steele, L.G., & Lynch, S.M. (2013). The pursuit of happiness in China: Individualism, collectivism, and subjective well-being during China's economic and social transformation. *Social Indicators Research*, *114*(2). https://doi.org/10.1007/s11205-012-0154-1

Sullivan, J., & Xie, L. (2009). Environmental activism, social networks and the internet. *China Quarterly, 198*, 422–32. https://doi.org/10.1017/S0305741009000381

Sun, H. (2011). Designing for social commerce experience as cultural consumption. In *International Conference on Internationalization, Design and Global Development* (pp. 402–6). Springer.

Sun, W. (2012). Desperately seeking my wages: Justice, media logic, and the politics of voice in urban China. *Media, Culture & Society, 34*(7), 864–79. https://doi.org/10.1177/0163443712452773

Szablewicz, M. (2014). The "losers" of China's Internet: Memes as "structures of feeling" for disillusioned young netizens. *China Information, 28*(2), 259–75. https://doi.org/10.1177/0920203X14531538

Tai, Z. (2006). *The Internet in China: Cyberspace and civil society.* Routledge.

Tai, Z. (2015). Networked resistance: Digital populism, online activism, and mass dissent in china. *Popular Communication, 13*(2), 120–31. https://doi.org/10.1080/15405702.2015.1021469

Tang, L., & Yang, P. (2011). Symbolic power and the internet: The power of a "horse." *Media, Culture & Society, 33*(5), 675–91. https://doi.org/10.1177/0163443711404462

Taylor, C. (1990). Modes of civil society. *Public Culture, 30*(1), 5–18.

Thompson, J.B. (1995). *The media and modernity: A social theory of the media.* Stanford University Press.

Thornton, P.M. (2008). Manufacturing dissent in transnational China: Boomerang, backfire or spectacle? In K. O'Brien (Ed.), *Popular protest in China* (pp. 179–204). Harvard University Press.

Thornton, P.M. (2010). The new cybersects: Popular religion, repression and resistance. In E. Perry & M. Selden (Eds.), *Chinese society: Change, conflict and resistance.* (pp. 215–38). Routledge.

Thornton, P.M. (2011). Retrofitting the steel frame: From mobilizing the masses to surveying the public. In S. Heilmann & E. Perry (Eds.), *Mao's invisible hand: The political foundations of adaptive governance in China.* Harvard University Press.

Tian, K., & Dong, L. (2010). *Consumer-citizens of China: The role of foreign brands in the imagined future China.* Taylor & Francis.

Tobak, S. (2014, 23 September). How Alibaba's Jack Ma became the richest man in China. Enterpreneur. https://www.entrepreneur.com/article/237692

Tok, S.K. (2010). Nationalism-on-demand? When Chinese sovereignty goes online. In S. Shen and S. Breslin (Eds.), *Online Chinese nationalism and China's bilateral relations.* Lexington Books.

Tong, S., & Walther, J.B. (2011). Relational maintenance and CMC. In K.B. Wright & L.M. Webb (Eds.), *Computer-mediated communication in personal relationships* (pp. 98–118). Peter Lang.

Tong, Y., & Lei, S. (2013). War of position and microblogging in China. *Journal of Contemporary China, 22*(80), 292–311. https://doi.org/10.1080/10670564.2012.734084

Townsend, J. (1996). Chinese nationalism. In J. Unger (Ed.), *Chinese nationalism* (pp. 1–30). Routledge.

Townsend, J.R. (1967). *Political participation in communist China.* University of California Press.

Tu, W., & Du, W. (Eds.). (1994). *China in transformation.* Harvard University Press.

Turner, J., & Markovsky, B. (2007). Micro-macro links. *The Blackwell Encyclopedia of Sociology.*

Unger, J. (Ed.). (1996). *Chinese nationalism.* Routledge.

Van Dijck, J. (2013). *The culture of connectivity: A critical history of social media.* Oxford University Press.

Vann, E.F. (2006). The limits of authenticity in Vietnamese consumer markets. *American Anthropologist, 108*(2), 286–96. https://doi.org/10.1525/aa.2006 .108.2.286

Wakeman Jr., F. (1993). The civil society and public sphere debate: Western reflections on Chinese political culture. *Modern China, 19*(2), 108–38. https://doi.org/10.1177/009770049301900202

Walasek, L., & Brown, G.D. (2015). Income inequality and status seeking: Searching for positional goods in unequal US states. *Psychological Science, 26*(4), 527–33. https://doi.org/10.1177/0956797614567511

Wallace, J.L., & Weiss, J.C. (2015). The political geography of nationalist protest in China: Cities and the 2012 anti-Japanese protests. *China Quarterly, 222*, 403–29. https://doi.org/10.1017/S0305741015000417

Wang, F.Y. (2009). Beyond x 2.0: Where should we go? *IEEE Intelligent Systems, 24*(3), 2–4.

Wang, H. (2012, 10 May).The rumor machine: Wang Hui on the dismissal of Bo Xilai. *London Review of Books, 34*(9), 13–14.

Wang, J. (2001). Culture as leisure and culture as capital. *Positions: East Asia Cultures Critique, 9*(1), 69–104. https://doi.org/10.1215/10679847-9-1-69

Wang, K.W., Lau, A., & Gong, F., (2016). How savvy, social shoppers are transforming Chinese e-commerce. http://www.mckinsey.com/industries /retail/our-insights/ how-savvy-social-shoppers-are-transforming-chinese-e-commerce

Wang, S. (2008). Changing models of China's policy agenda setting. *Modern China, 34*(1), 56–87. https://doi.org/10.1177/0097700407308169

Wang, Z. (2014). The Chinese dream: Concept and context. *Journal of Chinese Political Science, 19*(1), 1–13. https://doi.org/10.1007/s11366-013 -9272-0

Wang, Z. (2019). *"We are all Diba members tonight"*: Cyber-nationalism as emotional and playful actions online. In H. Liu (Ed.), *From cyber-nationalism to fandom nationalism: The case of Diba Expedition in China* (pp. 72–91). Routledge.

Wasserstrom, J. (2012). Learning from Chinese national and nationalist spectacles. *International Journal of China Studies, 3*(3), 315–23.

Watson, R.T., Pitt, L.F., Berthon, P., & Zinkhan, G.M. (2002). U-commerce: Expanding the universe of marketing. *Journal of the Academy of Marketing Science, 30*(4), 329–43. https://doi.org/10.1177/009207002236909

Wei, X. & Croft, W.B. (2006). LDA-Based Document Models for Ad-Hoc Retrieval. *Proceedings of the 29th Annual International ACM SIGIR Conference on Research and Development in Information Retrieval*: 178–85.

Wellman, B., Quan-Haase, A., Boase, J., Chen, W., Hampton, K., Díaz, I., & Miyata, K. (2003). The social affordances of the Internet for networked individualism. *Journal of Computer-Mediated Communication, 8*(3). https://doi.org/10.1111/j.1083-6101.2003.tb00216.x

Weng, J., Lim, E-P., Jiang, J., and He, Q. (2010). Twitterrank: Finding Topic-Sensitive Influential Twitterers. *Proceedings of the Third ACM International Conference on Web Search and Data Mining*: 261–70. 13

Weng, L., Menczer, F., & Ahn, Y.Y. (2014, March). Predicting successful memes using network and community structure. https://arxiv.org/abs/1403.6199

Wessler, H. (Ed.) (2008). *Public deliberation and public culture: The writings of Bernhard Peters, 1993–2005*. Palgrave Macmillan.

Westin, A.F. (1967). *Privacy and freedom*. Atheneum.

Westin, A.F. (2003). Social and political dimensions of privacy. *Journal of Social Issues, 59*, 431–53. https://doi.org/10.1111/1540-4560.00072

Williams, R. (1977). *Marxism and literature* (Vol. 1). Oxford University Press.

Wittel, A. (2001). Toward a network sociality. *Theory, Culture & Society, 18*(6), 51–76. https://doi.org/10.1177/026327601018006003

Wu, C. (2012). Micro-blog and the speech act of China's middle class: The 7.23 train accident case. *Javnost – The Public, 19*(2), 43–62. https://doi.org/10.1080/13183222.2012.11009084

Wu, J., Li, S., & Wang, H. (2019). From Fans to "Little Pink": The production and mobilization mechanism of national identity under new media commercial culture. In H. Liu (Ed.), *From cyber-nationalism to fandom nationalism: The case of Diba Expedition in China* (pp. 48–71). Routledge.

Wu, X. (2007). *Chinese cyber nationalism: Evolution, characteristics, and implications*. Lexington Books.

Wu, Y., Lau, T., Atkin, D.J., & Lin, C.A. (2011). A comparative study of online privacy regulations in the US and China. *Telecommunications Policy, 35*(7), 603–16. https://doi.org/10.1016/j.telpol.2011.05.002

Xia, Q. & Yuan, G. (2014a). "Guojia" de fenhua, kongzhi wangluo yu chongtuxing yiti chuanbo de jihui jiegou. [Fragmented "state," network control, and the opportunity structure for reporting contentious topics.] Open Times. http://www.opentimes.cn/Abstract/1935.html

Xing, G. (2012). Online activism and counter-public spheres: A case study of migrant labour resistance. *Javnost – The Public, 19*(2), 63–82.

Xinhua News Agency. (2014, 9 November). Xi's "new normal" theory. http://en.people.cn/n/2014/1110/c90883-8807112.html

Xinhua News Agency. (2015a, 6 March). China Focus: "Internet Plus" to fuel innovation, development. http://www.chinadaily.com.cn/business/tech/2015-03/06/content_19740249.htm

Xinhua News Agency. (2015b, 11 March). China issues opinions to encourage mass entrepreneurship, innovation. http://www.chinadaily.com.cn/regional/bda/2015-03/12/content_19794872.htm

Xinhua News Agency. (2015c, 15 March). Premier promises to pave way for entrepreneurs. http://en.people.cn/business/n/2015/0315/c90778 -8863208.html

Xinhua News Agency. (2015d, 22 December). Backgrounder: What is China's supply-side reform? http://usa.chinadaily.com.cn/china/2015-12/22 /content_22777212.htm

Xinhua News Agency. (2016a, 19 January). Xinhua Insight: China growth dips, more supply-side reforms signaled. http://www.scio.gov.cn/32618 /Document/1464778/1464778.htm

Xinhua News Agency. (2016b, 4 February). China vows better platforms for entrepreneurship and innovation. http://en.people.cn/n3/2016/0204 /c90882-9014113.html

Xinhua News Agency. (2016c, 12 May). Guowuyuan bangongting guanyu jianshe dazhongchuangye wanzhongchuangxin shifan jidi de shishi yijian. [The State Council: The opinion on establishing model bases of mass entrepreneurship and innovation.] http://news.xinhuanet.com /politics/2016-05/12/c_128978834.htm

Xu, J. (2015). Evolving Legal Frameworks for Protecting the Right to Internet Privacy in China. In J.R. Lindsay, T.M. Cheung, D.S. Reveron (Ed.), *China and Cybersecurity: Espionage, Strategy, and Politics in the Digital Domain*. Oxford University Press.

Xu, Y. & Denyer, S. (2015, 10 April). Wanted: Ten million Chinese students to "civilize" the Internet. *Washington Post*. https://www.washingtonpost. com/news/worldviews/wp/2015/04/10/wanted-ten-million-chinese -students-to-civilize-the-internet/?utm_term=.0dafadc73df4

Yan, Y. (2002). Managed globalization: State power and cultural transition in China. In P.L. Berger & S.P. Huntington (Eds.), *Many globalizations: Cultural diversity in the contemporary world* (pp. 19–47). Oxford University Press.

Yan, Y. (2009). *The individualization of Chinese society*. Berg.

Yan, Y. (2010). The Chinese path to individualization. *British Journal of Sociology, 61*(3), 489–512. https://doi.org/10.1111/j.1468-4446.2010.01323.x

Yan, Y. (2011). Dingxin Zhao: Weibo has changed China. *Time Weekly 155*. http://time-weekly.com/story/2011-11-17/120430.html

Yan, Y. (2012). Food safety and social risk in contemporary China. *Journal of Asian Studies, 71*(3), 705–29. https://doi.org/10.1017/S0021911812000678

Yang, F. (2015). *Faked in China: Nation branding, counterfeit culture, and globalization*. Indiana University Press.

Yang, F., & Xu, J. (2018). Privacy concerns in China's smart city campaign: The deficit of China's cybersecurity law. *Asia and the Pacific Policy Studies, 5*(3), 533–43.

Yang, G. (2003). The Internet and civil society in China: A preliminary assessment. *Journal of Contemporary China, 12*(36), 453–4. https://doi.org/10.1080/10670560305471

Yang, G. (2009). *The power of the Internet in China: Citizen activism online.* Columbia University Press.

Yang, G. (2011). Technology and its contents: Issues in the study of the Chinese Internet. *Journal of Asian Studies, 70*(4), 1043–50. https://doi.org/10.1017/S0021911811001598

Yang, G. (2012). A Chinese Internet? History, practice, and globalization. *Chinese Journal of Communication, 5*(1), 49–54. https://doi.org/10.1080/17544750.2011.647744

Yang, G. (2019). Performing cyber-nationalism in twenty-first-century China: The case of Diba Expedition. In H. Li (Ed.). *From cyber-nationalism to fandom nationalism* (pp. 1–12). Routledge.

Yang, P., Tang, L., & Wang, X. (2014). *Diaosi* as infrapolitics: Scatological tropes, identity-making and cultural intimacy on China's Internet. *Media, Culture & Society, 37*(2) 197–214. https://doi.org/10.1177/0163443714557980

Ye, W., Sarrica, M., & Fortunati, L. (2014). A study on Chinese bulletin board system forums: How Internet users contribute to set up the contemporary notions of family and marriage. *Information, Communication & Society, 17*(7), 889–905. https://doi.org/10.1080/1369118X.2013.854823

Yu, H. (2009). *Media and cultural transformation in China.* Routledge.

Yu, L.L., Asur, S., & Huberman, B.A. (2015). Trend dynamics and attention in Chinese social media. *American Behavioral Scientist, 59*(9), 1142–56. https://doi.org/10.1177/0002764215580619

Yuan, E.J. (2014). The new political of mediated activism in China: A critical review. In W. Chen & S.D. Reese (Eds.), *Networked China: Global dynamics of digital media and civic engagement* (pp. 215–31). Routledge.

Zapalska, A.M., & Edwards, W. (2001). Chinese entrepreneurship in a cultural and economic perspective. *Journal of Small Business Management, 39*(3), 286–92. https://doi.org/10.1111/0447-2778.00026

Zarrow, P. (2002). The origins of modern Chinese concepts of privacy: notes on social structure and moral discourse. In B. McDougall, and Hanson, (Eds), *Chinese concepts of privacy* (pp. 121–46). Brill.

Zelizer, V. (1988). Beyond the polemics on the market: Establishing a theoretical and empirical agenda. *Sociological Forum, 3*(4), 614–34. https://doi.org/10.1007/BF01115419

Zhang, D., Bi, P., Lv, F., Tang, H., Zhang, J., & Hiller, J.E. (2007). Internet use and risk behaviours: An online survey of visitors to three gay websites in China. *Sexually Transmitted Infections, 83*(7), 571–76. https://doi.org/10.1136/sti.2007.026138

Zhang, L., & Ong, A. (Eds.). (2008). *Privatizing China: Socialism from afar.* Cornell University Press.

Zhang, T. (2013). Governance and dissidence in online culture in China: The case of anti-CNN and online gaming. *Theory, Culture & Society, 30*(5), 70–93. https://doi.org/10.1177/0263276413486839

Zhang, X. (1998). Nationalism, mass culture, and intellectual strategies in post-Tiananmen China. *Social Text, 55,* 109–40. https://doi.org/10.2307/466689

Zhang, X. (2006). From institution to industry: Reforms in cultural institutions in China. *International Journal of Cultural Studies, 9*(3), 297–306. https://doi.org/10.1177/1367877906066876

Zhang, X., & Zheng, Y. (Eds.). (2009). *China's information and communications technology revolution: Social changes and state responses.* Routledge.

Zhao, S. (1997). Chinese intellectuals' quest for national greatness and nationalistic writing in the 1990s. *China Quarterly, 152,* 725–45. https://doi.org/10.1017/S0305741000047536

Zhao, S. (1998). A state-led nationalism: The patriotic education campaign in post-Tiananmen China. *Communist and Post-Communist Studies, 31*(3), 287–302. https://doi.org/10.1016/S0967-067X(98)00009-9

Zhao, S. (2006). The Internet and the transformation of the reality of everyday life: Toward a new analytic stance in sociology. *Sociological Inquiry, 76*(4), 458–74. https://doi.org/10.1111/j.1475-682X.2006.00166.x

Zhao, S. (2007). Internet and the lifeworld: Updating Schutz's theory of mutual knowledge. *Information Technology & People, 20*(2), 140–60. https://doi.org/10.1108/09593840710758059

Zhao, W.X., Jiang, J., Weng, J., He, J., Lim, E. P., Yan, H., & Li, X. (2011) Comparing Twitter and traditional media using topic models. In P. Clough P. (Eds.), Advances in information retrieval: ECIR 2011. Springer. https://doi.org/10.1007/978-3-642-20161-5_34

Zhao, Y. (1998). *Media, market, and democracy in China: Between the party line and the bottom line.* University of Illinois Press.

Zhao, Y. (2003). Transnational capital, the Chinese state, and China's communication industries in a fractured society. *Javnost – The Public, 10*(4), 53–74.

Zhao, Y. (2008). *Communication in China: Political economy, power, and conflict.* Rowman & Littlefield.

Zhao, Y. (2010). China media colloquium | for a critical study of communication and China: Challenges and opportunities. *International Journal of Communication, 4*(8), 544–51.

Zhao, Y. (2011). Sustaining and contesting revolutionary legacies in media and ideology. In S. Heilmann & E.J. Perry (Eds.), *Mao's invisible hand: The political foundations of adaptive governance in China* (pp. 201–36). Harvard University Press.

Zhao, Y. (2012). Introduction to "Communication and Class Divide China." *Javnost –The Public, 19*(2), 5–22. https://doi.org/10.1080/13183222.2012.11009082

Zheng, J., & Pan, Z. (2016). Differential modes of engagement in the Internet era: A latent class analysis of citizen participation and its stratification in China. *Asian Journal of Communication, 26*(2), 95–113. https://doi.org/10.1080/01292986.2015.1083598

Zheng, Y., & Wu, G. (2005). Information technology, public space, and collective action in China. *Comparative Political Studies, 38*(5), 507–36. https://doi.org/10.1177/0010414004273505

Zhou, L., Zhang, P., & Zimmermann, H.D. (2013). Social commerce research: An integrated view. *Electronic Commerce Research and Applications, 12*(2), 61–8. https://doi.org/10.1016/j.elerap.2013.02.003

Zhou, Y. (2006). *Historicizing online politics: Telegraphy, the Internet, and political participation in China.* Stanford University Press.

Zhu, H., Liu, P. & Shan, X. (2012, December). 2012 China Internet public opinion analysis report. (*2012 nian Zhongguo hulianwang yuqing fenxi baogao*) http://yuqing.people.com.cn/n/2012/1221/c210123-19974822.html

Zhu, H., Pan, Y., & Chen, X. (2015, December). 2015 China Internet public opinion analysis report. (*2015 nian Zhongguo hulianwang yuqing fenxi baogao*) http://yuqing.people.com.cn/GB/392071/401685/index.html

Zhu, H., Pan, Y., & Chen, X. (2016, December). 2016 China Internet public opinion analysis report. (*2016 nian Zhongguo hulianwang yuqing fenxi baogao*) http://yuqing.people.com.cn/GB/401915/408999/index.html

Zhu, H., Shan, X., and Hu, J. (2011, 23 December). 2011 China Internet public opinion analysis report. (*2011 nian Zhongguo hulianwang yuqing fenxi baogao*). http://www.cac.gov.cn/2014-08/01/c_1111902885.htm

Zhuang, J., & Bresnahan, M. (2012). HIV/AIDS stigma in Chinese Internet forums: A content analysis approach. *Chinese Journal of Communication, 5*(2), 227–42. https://doi.org/10.1080/17544750.2012.664443

Zywica, J., & Danowski, J. (2008). The faces of Facebookers: Investigating social enhancement and social compensation hypotheses – Predicting FacebookTM and offline popularity from sociability and self-esteem, and mapping the meanings of popularity with semantic networks. *Journal of Computer-Mediated Communication, 14*(1), 1–34. https://doi.org/10.1111/j.1083-6101.2008.01429.x

Index

privacy (*continued*)
(*mama*), 72; neglect (*hulue*), 74; pry
(*datan*), 74; respect (*zunzhong*), 73;
rooms (*fangjian*), 77; sad (*shangxin*),
77; superiors (*shangsi*), 73;
viewpoints (*guandian*), 74; villains
(*xiaoren*), 73; wife (*laopo*), 72
—privacy in public domains:
actress (*nvxing*), 78; boss (*laoban*),
77; civil servants (*gongwuyuan*),
77; classrooms (*jiaoshi*), 77;
customers (*kehu*), 77; detention
(*jvliu*), 82; dignity (*zunyan*),
82; dormitories (*sushe*), 77;
fines (*fakuan*), 82; governments
(*zhengfu*), 77; hospitals (*yiyuan*),
77; human rights (*renquan*), 82;
infringement (*qinfan*), 82; laws
(*falv*), 82; offices (*bangongshi*), 77;
officials (*guanyuan*), 77; others
(*bieren, taren, duifang, renjia*), 81;
the people (*renmin*), 82; police
(*jingcha*), 82; police station
(*jingchajv*), 82; programs (*jiemu*),
78; right to privacy (*yinsiquan*), 82;
rules (*faze*), 82; safety (*anquan*), 82;
the scandal (*chouwen*), 77; society
(*shehui*), 82; standards (*biaozhun*),
82; the state (*guojia*), 82; students
(*xuesheng*), 77; survival (*shengcun*),
82; teachers (*laoshi*), 77; top
secrets (*jimi*), 82; value (*jiazhi*), 82;
venereal disease (*xingbing*), 77
—privacy in socio-technological
domains: cellphone (*shouji*),
85; city (*chengshi*), 85; deleting
(*shanchu*), 85; displaying (*zhanshi*),
85; download (*xiazai*), 85; familiar
(*shuxi*), 85; forwarding (*zhuanfa*),
85; the media (*meiti*), 85; network
(*wangluo*), 85; news (*xinwen*), 85;
photos (*zhaopian*), 85; records (*jilu*),

85; report (*baodao*), 85; reporters
(*jizhe*), 85; shooting (*paizhao,
paishe*), 85; software (*ruanjian*), 85;
strangers (*moshengren*), 85; user
(*yonghu*), 85; website (*wangye*), 85
proletariat, 23
propaganda, 22, 100–1
properties, 53, 106, 118, 146
prosumer, 13, 131–4, 137–40
public service units (PSUs), 41–3
publics, 10, 13, 149, 151; cyber-
nationalism, 105; social change,
24; symbolic space, 40, 44, 50, 52,
54, 58
pushing hands (*tuishou*), 54
Putin, V., 98

qianxian, 126
Qifeng II, 100
Qing Dynasty, 98
Qingdao, 105
qiye, 118, 129
QQ, 48, 76, 94
qunti, 37

ratings, 48
rational patriotism, 105–6
rearticulation, 25, 34, 40
referendum, 92
regulations/regulatory, 30, 34, 53, 59,
66, 77, 123, 127, 128, 134, 136, 147
repertoire(s), 27, 67, 144
reposting, 79, 99, 104, 111
representations, 4, 7, 9–11, 145,
148–9; cyber-nationalism, 93;
privacy, 67, 71, 85; social change,
16–18, 20, 22, 25, 29, 36–7;
symbolic space, 49, 52, 58, 60
reproduction, 5, 7–8, 13–14, 59, 97, 151
republic, 110, 117
republican, 44
retweets, 55